Irish Masculinity on Screen

Irish Masculinity on Screen

*The Pugilists and Peacemakers
of John Ford, Jim Sheridan
and Paul Greengrass*

JOSEPH PAUL MOSER

McFarland & Company, Inc., Publishers
Jefferson, North Carolina, and London

"Land of Hope and Dreams" by Bruce Springsteen. © 2001 Bruce Springsteen (ASCAP). Reprinted by permission. International copyright secured. All rights reserved.

Library of Congress Cataloguing-in-Publication Data

Moser, Joseph Paul, 1978–
 Irish masculinity on screen : the pugilists and peacemakers of John Ford, Jim Sheridan and Paul Greengrass / Joseph Paul Moser.
     p.   cm.
 Includes bibliographical references and index.

 ISBN 978-0-7864-7416-5
 softcover : acid free paper ∞

 1. Masculinity in motion pictures. 2. Irish in motion pictures. 3. Ireland—In motion pictures. 4. Ford, John, 1894–1973—Criticism and interpretation. 5. Sheridan, Jim, 1949– —Criticism and interpretation. 6. Greengrass, Paul—Criticism and interpretation. I. Title.
 PN1995.9.M34M89   2013
 791.43'6529162–dc23   2013010877

British Library cataloguing data are available

© 2013 Joseph Paul Moser. All rights reserved

No part of this book may be reproduced or transmitted in any form or by any means, electronic or mechanical, including photocopying or recording, or by any information storage and retrieval system, without permission in writing from the publisher.

On the cover: James Nesbitt in *Bloody Sunday*, 2002 (Paramount Classics/Photofest); background image © 2013 Shutterstock

Manufactured in the United States of America

McFarland & Company, Inc., Publishers
 Box 611, Jefferson, North Carolina 28640
 www.mcfarlandpub.com

*For my wife, Jennifer, who has given me love,
support, and the freedom to be myself*

Table of Contents

Acknowledgments	ix
Preface	1

CHAPTER 1
A Fragile Liberalism: Gender in John Ford's Pre–World
    War II Cinema   21

CHAPTER 2
The Persistence of Patriarchy: Gender and Politics in John
    Ford's Later Films   49

CHAPTER 3
Assimilation, Integration, Continuity and Critique: Gender
    and Genre in the Hollywood Irish Cinemas of John Ford
    and Jim Sheridan   83

CHAPTER 4
Jim Sheridan: Reconstructing the Family, Redefining the Nation   113

CHAPTER 5
Alternative Masculinity and Irish Historical Trauma in Paul
    Greengrass's *Bloody Sunday* and *Omagh*   139

Conclusion	165
Chapter Notes	175
Bibliography and Filmography	187
Index	197

Acknowledgments

I owe many people a huge debt for helping me complete this book. At the University of Texas at Austin, where this project began, John Ruszkiewicz influenced and supported my teaching and shaped my ideas about analytical thinking and writing; Neville Hoad gave me a crash course in critical theory on gender; James Loehlin offered invaluable feedback on the overall structure and tone of the study; and Alan Friedman's meticulous editing improved my writing immeasurably.

I am lucky to have had the chance to study under Charles Ramírez Berg, who is as great a teacher and person as he is a scholar. He played a crucial role in shaping the chapters on John Ford and my overall understanding of film narrative, representation, and genre. By the same token, I am fortunate to have worked with Elizabeth Butler Cullingford, who has been an extraordinary mentor. Her humility, wit, and generosity, as well as her brilliance and tenacity, have been a continual source of inspiration. I am grateful for all her guidance and support throughout the past decade.

Donald Perret, a great friend and mentor, passed away in the summer of 2006. More than any single person, Donald helped put me on the path to graduate study and academic work, even as he repeatedly warned me against them. He was an erudite, irreverent, hilarious man, and he died too young.

I would also like to acknowledge my extraordinary friends and colleagues at the University of Texas, particularly Wooseong Yeom, Lacey Donohue, and Gregory and Patricia Foran. They were constantly supportive, generous, and forgiving. Additionally, my new colleagues at Fitchburg State University in Massachusetts have made me feel very much at home over the past five years, and I'm especially grateful to Eric Budd, Chola Chisunka, Michael Hoberman, Ben Railton, Peter Staab, Jennifer Berg, Judith Budz, Chris Cratsley, Rala Diakité, Jenny Fielding, Petri Flint, Lisa Gim, Sean Goodlett, Liz Gordon, Patrice Gray, Pam Hill, Kate Jewell, Aruna Krishnamurthy, Zak Lee, Margarite

Landry, Sara Levine, Ben Lieberman, Diane Lucas, Frank Mabee, Carl Martin, Irene Martyniuk, Tom Murray, Sarah Sadowski, Kisha Tracy, Michael Turk, Nancy Turnbull, Jean Varchol, Jeff Warmouth, David Weiss, Susan Williams, and Ian Williams. My thanks as well to all the hundreds of students I have had the privilege of working with over the past ten years—at the University of Texas at Austin and Fitchburg State University—and special thanks to Michael Bober, a great student who also served as my teaching assistant.

My profound thanks go to my parents, Colleen and Gary Moser, for their unconditional support. My sisters and brother, along with their spouses, have always helped and encouraged me: thank you Jill, Jim, Kate, Steve, Matt and Lynne. And my grandmother, Iris Cromett, who passed away in March of 2008, was wonderful to me my whole young life. Furthermore, I am grateful for the enduring friendship of Shawn Lupella, Zac Nagel, and Nathan Odegard.

I would like to thank all of my wife's family, especially Jean Hawsey, Rose Ewer, John Heller, Dorothy Heller, Mike Halay and Janet Hickey, for their kindness and acceptance. Finally, my deepest gratitude and love are to my wife and partner, Jennifer Heller. She has been patient, kind, and loving even when times were hardest.

Preface

Over two semesters in 2004–05, as a graduate student at the University of Texas at Austin, I taught a course on rhetoric and representations of gender, focusing on examples of alternative masculinity within the context of dominant genres and popular culture. This was my first attempt at combining my scholarly interests in gender and film studies with my teaching work, and this book continues in that vein. At the time I was consistently amazed by my students' tendency to use terms and expressions like "masculinity," "manliness," and "real man" completely unselfconsciously. And yet this should not have surprised me at all. Like me, these young men and women had been conditioned to take their defining ideas of gender for granted.

For those students, identifying what is not, or fails to be, "manly" was much easier than giving a compelling description of what they believed a man *is*. In dealing with various kinds of texts and representations—fiction, essays, drama, film — most of my students found men who cry or show strong emotion other than anger, who are hesitant or indecisive about committing violent acts, or who are sexually ambiguous, to be less than "what a man should be." These young people were not, however, especially regressive in their ideas about gender. In fact, they almost all agreed that we continue to live in a markedly patriarchal, sexist society, and for the most part they responded enthusiastically to women writers who openly, forcefully critiqued constrictive gender roles. Many of them were comfortable with voices and images of "strong" women. It was "weak" men they had a problem with, and against whom they had constructed their fundamental ideas of masculinity, in part because of the way in which they had been conditioned by the media and their peers to respond to unconventional male behaviors and identities.

I empathized with these students, as I continue to empathize with those who persist in viewing masculinity and femininity as strictly defined, mutually exclusive codes of moral, social and sexual conduct. I, too, was raised with no clear idea as to what being a man was. No one told me what to do to be or become a man, but I quickly learned what behaviors were unacceptable and essentially unavailable to me as a male in a patriarchal society. In her compelling essay "Putting Down the Gun," which anticipates her own son's impending manhood, Rebecca Walker explains:

> In what seemed like a movement but what was actually a slow buildup over time, an insidious and deceptively gradual occupation of psychic territory, young men were expected to change, to follow spoken and unspoken cues: don't feel, take control, be physically strong, find your identity in money and work, do not be afraid to kill, distrust everything that you cannot see. Don't cry [4].

In this way, patriarchal masculinity is defined almost completely in the negative.

I would call myself, and the vast majority of men I know, products of a system that devalues and dehumanizes us, a system that compels us to conform to a mode of living that is at best unfulfilling and at worst a recipe for dysfunction and discord in our relationships, so many of which in this country are tainted by emotional and in many cases physical abuse. As Walker puts it:

> What many men today are missing is themselves, the complex and unique experience of self that has been rerouted and suppressed in the name of work, war, and the arduous task of "being a man." This mandate to repress or obliterate anything and everything expansive or off the grid has defined generations, so much so that most men cannot even perceive the extent to which they have been robbed [5].

Lacking affirmative notions of manhood, men are susceptible to the allure of ruthless ambition, power, and domination. Feminist cultural critic bell hooks asserts, "Cultures of domination attack self-esteem, replacing it with a notion that we derive our sense of being from dominion over another. Patriarchal masculinity teaches men that their sense of self and identity, their reason for being, resides in their capacity to dominate others" (*Feminism Is for Everybody* 70). Reinforcing this repressive and dangerous mandate, popular culture, from military recruitment ads ("There's strong, and then there's Army strong"), to immersive, gory video games, to film after film featuring comic book action heroes, reaches us via ever more advanced digital technology. Violence and domination keep appearing sexier all the time.

Thus, this project has resulted from my desire to seek out and draw attention to films that break from popular generic patterns in their representations of gender, violence, and the family. Like advertisements and video games, screen narratives and images have enormous sociocultural power. As viewers, teachers, and critics of film, it is easy enough for us to recognize some of the persistent myths and social distortions that are both reflected in and perpetuated by mainstream movies and television. Cinematic testaments to the glories of war, the patriarchal family, and colonial expansion are not hard to come by, and Hollywood westerns often manage to celebrate all three at once. Furthermore, in recent years U.S. journalists have brought to light how military interrogators at Guantánamo Bay drew on the television show *24* to find new methods of torturing their captives (Herbert). These abuses occurred despite the U.S.'s longstanding commitment to the Geneva Conventions and the substantial scholarly evidence attesting to the inefficacy of torture as a means of extracting reliable intelligence.[1]

Yet screen stories and images can also open up new, affirmative possibilities. Postcolonial films from countries such as India, South Africa, and Ireland, as well as recent German, English, Israeli and American anti-war features and documentaries, critically engage with historical dogma by focusing on marginal figures and narratives, revealing alternative ways of thinking and acting. Investigating and exposing the hegemonic, deeply conventional, and at times insidiously regressive agenda of most popular culture and cinema is indeed an essential enterprise. It is equally important, however, that we put our energies into valorizing dissenting voices and dissonant texts: those artists and films that challenge the status quo, whether within the frameworks of established genres or by radically deviating from dominant narrative forms.

Examining images of gender and violence through the lens of representation studies, this book analyzes select works of three popular filmmakers whose careers, taken together, span the period from 1939 to the present.[2] I argue that these three artists—John Ford, Jim Sheridan, and Paul Greengrass—explore fundamental questions about patriarchy and violence within Irish and Irish-American contexts, and that, in the process, they upset conventional notions of masculine authority. Investigating alternative conceptions of manhood presented in these films, as well as these filmmakers' complex engagement with Hollywood film genres, I offer a fuller understanding of their subtle critiques of patriarchy and violence. I contend that their illustrations of socially sanctioned male dominance in the lives of women, as well as their portrayals of male and female resistance to patriarchy, constitute a subversive challenge to traditional order.

In the process, I address gendered archetypes prevalent in Irish and American cinemas, and analyze the ways in which Ford, Sheridan, and Greengrass employ and critique these masculine types through their portrayals of fathers, sons, boxers and pacifists. Ultimately, I argue that the recent Irish films of Sheridan and Greengrass gesture toward future modes of manhood that completely disavow patriarchy and violence. In sum, this project plots a trajectory of Irish cinema during the twentieth and early twenty-first centuries, charting a progression from ambivalent critique of patriarchy (in the films of John Ford) to outright rejection of patriarchal masculinity (in Jim

Sheridan's work) to reconceptualization of manhood and the family (in the films of Sheridan and Paul Greengrass).

Defining Key Terms

At the outset I should explain what exactly I mean by "patriarchy" and "progressive," two terms that show up frequently throughout this text. "Patriarchy," by my definition, is not simply "a form of social organization in which the father or oldest male is the head of the family, and descent and relationship are reckoned through the male line; government or rule by a man or men" (*Oxford English Dictionary*), but, more precisely, an institutionalized network of relationships (familial, social, professional, political) predicated on and maintained by an unequal distribution of power (financial, political, physical) among men and women.

According to Maria Mies, feminists such as Kate Millet began to prefer "patriarchy" to more problematic terms like "male dominance" in the early 1970s (25). As Mies explains, "[T]he term 'patriarchy' denotes the historical and societal dimension of women's exploitation and oppression, and is thus less open to biologistic interpretations" (36). Mies also makes the crucial link between patriarchy and capitalism:

> The fact that patriarchy is today an almost universal system which has affected and transformed most pre-patriarchal societies has to be explained by the main mechanisms which are used to expand this system, namely robbery, warfare and conquest.... It is my thesis that capitalism cannot function without patriarchy, that the goal of this system, namely the never-ending process of capital accumulation, cannot be achieved unless patriarchal man-woman relations are maintained or newly created [37].

Making this connection is essential for feminist film scholars due to the fact that screen narratives typically portray male protagonists both at work and in love—engaged in public acts as well as those in the intimate spheres of romance and/or the family. When the goal-oriented male protagonist of a Hollywood (or other genre-driven) film pursues a woman, she becomes a symbolic part of his quest for self-determination and thereby a commodified object. Thus, patriarchy and capitalism inflect virtually every aspect of mainstream cinema, and therefore my use of "patriarchy" is really shorthand for "capitalist-patriarchy," the term that Mies frequently employs.

The word "progressive" describes both my political orientation and the kind of cinema I most value—that which portrays complex gender identities. Linguist and political guru George Lakoff has proposed six distinct categories of progressives, and the one that best describes me is "anti-authoritarian progressive." I see enormous productive potential in texts (films or otherwise) that question inequality and structures of power, particularly in terms of gender. Such interrogation can be accomplished by films mainly concerned with demystifying the operation of patriarchy and portraying the victims of this repressive system; in addition to Sheridan's *The Field*, Peter Mullan's *The Magdalene Sisters* (2002) and Clint Eastwood's *Mystic River* (2003) — to offer just two recent examples of Irish and Irish-American–themed films — succeed exceptionally well in this regard.

In my view, however, the most progressive cinema is that which critiques patriarchy while offering productive alternatives: modes of masculinity and femininity endowed with revolutionary potential. As Kaja Silverman argues, alternative gender identities expose the "dominant fiction" of phallic, patriarchal masculinity and "say 'no' to power" (2–3). The majority of the films by Ford, Sheridan, and Greengrass that I analyze in Chapters 1, 3, 4, and 5 accomplish this kind of vital cultural work.

Why These Filmmakers?

John Ford is a towering figure in the histories of both Irish and American film. In terms of his professional cinematic practice, Ford was always a Hollywood filmmaker first and foremost, and most critics regard him as one of the greatest practitioners of this dominant aesthetic. Technically, Ford is virtually peerless in terms of his shot compositions. His striking dearth of camera movement and signature frame-within-the-frame shots, often involving windows and doorways, endow his work with a visual style that is more immediately identifiable than any other Classical Hollywood filmmaker beside Alfred Hitchcock.

On a basic narrative level, his films are perhaps most notable for their exceptional attention to character development and a refusal to rely on big action set-pieces to bolster their stories, though Ford was remarkably adept at choreographing and capturing such sequences. His films are often oddly paced, with sprawling first acts that leisurely establish a setting and group of characters; such is the case in *Fort Apache* (1948) and *The Quiet Man* (1952), for example. As Orson Welles put it, "With Ford at his best you get the sense of what the Earth is made of, even if the script is by Mother Machree"[3] (*Directed by John Ford*). Welles aptly underscores what made Ford such an inspiration to filmmakers around the world: his ability to do extraordinarily expressive work within Hollywood's restrictive system, one which would tragically addle Welles' own career at almost every turn.

Although Ford liked to tout himself as an Irish rebel, he still did the bidding of Hollywood producers, and he rarely retained the right of final cut on his films. The classic 1970 article "John Ford's *Young Mr. Lincoln*," by the editors of *Cahiers du Cinéma*, cites the fact that "as early as 1935, the five Major Companies (Paramount, Warner, MGM, Fox, RKO) and the three Minor (Universal, Columbia, United Artists) were totally controlled by bankers and financiers" (497). The editors go on to declare:

> In Hollywood, more than anywhere else the cinema is not "innocent." Creditor of the capitalist system, subject to its constraints, its crises, its contradictions, the American cinema, the main instrument of the ideological super-structure, is heavily determined at every level of its existence. As a product of the capitalist system and its ideology, its role is in turn to reproduce the one and thereby to help the survival of the other [499].

Nevertheless, in some instances, Ford pushed the ideological limits of Hollywood cinema quite far, particularly in the work he did from 1939 to 1941 while under contract with 20th Century–Fox; this was his first period of "full-blown maturity as an artist" (McBride 269). Ford's representations of gender in the films he made during this time are the focus of Chapter 1.

While eloquently describing Ford's creative strength, Orson Welles' comment above also points out the quality of Ford's cinema that critics most frequently cite as his major flaw: his tendency toward maudlin sentimentality. Most of the deeply sentimental passages in Ford films, however, center on at least one of the following elements: the working class family, Irish (and sometimes other white ethnic) identity, patriotic Americanism, and, most particularly in his later films, male leadership distinguished by enlightened paternalism — usually endorsed by the institutional authority of the U.S. military, or religious or political position. Furthermore, scenes of dancing, singing, drinking, and brawling are in almost every Ford film released between 1939 and 1966, and by and large they are moments of community building and "expressions of ethnicity" (Ramírez Berg, "The Margin as Center" 130). These scenes are silly, corny, and sometimes come at the expense of narrative continuity — most egregiously in the case of *The Searchers*— but Ford uses them to highlight the fun-loving, unpretentious qualities of "his people," often in stark contrast to the uptight, self-deluded WASP villains of his films.

Ford's deep emotionality is somewhat veiled by the fact that so many of his films are ostensibly westerns and war movies. In my view, though, Ford often made family melodramas masquerading as macho genre pictures,[4] and thus the sentimental, ritualistic expressions of community are not curious interludes but sequences absolutely integral to the director's artistic and cultural statements.[5] In a sense, Ford had it both ways. Since melodramas were "gendered female," and "action genres ... were just movies" (Ramírez Berg, "Gendered Actions..." 2), he managed time and again to shoehorn melodrama and sentimentality into narratives that were safely generic.[6] This strategy allowed Ford to ask serious questions about gender and the family while keeping his films commercially viable. In turn, it enabled him to occasionally attempt ambitious projects that were more openly concerned with social and political problems, including the progressive-oriented novel adaptations *The Grapes of Wrath* (1940) and *How Green Was My Valley* (1941), both of which I analyze in Chapter 1.

Apart from a few notable exceptions, like *The Informer* (1935), *The Plough and the Stars* (1936), *The Quiet Man* (1952), *The Long Gray Line* (1955), *The Rising of the Moon* (1957), and *The Last Hurrah* (1958), the Irish experience was not integral to the plots of Ford's films.[7] Yet Irishness, along with other kinds of working class cultural identity, almost invariably found its way into the director's work, particularly through his sequences of communal celebration and his frequent casting of Irish-American and Irish actors, including John Wayne, Maureen O'Hara, Barry Fitzgerald and Arthur Shields, as well as Victor McLaglen (an Englishman who specialized in Irish roles). Additionally, Ford was well known for playing up his Irish identity on set and off: he had a shamrock emblazoned on his director's chair and usually called a tea break at 4:00 each day (Eyman 292); in his dealings with Hollywood executives, Ford would often act the part of a "mad Irish" philistine, playing dumb in order to avoid following the commands of money men (McBride 5).

Ford's sense of ethnic heritage had a darker, more reflective aspect as well. Writing to a nephew fighting on the side of the Spanish Loyalists in 1937, Ford declared, "I am glad you got the good part of the O'Feeney blood [Feeney was Ford's given name]. Some of it is *very* god-damned awful. We are liars, weaklings and selfish drunkards, but there has always been a stout rebel quality in the family and a peculiar passion for justice" (Eyman 187). Even if Ford was as ambivalent about the country of his parents as he was about the land of his birth, he generally romanticized Irish and working folk in his films, whereas he was often willing to hold up American history and society to harsh scrutiny.

Like Ford's life, his art sits astride these two nations and cultures. Recent scholarship on the history of Irish film — most notably, Martin McLoone's *Irish Film: The Emergence of a Contemporary Cinema* (2000) and Ruth Barton's *Irish National Cinema* (2004) — inevitably addresses the impact of Ford's work, particularly the landmark cinematic depiction of the Emerald Isle in *The Quiet Man*, a film that seems to inspire an equal measure of admiration and exasperation in critics. Taking into account financial and political realities, Barton clearly establishes that any definition of Irish cinema must necessarily be an expansive one:

> In the Irish case, the absence of a local film production industry for most of the twentieth century means that if we are to talk of a national cinema, or a national film text even, we have to engage in a series of acts of creative bricolage; that is, to see how an image of Ireland on screen emerged out of the national industries of other countries.... An Irish national cinema is thus defined here firstly as a

body of films made inside and outside Ireland that addresses both the local and diasporic cultures [4–5].

Viewed from this perspective, Ford is unquestionably the first great Irish feature filmmaker of the Sound Era. Yet there is a surprising lack of in-depth critical work connecting Ford with later Irish cinema and considering his impact on particular filmmakers.

Thus, the main contribution of this project is two-fold. First, it makes original use of the methodologies of representation, gender, and *auteur* studies to illuminate how John Ford's films—most particularly his non-western movies from 1939 to 1966—represent men and women. I analyze Ford's radically unconventional representations of masculinity and, to a lesser extent, femininity, particularly in the contexts of marriage, war, labor struggle, and religious practice, in several of his films from 1939 to 1941. Then I proceed to chart the increasingly reactionary and militaristic bent of his subsequent films, which is most notable in his "cavalry trilogy," *The Quiet Man* and other works from the late '40s, '50s and '60s. Second, this book considers how Ford's movies and his depictions of Irish identity and gender have influenced Irish films of the late 20th and early 21st centuries, especially those of Jim Sheridan.[8] To my knowledge, no detailed study has yet pursued either one of these lines of inquiry.

Beyond addressing the strong similarities between *The Quiet Man* and Jim Sheridan's *The Field* (1990), scholars have seldom explored Ford's enormous influence on Sheridan's films in terms of his use of genre conventions, and in particular his representations of gender and the family. Much like Ford, Sheridan occasionally verges on the banal in his earnest, often sentimental valorizations of the Irish family, though, as I will argue, his overall agenda is more progressive than Ford's. In all of Sheridan's films, "the family becomes metonymic for the nation" (Barton 77), as he attempts to enact its liberation from the ideological confines of nationalism, patriarchy and colonialism, most notably in his last three Irish films, *In the Name of the Father* (1993), *The Boxer* (1997), and *In America* (2002).

Paul Greengrass, although not stylistically beholden to Ford or Sheridan, is equally concerned with examining the impact of social and historical upheaval on Irish masculinity and the family in both *Bloody Sunday* (2002) and *Omagh* (2004). Furthermore, with his background in television documentary filmmaking, Greengrass has infused his Irish films with a riveting sense of immediacy, creating cathartic, challenging cinematic reconstructions of pivotal atrocities of the Troubles. With Sheridan having helped to carve out a commercial niche for nuanced film treatments of Irish political and social problems, Greengrass continues in this vein by dramatizing Irish communities in conflict and collaboration with amazing sensitivity and specificity.

Additionally, focusing on these three directors allows me to illuminate not just three phases in the development of Irish cinema, but three distinct perspectives on masculinity and Ireland: those of Ford, the second-generation Irish-American; Sheridan, the Dubliner; and Greengrass, the Englishman.

Why These Figures?

Patriarchs

In addition to examining pugilists and peacemakers in these works, I focus extensively on the representation of patriarchs, which applies to screen fathers in a wide range of familial capacities: husband, parent, family head, disciplinarian, role model, wage earner. Furthermore, my intention is not to restrict my analysis to fathers alone but to give broad critical assessments of male figures and their intimate relationships as portrayed in these films, paying particular attention to bonds between fathers and sons (of whatever age), and husbands and wives. In his study of Hollywood film genres, Thomas Schatz asserts that when films place families at the narrative center (like family melodramas, and many musicals and screwball/romantic comedies), normally they are enacting plots of "social integration" in settings of "civilized space," while action-oriented pictures (like westerns and gangster and detective films) are generally concerned with "social order" and play out in "contested space" (29). The works of Ford, Sheridan, and Greengrass provocatively confound these generic categories by inserting family drama into contested political and cultural spaces.

Ford's cinema illuminates social values and problems by depicting families—traditional and non-traditional, nuclear and military—and communities surviving and disintegrating in the face of war, dislocation, and modernization, often on the nineteenth-century American frontier. Even when dealing with more static settings, however, Ford could illuminate contested ideological territory, as he does to powerful effect in *How Green Was My Valley*, which takes place in a Welsh mining town in the early twentieth century. This film deals so openly with labor and religious conflict that it is a miracle it was ever made during the Classical Hollywood era, and that it won the 1941 Oscar for Best Picture is utterly astounding.[9] By registering the effects of ideological clashes in the life of one family, however, Ford cleverly cloaks his potent political statement in a narrative that ostensibly focuses on the encroachment of modernization and childhood innocence lost.

Jim Sheridan has remarked upon the absence of "Good Father" stories in Irish culture (Barton, *Jim Sheridan* ... 144). John Ford's good fathers mainly appear in his pre–World War II films, particularly *Drums Along the Mohawk*

(1939), *The Grapes of Wrath* (1940), and *How Green Was My Valley*, which features two good fathers for Huw, the protagonist: his biological father, Mr. Morgan, and Mr. Gruffydd, the pastor who serves as Huw's teacher and spiritual mentor. After World War II, Ford tended toward hard-assed militarist fathers, like those played by Robert Montgomery in *They Were Expendable* (1945), Henry Fonda in *Fort Apache*, and John Wayne in most of his many collaborations with Ford.

Conversely, in Sheridan's cinema, father figures grow progressively kinder and less autocratic. From the tyrannical patriarchs in *My Left Foot* and *The Field*, whose destructive impact on their families he portrays in harrowing detail, Sheridan shifts his focus to the sensitive, nurturant father figures of *In the Name of the Father*, *The Boxer*, and *In America*. Although these films all portray families in crisis—taken together, they deal with unjust imprisonment, the legacy of paramilitary violence, and emigration following the loss of a child—the director emphasizes the need for reconciliation and humane methods of conflict resolution in each case. In the course of these five films Sheridan reconfigures the Irish family as a model of peaceful, egalitarian coexistence. By the same token, Ford's representations of women go from somewhat progressive to fairly misogynistic during the second half of his career (1939–66), while in the case of Sheridan, his latest Irish film, *In America*, features Samantha Morton as his most complex and compelling female character to date.

Like Ford and Sheridan, Paul Greengrass interrogates notions of gender, family, and community as he dramatizes Irish historical shifts and traumas. *Bloody Sunday* portrays the tragic failure of an actual political and spiritual father figure, Ivan Cooper, whose nonviolent protest movement for Catholic civil rights in Northern Ireland is undermined and ultimately destroyed by the colonial atrocity that occurred on January 30, 1972. The film indicates how British violence on that day (resulting in the murders of 14 unarmed civilians) became a rallying point for Irish paramilitary violence in the form of the IRA and other groups, thus neutralizing the potentially productive impact of a peaceful Irish Catholic movement for equality and justice.

As a bookend to *Bloody Sunday*, *Omagh* focuses on the members of the Gallagher family—who did in fact lose Aiden Gallagher, their son and brother, in the 1998 terrorist bombing of the titular Northern Irish town—as they deal with their grief and desire for justice in often conflicting ways. The protagonist, Michael Gallagher, struggles to reconcile his roles as husband and father to his surviving wife and daughters with his leadership responsibilities in a grassroots community group seeking redress against both the criminals who committed the bombing and the bureaucrats who bungled the investigation. The film is a fitting, respectful testament to the suffering of those afflicted by political violence and accurately attests to the open psychic wounds they carry with them, the lack of finality and justice that is an everyday fact of their lives. Through its attention to human vulnerability and loss in the lives of one man and his family, *Omagh* captures the enormous personal costs of impersonal political atrocity and illustrates the futility of violent revenge.

All three filmmakers covered in this study explore the cultural implications of families in mourning. In Ford's work, funeral scenes are most often solemn rituals that affirm the transcendence of lost loved ones; in *The Searchers* (1956), however, the protagonist's grief at the loss of his family is foregone in the interest of revenge, the pursuit of which turns Ethan Edwards into a kind of social savior, but an exile from his own loved ones. With *In America*, Sheridan considers the impact of historical trauma from the Great Famine to the Troubles on the Irish family, responding to what he views as the Irish "death culture" by depicting family members helping each other face grief in order to "say goodbye" and have a future. Greengrass reconstructs harrowing atrocities in chilling detail, yet puts equal dramatic investment into documenting the human consequences, affirming life while contributing to the demystification of violence.

Pugilists

Apart from political leaders and iconic poets and writers—Oscar Wilde, W.B. Yeats, James Joyce, Seamus Heaney—no male public figure has been as prominent in nineteenth- and twentieth-century Irish culture as that of the pugilist.[10] Since the late nineteenth century the Irish on both sides of the Atlantic have maintained an unflagging fascination with boxers, many of whom they have called their own. Celebrated Irish-Americans John L. Sullivan (1858–1918), James J. "Gentleman Jim" Corbett (1866–1933), Jack Dempsey (1895–1983),[11] Gene Tunney (1897–1978), and James J. Braddock (1905–1974) were all world heavyweight champions. They collectively dominated the sport from the 1880s through the mid–1930s, a period when the heavyweight crown represented the epitome of masculine strength and success in Western culture.[12] Belfast's John "Rinty" Monaghan (1920–1984) and John Caldwell (b. 1938) are two of the most famous Northern Irish boxers of all time; Monaghan held the World Flyweight Championship from 1947 to 1950, and Caldwell the World Bantamweight Championship from 1961 to 1962.[13] More recently, the Irishman Barry McGuigan (b. 1961) won the World Featherweight Championship in 1985; his life story and outspoken support for peace between Irish Catholics and Protestants was part of the inspiration for Sheridan's *The Boxer* (*BoxRec*).

One can easily argue that the sport of boxing is a regressive, patently patriarchal subculture. Indeed, it is responsible for brutal spectacles in which male and female fighters are periodically killed, and frequently maimed and disabled.[14] As a cinematic milieu, however, boxing has often functioned symbolically to productively challenge conceptions of gender and capitalism. Hollywood boxing films reached their artistic and popular peak in the 1940s and '50s. Influenced by the existential angst of the *film noir* movement, many of these pictures highlighted the social and personal corruption engendered by the sport, which was tarnished by its enduring ties to the mafia and by boxers' often precipitous falls from grace, financially as well as physically.

A great many boxing pictures, such as *Body and Soul* (Robert Rossen, 1947), *The Ring* (Kurt Neumann, 1952), and *Requiem for a Heavyweight* (1956; 1962), stress the humanity and integrity of individual fighters caught up in a business that ruthlessly exploits them. *The Harder They Fall* (Mark Robson, 1956), Humphrey Bogart's final film, addresses the manner in which callous managers and promoters essentially eat up and spit out boxers, ending with an explicit call for the abolition of the sport. *On the Waterfront* (Elia Kazan, 1954) features Marlon Brando's immortal performance as Terry Malloy, an Irish-American ex-boxer who "coulda been a contender" had his brother and his mob cronies not ruined Terry's career by inducing him to "take a dive," thereby giving him "a one-way ticket to palookaville."

John Ford's *The Quiet Man*, which I dissect at length in Chapter 2, is another 1950s film about an ex-professional boxer, one who flees the U.S. to pristine Western Ireland after having killed his last opponent in the ring. Although Sean Thornton (John Wayne) vows to never fight again, he is finally compelled to take on his bully of a brother-in-law in order to prove his love to his fiery Irish wife and his manliness to his new community. The first three-quarters of *The Quiet Man*, much like other outstanding boxing-themed films of its era, conducts a probing examination of the cultural links between masculinity, violence, and capitalism; at one point Sean Thornton confesses his shame for having committed "murder" in the name of "lousy money." From there, however, the film regresses to an endorsement of not just brawling and drunkenness—par for the course in Ford's cinema—but spousal abuse, while making clear that Sean's wife had wanted him to put her in her place all along. A star vehicle for John Wayne at his commercial peak, the film could hardly have been viable had the protagonist not ultimately abandoned his pacifism. Yet the film's abrupt thematic and tonal reversal remains deeply problematic as a validation of the Irish-American patriarchal status quo, a narrative turn very indicative of Ford's own post-war ideological shift toward social conservatism.

In *The Boxer*, the main subject of Chapter 4, Jim Sheridan uses the sport as a vehicle for examining the Troubles and the legacy of British colonialism in 1990s Northern Ireland. In this context, boxing serves as a productive alternative to paramilitary violence for young men, reinforcing the crucial distinction between the "hard man" and "gunman" in Irish history and culture (Feldman). As Jack Dempsey famously stated, "You're in there for three-minute rounds with gloves on and a referee. That's not real fighting" (Oates). Sheridan compellingly dramatizes the affirmative potential of mediated aggression in a land riven by extremism and colonial exploitation; the transformation of the film's central figure from gunman to boxer represents a source of hope for peace and sectarian coexistence in Belfast. As the anti–Sean Thornton, Danny disqualifies himself from his only professional fight, relenting rather than continuing to pound an opponent who is no longer capable of defending himself.

Peacemakers

Clearly, peacemaking is a tough sell, an activity that is hard to portray as sexy and compelling onscreen. According to Charles Ramírez Berg, since the era of silent film, along with pushing female characters to the margins, "Hollywood's action-centered storytelling practice impacted male characters as well. Boosting physical male prowess, it discounted everything else." Thus, the difficulty inherent in placing peaceful men at the narrative center is that "protagonists whose goals were neither concrete nor physical, whose quests existed on an emotional or spiritual plane, did not appear, by Hollywood's gender definition, very masculine" ("Gendered Actions..." 6).[15] This macho gender bias has had far-reaching implications for cinema, and very few films have managed to valorize peacemakers while achieving mainstream commercial success. Two of the most exceptional works in this regard are *Gandhi* (Richard Attenborough, 1982) and *The Passion of the Christ* (Mel Gibson, 2004),[16] which depict violence erupting around and inflicted upon their protagonists, both of whom are finally martyred.

Sheridan's *In the Name of the Father* and *The Boxer*, and Greengrass's *Bloody Sunday* and *Omagh*, largely follow the *Gandhi* blueprint of placing peacemakers at the center of intense political and personal conflict. Additionally, Ford's pre-war work features peacemakers, most centrally in *Young Mr. Lincoln* and *How Green Was My Valley*. In the case of *The Grapes of Wrath*, while Tom Joad, the protagonist, resorts to violence in crisis, his spiritual and political mentor, Jim Casy, preaches peaceful resistance in the form of labor strikes.

My focus on this figure is an attempt to underscore the artistic possibilities of films about peacemakers and to trace a trend in Irish cinema toward increasingly complex engagements with notions of masculinity, colonialism, and the nation's history of internecine conflict. I ultimately posit Irish film as an exemplary model for other postcolonial national cinemas. Furthermore, analyzing peacemakers in film is my way of uniting the political projects of feminist cultural criticism and peace studies scholarship, which I see as an essential task.

While the aims of feminists and peace activists might seem complementary, however, the latter have often served to reinforce sexist hierarchies. As international peacemaking expert David Cortright makes clear, many prominent male leaders of nonviolent movements for social and political change have been unenlightened, even misogynistic, in their views on gender. While praising Martin Luther King's high ideals and effective leadership, Cortright also examines his deep flaws, particularly King's role in the "male chauvinist culture of the civil rights movement," including his rampant marital infidelity and refusal to grant his dynamic wife, Coretta Scott King, the "more active role" in the movement that she craved.[17] Cortright challenges us to build on the legacy of King by expanding his humanitarian vision to include feminist ideals: "King did not realize that the giant triplets of which he spoke contain a sibling, sexism. The struggle against racism, poverty, and militarism means struggling against patriarchy as well. All must be overcome if the beloved community is to be realized" (182–3).

Intellectually as well as socially, scholars and activists must continue to build bridges between these two vital movements. Feminist goals can only be achieved through peaceful means—not because feminists aren't the fighting kind, but because violence is antithetical to the egalitarian ethos of the cause. As Walter Wink writes, "Violence is simply not radical enough, since it generally changes the rulers but not the rules. What use is a revolution that fails to address the fundamental problem: the existence of domination in all its forms, and the myth of redemptive violence that perpetuates it?" (72). Ireland's own bloody early-twentieth-century revolution confirms how violence tends to legitimize patriarchy and its attendant hierarchical power relations, in this case substituting one form of oppression (English colonialist) for others (religious, nationalist, and capitalist).

Furthermore, as Cortright defines Gandhi's philosophy of resisting injustice, "[T]he means are the ends" (18); if their means are just, movements will have success, even when they fail to achieve short-term goals. Activists can build enduring professional and personal bonds founded on abiding mutual beliefs, rather than shared antipathies that are often fleeting and self-defeating. According to Wink, "The issue ... is not just which [means of resistance] *works* better, but also which *fails* better. While a nonviolent strategy also does not always 'work' in terms of preset goals—though in another sense it always 'works'—at least the casualties and destruction are far less severe" (54). As Samuel Beckett wrote late in life, "All of old. Nothing else ever. Ever tried. Ever failed. No Matter. Try again. Fail Again. Fail better." Combining feminist cultural inquiry with ideas from peace studies scholarship allows us to learn from the mistakes of our forebears, reexamine our principles, and hopefully become increasingly effective in our progress toward social justice and human rights for all.

Through dramatizations of humane, alternative modes of masculinity and femininity, films can play a crucial part in molding popular consciousness and raising awareness about marginalized historical figures. In my view, the greatest films in Irish cinema reflect the experience of a "defeated people" interrogating their own past (Cullingford 7), not as exercises in jingoism, but as a dialectical challenge to received dogmas. Sheridan and Greengrass lead the way in this respect, creating politically engaged cinema that validates ethical modes of human agency rather than any faction in national, social, or religious conflicts.

Methodology

As Thomas Schatz indicates, looking critically at movie genres helps us understand what these narrative formulas reveal about particular societies. As part of a cinematic dialogue with their audiences, westerns, family melodramas, and boxing films repeatedly pose and answer the same troublesome questions, usually revolving around love, success, and violence. In recent years genre approaches have combined with other scholarly approaches with productive results. Practitioners of representation studies, such as Charles Ramírez Berg, Donald Bogle, and Jack Shaheen, have done foundational work exploring how Hollywood films make meaning concerning race, specifically in the cases of Latinos, African-Americans, and Arab peoples. These scholars reveal the cultural implications of Hollywood's generic queries and responses; they track the way a hegemonic, and still overwhelmingly white American male, media juggernaut persistently marginalizes and stereotypes ethnic and racial Others.

Ramírez Berg's scholarship, however, is particularly exemplary in that, in addition to analyzing the problem of Hollywood's stereotyping of Latinos, it notes instances of resistance to these hegemonic portrayals and considers strategies for preventing stereotyping of all minority groups in the future. In the conclusion to *Latino Images in Film*, he states, "As we near the downturn of or even the end of Latino stereotyping, we need to be more, not less, vigilant. Film stereotypes are not dead, they just take on Other forms, targeting Other groups from society's margins" (271). As the example of the Irish in America has shown, some ethnic groups succeed collectively at the expense of other marginalized groups—just as men have often succeeded (on screen and in our society) at the expense of equally capable women. Recognizing and learning from such sociohistorical repercussions is an essential imperative for those engaged in representation studies.

This analytical model can and should be used as an approach to studies of gender in mainstream cinema. Indeed, critics like Laura Mulvey, Kaja Silverman and bell hooks have been doing this type of work, in one form or another, for decades: Mulvey investigates the male gaze in *film noir* in her seminal 1975 article "Visual Pleasure and Narrative Cinema"; Silverman does a psychoanalytic reading of social melodramas, such as William Wyler's *The Best Years of Our Lives* (1946), in her 1992 book *Male Subjectivity at the Margins*; and hooks analyzes images of gender and race in films as part of her overall critique of "white supremacist capitalist patriarchy" in popular culture and society. These are important touchstones for any film and cultural studies scholar. What such representation studies generally have not done, however, is to read gender across the works of individual mainstream filmmakers, or *auteurs*.

By the same token, scholars of Irish cinema have rarely combined gender studies with an *auteur* approach, particularly with respect to two of the three Irish filmmakers generally acknowledged as canonical: John Ford and Jim Sheridan (the other being Neil Jordan, whose representations of gender have often been dissected critically). The one excellent work in this vein so far is Elizabeth Butler Cullingford's chapter on "The Irish Western" in her 2001 book *Ireland's Others*, which includes a substantial consideration of Ford's *oeuvre* in terms of gender and ethnicity. Scholars such as Ruth Barton, Martin McLoone, and Brian McIlroy have analyzed Sheridan's cinema in terms of politics and its portrayal of the Troubles in Northern Ireland, and Luke Gibbons, Barton and McLoone have contributed to the discourse on Ford's depiction of Irishness in *The Quiet Man*. In these works, however, gender is a secondary concern.

Therefore, this book will apply the methodologies of representation studies and *auteur* studies to masculinity in the works of John Ford, Jim Sheridan, and Paul Greengrass. All three directors have been critically acclaimed and commercially successful. Achieving such a difficult artistic balance in the tremendously expensive enterprise of film production generally means that a filmmaker has done creative work within established genres, and this is certainly the case with these three directors, as well as other world-renowned *auteurs* of the twentieth century, like Alfred Hitchcock, Akira Kurosawa, and Martin Scorsese.

The guiding questions of Chapters 1 through 4 are the following: 1. How do Ford and Sheridan portray men and women in their generic narratives, and how do their often original engagements with Hollywood formulas affect their representations of gender? 2. What are Ford and Sheridan's engagements with the traditions of Irish and Hollywood cinemas (both of which have consistently favored a handful of gendered types in their narratives)? 3. How do these directors portray violence and its impact on perpetrators and victims, and what are the political implications of these representations? 4. What are the cultural and political implications of Ford and Sheridan's dramatic renderings of family life?

In approaching Paul Greengrass's early twenty-first century Irish cinema, I am principally concerned with his narrative focus on male peacemakers, as well as his use of documentary filmmaking techniques to "dramatically reconstruct" Irish historical trauma and the implications this practice has in terms of gender and politics. The deeply unsettling, richly contextualized representation of political violence in his work comes as a welcome, radical departure from the simplistic depictions of violent conflict typical of Hollywood cinema. I view his work as an extension of the dialogue about gender, conflict resolution and Irish identity that Ford treated seriously from 1939 to 1966 and that Sheridan continued in the five films he made from 1989 through 2002.

Therefore, I am interested equally in how filmmakers have worked within generic formulas to create complex, progressive representations of masculinity, and the potential for *auteurs* to successfully craft experimental narratives featuring alternative conceptions of gender outside the mainstream. In my view, these two kinds of cinematic narratives have a symbiotic relationship. For example, there is a way in which prominent big-budget historical epics from the early 1980s, such as *Reds* (Warren Beatty, 1981) and *Gandhi*, with their unconventionally heroic male protagonists (neither kills anyone and both finally die onscreen), helped condition Western culture to look favorably upon the peaceful male figures in Sheridan's genre-driven Irish films, which in turn paved the way for the pacifist heroes in Greengrass's low-budget, experimental Irish historical narratives. Subsequently, both Sheridan and Greengrass have "gone Hollywood," and while Sheridan has yet to achieve great success with a film outside the Irish context, Greengrass has directed two massive hits for Universal Studios: *The Bourne Supremacy* (2004) and *The Bourne Ultimatum* (2007). Both of these movies have reinvigorated the genre of the political thriller by openly questioning American foreign policy.

At the same time, the very concept of an Irish cinema remains tenuous due to Irish filmmakers' dependence on funding from English and American investors and producers. Therefore, I do not want to sound overly sanguine about the present or future condition of this national cinema. Making a sober assessment of the state of Irish film in 2002, the actor Stephen Rea contends, "We don't have a cinema of ideas, and if we completely latch ourselves onto the American cinema, we won't have one. They have a cinema of plots and effects. There are people like Altman, maybe the Coen brothers, who have ideas, but it's not how it is run" (*Keeping It Real* 200). However, considering the relatively tiny size of Ireland — 6.4 million people, if Northern Ireland is included — its creative impact on cinema, via both indigenous and foreign outlets, has been nothing short of astounding, and on the whole the artistic cross-pollination between Ireland and Hollywood has been amazingly productive for both nations.

What I hope the following study proves is that at least since the 1930s a select few filmmakers have engaged central questions of Irish history and identity, making provocative interventions into cultural and political discourse. With distinctive styles but similar thematic concerns, the works of John Ford, Jim Sheridan, and Paul Greengrass reflect the experience of colonialism and oppression while imagining alternative modes of manhood through portrayals of patriarchs, pugilists, and peacemakers. In my view, Ireland, in terms of its history as well as its cinema, has provided cultural critics an exemplary text for problematizing patriarchy and violence, as well as investigating and discovering nonviolent male identities and methods of peaceful conflict resolution.

In Chapter 1, "A Fragile Liberalism: Gender in John Ford's Pre–World War II Cinema," I place Ford's filmmaking practice within the dominant classical Hollywood paradigm and consider the director's narrative engagement with patriarchy and politics over the second half of his career (1939–66). Examining the exceptionally progressive masculine and feminine figures in several of his films from 1939–41, including *The Grapes of Wrath* and *How Green Was My Valley*, I contend that Ford achieved his most mature work with regard to both gender and politics during this short period.

Chapter 2, "The Persistence of Patriarchy: Gender and Politics in John Ford's Later Films," argues that the political transformation Ford underwent during World War II and the Cold War occasioned his movement toward a more militaristic view of American history in his films and a shift away from his earlier affirmations of complex gender identities. *The Quiet Man*, one of Ford's most successful post-war works, and one that remains perhaps the most influential film about Ireland, poses deeply troubling questions about patriarchy, capitalism and Irish identity, only finally to resolve them through a spectacular vindication of macho violence and female subordination. In addition, I address the meaning of John Wayne's star image and its relationship to Ford's work, and investigate other films in which Ford employs misogynistic images and themes, particularly *The Searchers* (1956) and his final feature, *7 Women* (1966).

In Chapter 3, "Assimilation, Integration, Continuity and Critique: Gender and Genre in the Hollywood Irish Cinemas of John Ford and Jim Sheridan," I begin by defining ten archetypes of masculinity and femininity that Ford habitually employs in his cinema, addressing their implications for Irish and American conceptions of gender. I then analyze direct artistic engagement with Ford's work, specifically Sheridan's *My Left Foot* (1989) and *In America*, distinguishing the latter director's representation of the Irish family from Ford's in terms of their use of Oedipal narratives and their dramatizations of matriarchal shifts in emigrant families.

Chapter 4, "Jim Sheridan: Reconstructing the Family, Redefining the Nation," analyzes the director's cinematic engagement with Irish history and politics, particularly the Troubles in Northern Ireland and the legacy of English colonialism. As Sheridan attests, his narratives address crucial voids in the nation's cultural discourse — such as stories about good fathers and strong, complex mothers. Sheridan endeavors to diagnose the ills of the colonized patriarchal family in *The Field*, and then reconstructs the family using alternative modes of masculinity, including the prisoner, the peacemaker, and the pugilist, with *In the Name of the Father* and *The Boxer*. Examining the director's deployment and negotiation of Hollywood formulas, I argue that his deft manipulation of various generic elements creates dynamic narrative hybrids, a strategy that has contributed to his films' international critical and box office success.

The final chapter, "Alternative Masculinity and Irish Historical Trauma in Paul Greengrass's *Bloody Sunday* and *Omagh*," investigates two recent Irish films that repudiate violence and patriarchy while cathartically revisiting deeply painful events at the heart of Irish and Northern Irish identity. I argue that Paul Greengrass's *Bloody Sunday* offers a "dramatic reconstruction" of the titular massacre both as a testament to the innocence of the victims and as a poignant elegy for a viable nonviolent resistance movement, which was also a casualty of brutal colonial repression on that day in 1972. Additionally, I examine the film *Omagh* (co-written and produced by Greengrass, and directed by Pete Travis) as another cinematic attempt to deal with political violence and trauma by advancing a mode of masculinity based on productive grieving and peaceful activism.

CHAPTER 1

A Fragile Liberalism: Gender in John Ford's Pre–World War II Cinema

> He always saw himself as a descendant of peasants, and loved nobility and fancy titles, surrounding himself with important people whenever he could. He was impressed by them and felt they legitimized him. Even his own tombstone reads "Admiral John Ford." It doesn't read "Director John Ford." — MAUREEN O'HARA[1]

Whether portraying Abraham Lincoln's coming-of-age, Wyatt Earp at the OK Corral, or the U.S. cavalry battling Apaches on the southwestern frontier, John Ford's films express profound ambivalence about American history and culture. As a patriotic — and at times, jingoistic — supporter of U.S. military and foreign policy, he believed in the greatness of his native country, but as a proud ethnic Irishman, he was exceptionally sensitive to the predicament of marginalized peoples and communities. Born in Maine to Irish immigrant parents in 1894, Ford (né John Martin Feeney) evinced an appreciation for Irish drama throughout his career: he filmed adaptations of Sean O'Casey's *The Plough and the Stars* (1936) and Lady Gregory's *The Rising of the Moon* (1957),[2] and he later developed a biopic, *Young Cassidy* (1965), which was based on O'Casey's life and dramatized the 1916 Easter Rising.[3] The tempestuous pastoral romance of *The Quiet Man* (1952) also strongly echoes the tragicomic tone, though not the subversive cultural critique, of J.M. Synge's *The Playboy of the Western World*.

While indisputably the first great director of Irish-themed feature films, Ford's principal cinematic endeavor was investigating the foundational dilemmas of American national identity, such as Manifest Destiny (in his westerns) and class stratification (in almost everything he did).[4] In the process he consistently placed markedly ethnic (though usually white) working- and middle-class characters at the center of his films. As Charles Ramírez Berg argues, "The progressiveness of Ford's cinema came from consistently taking the side of the oppressed against the mainstream." For Ramírez Berg, however, the filmmaker's liberalism was a double-edged sword: "[Ford's] overarching project was to elevate Irish and European ethnics above WASP elites, not to put people of color down. Unfortunately, in trying to accomplish the former he often ended up doing the latter" (152). While Ford's films privilege the experience of white ethnics in conflict with representatives of WASP hegemony, they often employ dangerous stereotypes in portraying people from other marginalized groups: specifically, African-Americans, Asians, Latinos, and Native Americans.[5]

In Chapter 2 I argue that, just as Ford's affirmative portrayals of ethnic (usually Irish-) Americans often wind up reinforcing racist ideas, his commitment to valorizing certain archetypes of masculinity frequently serves to uphold dominant Western attitudes about the legitimacy of patriarchy and the necessity of female subordination. Thus, Ford's limitations as a filmmaker are just as apparent in his representations of gender as in his conceptions of race, and in this respect his post–World War II works, particularly his collaborations with the Irish-American actor John Wayne, become increasingly reactionary. *The Quiet Man* (1952), one of the first Hollywood features to be shot (in part) on location in Ireland since the Silent Era, provides a particularly illustrative case in point, as the Irish nation itself becomes for Ford a therapeutic place of patriarchal and ethnic purity and completeness.

In this chapter, however, I analyze those Ford films that break from the Classical Hollywood pattern of privileging dominant masculinity. Particularly in several of the pictures he made just prior to the United States' entry into World War II, Ford seemed remarkably open to non-violent, egalitarian forms of masculinity, as well as female figures invested with significant power. Thus, in terms of portraying gender relations, Ford's most mature work came right in the middle of his career.

In recent years, Ford's westerns have been the focus of most scholarly attention devoted to his work: articles by Richard Maltby and Douglas Pye in *The Book of the Western* (1996); William Darby's *John Ford's Westerns* (1996); *John Ford Made Westerns* (2001), edited by Gaylyn Studlar and Matthew Bernstein; and *John Ford and the American West* (2004) by Peter Cowie. A handful of excellent articles specifically devoted to Ford and gender have also appeared fairly recently: Robert D. Leighninger's "The Western as Male Soap Opera: John Ford's *Rio Grande*" (1998) and Studlar's piece in *John Ford Made Westerns* and her subsequent article collected in *John Ford's Stagecoach* (2003).

My study addresses a void in Ford scholarship by focusing on the director's representations of gender outside the western genre and by analyzing his conflicting and ambivalent portrayals of men and women over about half of his career: 1939 through 1966. In particular, I will examine *Drums Along the Mohawk* (1939),[6] *Young Mr. Lincoln* (1939), *The Grapes of Wrath* (1940), and *How Green Was My Valley* (1941) in this chapter; and in Chapter 2 I will analyze *The Quiet Man* along with several other films from late in Ford's career. Critical touchstones include Luke Gibbons' book on *The Quiet Man*, as well as the two recent Ford biographies, Scott Eyman's *Print the Legend* (1999) and *Searching for John Ford* (2001) by Joseph McBride. Along the way, I will briefly discuss a few of Ford's most ideologically conflicted westerns, particularly *My Darling Clementine* (1946), his cavalry trilogy (*Fort Apache*, 1948; *She Wore a Yellow Ribbon*, 1949; and *Rio Grande*, 1950), *Two Rode Together* (1961), and *The Man Who Shot Liberty Valance* (1962), as they relate to recurrent themes and patterns in the narrative and cultural content of his films. In the second half of Chapter 2 I will go into some depth considering *The Searchers* (1956) in terms of its representations of race and gender, as well as its centrality to critical perceptions of Ford's *oeuvre* and dominant ideas concerning John Wayne's star image.

Ford and the Hollywood Aesthetic

In addition to his own sympathies and prejudices, Ford's cinematic cultural critique was always severely limited by his adherence to the Hollywood mode of production, which heavily favored films with happy, tidy endings. As the director himself explained in an interview in the mid–1930s,

> There's nothing surprising about the difficulty of doing things you yourself believe in in the movies ... when you consider that you're spending someone else's money. And a lot of money. And he wants a lot of profit on it. That's something you're supposed to worry about, too.... [The studio's like] a market. Got to fight it every time. (qtd. in Eyman 161)

Thus, Ford's filmmaking practice constantly reflects the conventions of what David Bordwell calls "The Classical Hollywood Style." For Bordwell this term refers to both an extrinsic set of cinematic norms, including the "Hollywood ending," and the period 1917–1960. Significantly, that era encompasses nearly the entirety of Ford's career as a director of fiction films, which began in 1917 with *The Tornado* and ended in 1966 with *7 Women*.[7]

With a few notable exceptions— such as *My Darling Clementine* and *The Man Who Shot Liberty Valance*— Ford's narratives conclude on an affirmative and strongly sentimental note. Nonetheless, he often leaves room for doubt and ambiguity in terms of the ideological implications of his work. According to Bordwell, within the classical Hollywood paradigm such lingering questions have subversive potential: "If the ending, especially the happy ending, is inadequately motivated, then the film creates a possibly productive split of story from narration. By including an ending that runs counter to what went before, deviant narration indicates certain extratextual, social, historical limits to its authority" (83). One of Bordwell's prime examples of "deviant narration" is Ford's *How Green Was My Valley*, and indeed, as I will discuss in more detail below, that film performs an amazing narrative feat by essentially placing a potent leftist political message within the context of a sweetly nostalgic evocation of youthful innocence and familial love.

In many cases, though, Ford's conflicted finales make for stilted cultural commentary and deeply flawed cinema. In his article "The Margin as Center: the Multicultural Dynamics of John Ford's Westerns," Ramírez Berg explains why the director's attempts to place African-Americans (in *Sergeant Rutledge*, 1960) and Native Americans (in *Cheyenne Autumn*, 1964) at the narrative center of two of his late westerns fail artistically: the final scenes of both films occlude Ford's anti-racist message by reverting to utterly conventional resolutions involving white heterosexual romance.

In a similar vein, Ford employs a tragicomic structure in *The Quiet Man*, using the first 106 minutes of the film as a vehicle for interrogating patriarchal norms of marriage, culture and violence before finally restoring the male-dominated status quo through scenes of spousal abuse, fighting and drunkenness in the final 20 minutes. That the film should ask such unsettling questions about male dominance only finally to drop them in favor of a happy romantic (and affirmatively patriarchal) ending renders it a deeply disturbing work as a whole. Indeed, a consistently troubling facet of Ford's post–World War II cinema is his tendency to use his films' endings to mute or dismiss the subversive thematic concerns raised by their narratives.

Critics such as Luke Gibbons and Joseph McBride read the final moments of *The Quiet Man* as articulating, within the male-dominated Hollywood paradigm, a progressive message of female empowerment. In my view, however, *The Quiet Man* is indicative of Ford's post–World War II shift toward blatant sexism. The "taming of the shrew" romantic plots he relies on in three of his post-war films, *Rio Grande*, *The Quiet Man*, and *Donovan's Reef* (1963), become increasingly misogynistic, culminating in *Reef*'s finale, in which Donovan (John Wayne) declares that he has "made a human being out of" the much younger woman (Elizabeth Allen) he's about to marry, before proceeding to take her over his knee and spank her.

Whitewash at Fort Apache

For Ford sexism often goes hand in hand with militarism. An earlier, emblematic example of a disconcerting ideological reversal in one of his films comes in *Fort Apache* (1948), when the Irish-American Captain York (John Wayne) finally takes up the mantle of his fallen but much-maligned WASP commander, Lieutenant Colonel Thursday (Henry Fonda).[8] During the first two hours of the film, Thursday is portrayed as the story's principal villain and the epitome of hubris, as he repeatedly dismisses York's superior tactical knowledge and thwarts the romantic pairing between his daughter, Philadelphia Thursday (Shirley Temple), and another Irish-American officer, Lieutenant O'Rourke (played by Temple's actual husband, John Agar). At the film's climax, Thursday leads his men into a patently unnecessary and disastrous battle against a superior Apache force — with whom York had earlier brokered peace — leading to the slaughter of the commander and most of his cavalrymen.

In the film's final five minutes, however, the narrative does an abrupt about-face and features York — first haltingly, then enthusiastically — valorizing Thursday (essentially, a dark-haired Custer) as a hero and martyr: "No man died more gallantly," he tells a group of gullible reporters, "nor won more honor for his regiment." The *coup de grâce* of this jarring ending comes when York picks up the cavalry hat once worn by the man he had despised and proudly places it on his own head, as the film score pipes in the solemn strains of French horns. Then York goes out to lead his men in a military campaign against the friend — the Native American Apache — that Thursday has now turned into a bitter enemy. York's capitulation is distressing as an inducement to historical amnesia — he tells the reporters of Thursday's "bravery" and they eat it up — and as cultural commentary, suggesting as it does that aristocratic, racist egotism is not only acceptable but can serve a vital purpose in building morale and courting public sentiment in support of imperialist, genocidal oppression. As historian and cultural critic Garry Wills argues,

> [A] passive or minimal acceptance of the Thursday legend is one thing. To take on his persona, his characteristic sayings and garb, is quite another. They are the things we have been taught to resent, in contrast with Wayne's more humane bearing. We are led, now, to think that Wayne may also take on Thursday's attitude toward Indians.... The Cold War would take on many more casualties than artistic integrity, but in this case it also victimized art. (175–6)

Ford's final shots depict the cavalrymen, led by York, filing out of Fort Apache to pursue their foe, but he undercuts the triumphalism of these moments just slightly by indicating the presence of two women left to wonder and worry: Philadelphia, holding her dubiously named baby boy, Michael Thursday York O'Rourke, and Philadelphia's mother-in-law, Mrs. O'Rourke, whose husband was killed in battle as a result of Thursday's blunders. In this low-angle medium shot, which contrasts sharply with the foregoing and succeeding long shots of the men riding on horseback, the young wife watches

In *Fort Apache* (Warner Bros., 1948, dir. John Ford), York (John Wayne) completes his capitulation to Thursday's legacy, as Mrs. O'Rourke (Irene Rich), Lieutenant O'Rourke (John Agar), and Philadelphia (Shirley Temple) look on.

her husband, Lieutenant O'Rourke, go off to battle, and as played by the frequently beaming Shirley Temple, Philadelphia looks uncharacteristically solemn in this moment. Even more remarkable is the widowed Mrs. O'Rourke, who stands in the foreground wrapped in a black shawl, looking forlorn as she watches her only child, the young Lieutenant, set off to meet an uncertain fate. This shot, coming in the final minute of the film, lasts only ten seconds, but it has the effect of slightly redeeming this overwhelmingly jingoistic whitewash of an ending. It acts as a small gesture toward acknowledging the human consequences of militarism and patriarchy in the lives of these two women.

Earlier Ford films, particularly his work in 1939–41, accomplish far more in depicting complexity in the inner lives of female characters, as well as in portraying relatively unconventional modes of masculinity. In this period Ford was at his most progressive in terms of representing gender. Even his most successful film from the mid–1930s, *The Informer* (1935), for which he won his first of four Best Director Oscars (the last was for *The Quiet Man*), starkly contrasts with his 1939–41 work with respect to gender. The main

1. A Fragile Liberalism 27

Ford briefly pays tribute to the sacrifices of Philadelphia (Shirley Temple) and Mrs. O'Rourke (Irene Rich), who must stay behind, anxiously awaiting the return of husband, son and father Lieutenant O'Rourke in *Fort Apache* (Warner Bros., 1948).

male characters in *The Informer* are either stage Irish drunks or pious revolutionaries, and the leading women include a whore with a heart of gold and two stereotypically good, wholesome women: the protagonist's devoted mother and sister (who is also the love interest of a dashing IRA leader).

Just a few years later, though, Ford's career entered a brief but prolific golden age — during the years 1939–41 he made seven feature films— marked by an extraordinary maturity in portraying gender relations. In his documentary homage *Directed by John Ford* (2006), Peter Bogdanovich judges Ford's work during these three years as his "greatest sustained artistic achievement." Bogdanovich also suggests that Katharine Hepburn, who during the period of 1936–38 became the greatest (extramarital) love of Ford's life, may have had a notable and overwhelmingly positive impact on the director's work in the ensuing years. As biographer Scott Eyman attests,

> Certainly, it's true that Hepburn helped unlock Ford's ambition, freed it up. Before Hepburn, he was a high-line workaday director, given to expressing himself only infrequently. After Hepburn, he would rarely do anything else. It's not

hard to imagine Hepburn exhorting Ford to live up to the responsibilities of his great gift [174].

One can only speculate about the degree to which the intermittently radical proto-feminist Hepburn influenced Ford's representations of gender, but by all accounts her feminine autonomy was one of the qualities that most enchanted him. Although, as Eyman declares, "Hepburn was one of the few people of either sex Ford couldn't cow" (169), according to Joseph McBride, "[Her] free-spirited nature affected [him] like an aphrodisiac" (231). It seems to be more than mere coincidence, then, that in the wake of this passionate relationship Ford's films (of 1939–41) tended to challenge traditional patriarchal gender roles to an exceptional extent. In certain cases, Ford even went so far as to invest women with a degree of agency far exceeding their traditional, and classically Hollywood, roles as men's helpmates. Both *Drums Along the Mohawk* and *How Green Was My Valley* feature two strong women defying patriarchal strictures to assert themselves in private and public spheres.

Before the Fall: Female Agency and Enlightened Masculinity in *How Green Was My Valley*

How Green Was My Valley is an exceptional Ford film for several reasons. First of all, it features an unusually small number of his usual stock company of actors—specifically, Maureen O'Hara, in her first collaboration with Ford, and the Irish brothers Barry Fitzgerald and Arthur Shields—and neither of the director's two most frequent leading men—Henry Fonda and John Wayne. *Valley* concerns residents of a small Welsh coal town, not Irish ethnics, although at times Ford seems to conflate the identities of the two peoples: like Ford's Irish and Irish-Americans elsewhere, these Welsh villagers love drinking, dancing, singing, and the occasional scrap. As the narrator (the adult Huw Morgan) declares early in the film, "Singing is in my people as sight is in the eye." In addition, with union agitation and mining accidents driving its narrative, *Valley* represents one of Ford's most sympathetic and politicized portrayals of working-class people—along with *The Grapes of Wrath* from the previous year.[9]

Furthermore, the director's rendering of family and gender conflict in *Valley* is one of his most nuanced and compelling. Judging it "[o]ne of John Ford's very best films," the critic and film historian Glenn Erickson views *Valley* as "the strongest expression of the 'family' theme that becomes the key to understanding many of Ford's later movies." Although Mr. and Mrs. Morgan, the protagonist's mother and father, have a marriage that is traditional in many respects (he works in the mine, she does all the domestic work), Mrs.

Morgan consistently asserts her independence by chastising her generous but stubborn husband. In addition, as played by the dynamic Abbey Theatre veteran, Irishwoman Sara Allgood, Mrs. Morgan never hesitates to voice her opinion or intervene in public affairs when she deems it necessary. After her initially anti-union husband (Donald Crisp) becomes the target of unemployed unionized miners in town, Mrs. Morgan goes up to their meeting in the hills to defend her husband, threatening to kill anyone who harms him. Like Jane Darwell's Ma Joad in *The Grapes of Wrath*, Allgood's Mrs. Morgan proves her willingness to step outside her traditional homemaking role and fight to protect her family.

Similarly, the Morgans' only daughter, Angharad (O'Hara), bravely defends a "fallen woman" in chapel near the middle of the narrative, an incident which foreshadows the church fathers' inquisition of her own virtue near the climax of the film. Explaining her protest to the town's progressive young parson, Mr. Gruffydd (Walter Pidgeon), she cites Jesus' benedictory command to an adulterous woman in John 8 to "Go, and sin no more" (8:11),[10] thereby upholding Christian principles of forgiveness and mercy and defying pious moralizing and patriarchal intolerance. Angharad's ultimate, unwarranted ostracism comes as a result of the narrative's main romantic thread, which concerns the ill-fated attraction she shares with Mr. Gruffydd. She propels this relationship by caressing his hand in an early scene and later visiting his home and initiating a kiss. Gruffydd resists acting on their mutual affection, however, because he feels he can't adequately provide for her: "No, I can bear with such a life for the sake of my work, but I think I'd start to kill if I saw the white come to your hair 20 years before its time ... I am no saint, but I have a duty towards you. Let me do it." It is only after Gruffydd rejects her that Angharad accepts a marriage proposal from the arrogant son of the local coal company baron, a tragic match that Ford underscores with a somber wedding scene punctuated by a long shot of Gruffydd standing in a cemetery, watching from afar as a frowning Angharad departs with her foppish groom. Thus, Angharad and Gruffydd's relationship represents not merely a repudiation of traditional gender roles, as she pursues him rather than vice versa, but the interaction of two unconventional and dynamic individuals constrained by their patriarchal community into denying themselves a lifetime of happiness together.

Throughout the film Gruffydd represents the antithesis of the positive but traditional masculine figures in the life of the film's young protagonist, Huw. While his father and brothers teach him to fist fight and ward off school bullies, Gruffydd helps him cultivate his mind through education and spirituality. For the parson the two realms are not mutually exclusive but one and the same: "Prayer is only another name for good, clean, direct thinking." As compellingly as any character in Ford's films, Gruffydd preaches and practices the two virtues the director held most dear: "justice and tolerance" (Ramírez Berg 152).

Portraying the opposition and ultimate ostracism that Gruffydd and Angharad face in their advocacy of community life based on equality, love and understanding, *Valley* enacts a potent critique of religion in its worst and most intolerant form: as a vehicle for upholding prudery, hypocrisy, and the socioeconomic status quo. When Gruffydd voices his support for the miners' union, stipulating that the workers should be careful to use "justice" in all their dealings, Mr. Parry (Arthur Shields), the senior parson in town, viciously upbraids him: "Are you coming outside your station in life, Mr. Gruffydd? Your business is spiritual.... The deacon shall hear that you've been preaching socialism."[11] Mr. Parry later leads the church fathers in denouncing, first the pregnant, "fallen woman" whom Angharad defends, and eventually Angharad herself. At the film's climax Gruffydd decries the scurrilous charges of Parry and the other church elders, urging them to accuse him of wrongdoing and leave Angharad alone: "You have forgotten the love of Jesus.... If you do this.... You blaspheme against Him and His word."

Along with industrialism and the gradual degradation of the green valley, intolerance spurred by religion spreads throughout the village and destroys the spirit of community. The adult Huw attests in voice over, "As the slag had spread over my valley, so now a blackness spread over the minds of its people." While the churchmen prepare to publicly impugn the virtue of his daughter, Huw's father, Mr. Morgan, up to this point a devoted parishioner, vows, "If they do this thing, I will never set foot in the chapel again." Both Gruffydd and Mr. Morgan protest the church's destructive ignorance, but to no avail. In stark contrast to Ford's affectionate portrayals of the Church, Catholic as well as Anglican, in *The Quiet Man*, *How Green Was My Valley* dramatizes religious institutions' collusion with capitalism to defame, defraud and divide the people of working-class communities. At the same time, the film poignantly illustrates the persistent marginalization of non-traditional gender identities in the figures of Angharad and Mr. Gruffydd. Ford's treatment of social underdogs and noble romantic outsiders is never more inspired and affecting than in *Valley*.

According to Scott Eyman, during the making of this extraordinary picture Ford was uncharacteristically gentle, refraining from his frequent practice of dysfunctional manipulation and capricious tyranny on set: "Ford reined in most of his native sarcasm, because he couldn't afford to do or say anything that might cause [12-year-old actor] Roddy McDowall to freeze up. The story was told through his eyes, and he needed the boy emotionally open" (Eyman 239–40). McDowall himself later reflected that "Ford had created such an extraordinary sense of being together ... a total belonging" during the shoot (Eyman 241). The director's less autocratic approach in this case was very much tied to professional expediency — and he was notorious, by his own and others' accounts, for doing whatever he believed was necessary to elicit strong performances from his actors. Yet the idea of Ford as the magnanimous taskmaster at the helm of *Valley* fits perfectly with the spirit of the film.

Drums Along the Mohawk: Negotiating Gender Identity on the Frontier

During the late 1930s and early '40s, Ford frequently represented unconventional heroines and heroes, even in a genre piece like *Drums Along the Mohawk*. In this Technicolor adventure film about frontier life and warfare circa 1776, Lana Martin's (Claudette Colbert) narrative significance equals, and in some respects surpasses, that of Gil, her husband, played by Henry Fonda.[12] With respect to gender equity, however, Ford's historical drama starts off unpromisingly, to say the least. After the main title sequence, the first shot of the film features a close-up of Lana's marital bouquet quivering in her unsteady hands before zooming out to reveal her nervous face as she takes her wedding vows. Gil, on the other hand, takes his vows with a placid smile.

Although Lana does show sexual agency by beckoning Gil up to bed (at a wayside inn) on their wedding night, she loses her composure again once they arrive at their new home, a cabin Gil has built in the wilderness of New York's Mohawk Valley. When Gil's Native American friend, Blue Black,[13] comes into their place unannounced in the dark of night, Lana becomes hysterical. She screams uncontrollably until Gil intervenes and slaps her. He immediately displays batterer's remorse, explaining, "I'm sorry, Lana, I had to." Then Gil apologizes to Blue Black, who goes off and returns shortly thereafter to present Gil with a large varnished stick. Blue Black instructs, "You got fine woman. But you young man. You use this on her. Lick her good! Make fine woman." Gil takes the stick, taps it in his hand several times, walks to the fireplace, and rather than throwing it into the fire, he places it on hooks right below the mantle.[14] He then turns to Lana and smiles as the scene ends, suggesting that he knows his power as a husband, but he will choose to use it benevolently — and indeed he does in the succeeding narrative. He never hits Lana again, perhaps because she has "learned her lesson"; however, it also seems reasonable to conclude from succeeding events that Gil grows to appreciate his wife as a relatively equal partner and learns to respect her autonomy.

After the opening scenes of *Drums Along the Mohawk*, Lana takes on a much more active role in the narrative and in her marriage. She works with Gil in their wheat fields, takes on domestic work outside the home, cares for her husband when he's wounded, and ultimately uses his gun to shoot an

"Indian" attacker. By the same token, one of the most poignant moments of the film comes at the end of the second act during a party and dance (a Ford film staple) when Gil slips away from the revelry to look in on their newborn son. Unbeknownst to Gil, Lana follows him upstairs and watches as he dotes on the baby. Outside the door in the shadows, Lana whispers a prayer: "Please, God. Please let it go on like this forever." Filmed from her point of view and representing her deepest desires, this scene shows Lana articulating her yearning for a marriage and family life in which her husband acts as a caregiver as well as a provider, just as she does.

This and other key sequences mark Lana as the film's protagonist — or, at least, as a dual protagonist, along with Gil. Earlier, after their local parson demands that every able-bodied man "16 to 60" serve in the militia or face summary hanging, Gil and the other men in their frontier community leave to fight encroaching Loyalist forces. Rather than emphasizing the martial bearing and exploits of the militiamen, however, Ford focuses on Lana and the other frontier women who must stay behind and wait. Thus, *Drums* much more effectively serves to underscore the full human toll of war — exacted on women as well as men — than the analogous farewell scene at the end of *Fort Apache*. As she watches Gil march off to battle, Lana seems to become the film's narrative center, a turning point that Ford emphasizes stylistically with a striking low-angle shot of his heroine looking on in stoic anguish. At this moment, Lana's emotions are the focus of the story, while Gil's are secondary. When the men do return, instead of depicting Gil's march home, the narrative stays with Lana as she searches for and finally finds him wounded and collapsed along the road.

In addition to Lana, the film features another of Ford's most compelling and independent female characters: Mrs. McKlennar (Edna May Oliver). After Indians torch Gil and Lana's house, they both go to work for the widow and live in an adjoining house on her farm. Mrs. McKlennar is a sagacious firecracker; she is irreverent, self-assured, and sensual. Upon meeting and employing them, she declares to Gil and Lana, "I hate any housework.... I took good care of my husband. Now he's gone, I do as I like. I've got a long face, and I poke it where I please." She also makes no secret of her matronly crush on Gil as she kisses him on the mouth before he goes off to battle; later, when she's mortally wounded, she tells him, "Good-bye, good-lookin.'" Like Lana, she does "men's work" and carries a gun. Only during the scene of her death does Ford soften the edge of her proto-feminist autonomy, as the widow finally calls out for "Barney," her late husband.

Along with its intermittent valorization of rugged femininity, *Drums Along the Mohawk* features a remarkably complex male hero, especially considering the film's genre. After utilizing patriarchal violence against his wife at the outset of the narrative, Henry Fonda's Gil proceeds to become a gentle

Lana (Claudette Colbert) tends to her wounded husband, as Gil (Henry Fonda) tells her about his harrowing experience of battle in *Drums Along the Mohawk* (20th Century–Fox, 1939, dir. John Ford).

husband and father, as well as a brave, but reluctant, soldier. After Lana finds him wounded and brings him home, Gil, while seemingly in a state of shock, relates in detail the atrociousness of battle as Lana cleans his wounds. He tells her of a fellow militiaman having his "head half blown off"; he describes his repulsion upon seeing his friend, Adam (Ward Bond), smiling amidst the carnage ("I was thinking, 'He's having a good time. He likes this'"); and he expresses empathy for his Native American enemies and anguish over having killed one of them at close range. Throughout the darkly lit scene, Fonda lies prone and his blue eyes pierce the shadows. Gil ends his account by saying, "Out of 600 of us, about 240 were still alive. But we'd won. We licked them. We showed them they couldn't take this valley. Lana, do you hear? We'd won." Then he passes out.

In typical Ford fashion, his hero ultimately justifies the use of violence on the frontier, but Gil's ambivalent emotions reflect the conscience of a sensitive man who has refused to become dehumanized, or to dehumanize his adversaries, as a result of traumatic, violent conflict. Gil never neatly conforms to the stoic avenger figure so prevalent in American action/adventure pictures.[15] In contrast to Mrs. McKlennar's description of her husband Barney as a man who had gone off to battle "loving it," Gil takes no pride or satisfaction in the act of killing, and Ford shows Gil shooting enemies only during one scene. Further attesting to his reluctance to fight, the morning after describing the horror of war to Lana, he declares, "While I was out there, I kept thinking about you all the time—about how good it'll be when everything's over and we can all go back home."

In the same vein, at the film's climax Gil's greatest act of bravery comes in the form of evasion rather than confrontation: he leaves the besieged fort, where he, Lana and the rest of the surviving militiamen and their families have been holding on for dear life, and he outruns three Indian braves for several hours to reach a neighboring fort and call in reinforcements. Ford uses this chase to mount a riveting action sequence (and capture a glorious Technicolor sunset), but the hero succeeds only by avoiding a fight, not courting one. Complementing the strong and independent female figures of Lana and Mrs. McKlennar, Gil Martin's predominantly humane conduct in love and war and Henry Fonda's youthfully vulnerable demeanor mark *Drums Along the Mohawk* as a remarkably progressive depiction of gender relations in a twentieth-century Hollywood war film.

Oedipal Romance and Spiritual Paternity in *The Grapes of Wrath*

With his 1940 film adaptation of John Steinbeck's classic novel *The Grapes of Wrath*, Ford posits the working class family as the heart and soul of the American nation, while his representations of women in this film adhere more closely to established Irish and American archetypes. As Ma Joad declares in her final speech, "Rich fellas come up and they die, and their kids ain't no good and they die out, but we keep a-comin.' We're the people that live. They can't wipe us out, they can't lick us. We'll go on forever ... 'cause we're the people." This piece of dialogue, which isn't in Steinbeck's book, acts as Ford's (and screenwriter Nunnally Johnson's) explicit statement of the narrative's populist politics.

Although Ford makes no overt references to ethnicity in *The Grapes of Wrath*, he had the Irish experience in mind as he was making the film. As he explained in his later years to Peter Bogdanovich,

> [It] appealed to me—being about simple people—and the story was similar to the Famine in Ireland, when they threw the people off the land and left them wandering on the roads to starve. That may have something to do with it—part of my Irish tradition—but I liked the idea of this family going out and trying to find their way in the world [qtd. in Cowie 8].

Accordingly, Ford places a great deal of narrative emphasis on investigating the causes of the displacement of the "Okies." Early in the film, when Tom Joad (Henry Fonda) and Jim Casy (John Carradine) encounter the self-described "graveyard ghost," Muley Graves (played by Ford regular John Qualen), he recounts the details of his eviction at the hands of bank agents. Ford uses extended flashbacks to emphasize Muley's anguish as he watches his house bulldozed to the ground in a matter of seconds. As he speaks to Tom and Casy, Muley is frequently shot in darkly lit close-ups with his shadow looming large on the wall behind him. He is the face of bereavement and desolation.

Ford invests Muley — who appears in only this one extended sequence — with great significance as a testament to the losses suffered by all kinds of emigrants, as well as the callousness of the rich and powerful amidst disaster. Later, Tom Joad attests to the indifference of the ruling elite when he declares, "It looks like a lot of times the government's got more interest in a dead man than a live one." In this way, as Ford suggests, his cinematic document of the Great Depression can be viewed as a modern meditation on the Great Famine.

Not surprisingly, then, the working class characters in *The Grapes of Wrath* parallel the more identifiably ethnic figures of *How Green Was My Valley* in significant ways.[16] Like Mr. Morgan and his sons, the Joad men are the salt of the earth, and, like Mrs. Morgan, Ma Joad is tough and outspoken in dealing with the men of the family. Although Ford made the former film a year before *Valley*, in a sense *The Grapes of Wrath* begins where the later picture ends: with the loss of a home and of community, and the sorrowful departure that ensues.

Throughout their long westward journey the Joads experience moments of community engagement — particularly during the dance at the government labor camp late in the film — but all these interactions are fleeting. Following Ma's "We're the people" speech, the final shot of the film captures the Joad family's rickety truck cruising down the road with a sign warning "DANGER!" foregrounded in the center of the frame and the sun setting on the horizon. The Joads have endured tremendous losses and face an uncertain future, but they remain determined to uphold blood ties. As long as the family survives, it seems, so does the American Dream.

Ford constantly emphasizes the role shifts and reconfigurations necessary to maintain familial bonds in hard times. The nature of the film's complex gender dynamics reveals its startling juxtaposition of radical and traditional ideas, which is most clearly evident in the narrative's two central relationships: those of Tom Joad and Ma, and Tom and Jim Casy. Like *How Green Was My Valley*, *The Grapes of Wrath* features a tragic romance. In this case, though, Ford explores not a story of star-crossed lovers, but an intimate bond between a mother and son. His choice of camera angles and use of music, in particular, underscore the Oedipal tension between Tom Joad and Ma.

The strong mother holding together a downtrodden family is an archetype of Irish drama, from O'Casey to Brian Friel, and viewed in this way Ma Joad is more mythical than realistic.[17] In the course of the film her only agency comes in the form of caring for and protecting her family as best she can. As opposed to Mrs. Morgan in *Valley*, Ma never asserts herself in the public sphere, and whenever the men do find work, she stays behind to keep the home fires burning. By the same token, as played by Jane Darwell — at 60 years old, the quintessential portly matron — Ma completely lacks sensuality, which helps to blunt the subversive edge of her intense relationship with Tom.

Nonetheless, Ma's role in the narrative and in the Joad family is extraordinarily complex. In addition to having the final word in the film, she is the first of the Joads to greet Tom when he returns home after seven years in prison: both of these details are changed from the novel to foreground Ma as a principal character. Ford composes this first scene involving Tom and Ma as if it were a reunion of two lovers. She sees Tom approaching and goes out on the porch; when she steps outside, she walks into a low-angle close-up. Her eyes glowing with joy, she says, "Oh, thank God, thank God," and calls out, "Tommy!"[18] The succeeding shot features Tom stepping into a low-angle close-up as well. His eyes light up, and he answers, "Ma!" They rush to each other and stop just short of embracing, as Tom reaches out to shake her hand. Ford captures mother and son in a conventional romantic two shot — a medium shot with both figures standing in profile — and one that parallels a key moment in the courtship of *How Green Was My Valley*'s Angharad and Mr. Gruffydd (see figures 4 and 5 below). Ma then touches Tom's chest and arm, as if to make sure he's physically whole, and she asks,

> Did they hurt you, son? Did they hurt you and make you mean-mad? ... Sometimes they do something to you. They hurt you, and you get mad and then you get mean. Then they hurt you again, and you get meaner and meaner, till you ain't no boy nor man anymore — just a walking chunk of mean-mad. Did they hurt you that way, son? Why, I don't want no mean son.

Her questions not only reflect her anxiety about Tom's mental health in the wake of his long confinement, but also imply that she is concerned about whether imprisonment has compromised his sexual integrity. Thus, in this sense she seems to look upon Tom as her sexual property.

Once the family sets out on their journey west and they have endured a series of misfortunes, Ma's love for Tom takes on increasing urgency as it becomes clear that she needs him to take over as head of the family. After Tom kills a policeman in retaliation for Casy's murder, Ma begs him to remain in hiding and not to flee, citing the breakdown of patriarchal hierarchy: "There was a time when we was on the land.... We was the family — kind of

Top: Ford captures the reunion of Tom (Henry Fonda) and Ma (Jane Darwell) in *The Grapes of Wrath* (20th Century–Fox, 1940). *Bottom:* In *How Green Was My Valley* (20th Century–Fox, 1941), Ford uses a similar shot composition to depict the two star-crossed lovers (Walter Pidgeon and Maureen O'Hara).

whole and clear. But now we ain't clear no more. There ain't nothing that keeps us clear.... Your pa's lost his place — he ain't the head no more. We're cracking up, Tom. We ain't no family now. Don't go, Tom. Stay and help. Help me." Acceding to her wishes, Tom does stay and briefly supplants his father. When the family arrives at the government-run camp, which turns out to be a kind of egalitarian paradise, Tom speaks with the head administrator and remarks, "Ma's sure gonna like it here. She ain't been treated decent for a long while," indicating his nigh-romantic fixation on his mother's health and happiness.

Throughout the film, Pa Joad becomes more and more marginalized within the family.[19] When Tom finally does leave to go it alone, he bids goodbye to his father by kissing him on the forehead while he sleeps. Clearly, Tom's masculine authority now far surpasses that of his declining father. Ultimately, Pa openly admits his own dissolution: "You're the one that keeps us goin,' Ma. I ain't no good no more, and I know it." In a unique moment in Ford's cinema, Ma responds by positing a fundamental difference between the sexes: "Well, Pa, a woman can change better than a man. A man lives sort of, well, in jerks. Baby's born or somebody dies, and that's a jerk. He gets a farm or loses it, and that's a jerk. With a woman it's all in one flow like a stream."[20] Here Ma describes a form of female empowerment, though a seriously limited one. She suggests that women are more durable because they are more accepting — and, essentially, more passive — even though her own pivotal role in the Joad family up to this point contradicts this assertion. In any case, this is the closest thing to a feminist pronouncement that Ford ever makes.[21]

Ford's use of music (both non-diegetic and diegetic) throughout the film reinforces the centrality of the Oedipal romance and Pa Joad's decline in authority. The main title and end title themes are instrumental variations on the American folk song "Remember the Red River Valley," which is also used frequently as score music throughout the narrative, including the memorable scene in which Ma sits alone going through her personal effects and burning them on the night before the family leaves for Oklahoma. The song has obvious geographical significance for the Joads, but in the dance scene in the film's final act, when a band plays the tune, and thus the music becomes diegetic, it takes on deeper significance. Tom pulls Ma out onto the floor (while his amorous brother Al dances with a young female non-relative), and as he dances with her he sings the chorus of the song:

> Come and sit by my side if you love me
> Do not hasten to bid me adieu
> And remember the Red River Valley
> And the boy who has loved you so true.[22]

As her son implicitly professes his love for her, Ma first giggles delightedly at all this attention; then, her expression turns from joy to longing, as she seems to be anticipating his permanent absence.

The scene of Tom's departure and his "I'll be everywhere" speech — the emotional high point of the film and a monumental moment in American cinema — provides the climax and resolution of the Oedipal romance as well. After Ma wakes to find Tom sneaking off in the night, she stops him. As they sit on the edge of the now-desolate dance floor, Tom tells her the reasons for his impending flight and his plans for the future. He avows that his main regret in leaving is missing Ma's American Dream come to fruition: "I'd like to be with you and see your face when you and Pa get settled in some nice new place. I'd sure like to see you then. But I won't never get that chance, I guess now."

After Tom finishes his political statement of purpose speech, the scene culminates with Ma kissing her son on the cheek and him reciprocating. Drawing a parallel to the earlier scene of their reunion, Ford once again uses the romantic two shot as the mother and son bid each other farewell. In a sense, they are consummating their love. As is their custom, Tom had simply taken her hand to say good-bye, but with the disclaimer, "Tom, we ... ain't the kissing kind, but—"Ma initiates the embrace and kiss.[23] As shown in Figures 6 and 7 below, mother and son's final, and only, embrace is staged in a manner remarkably similar to the one shared by Angharad and Mr. Gruffydd in *How Green Was My Valley*, which is also their most intimate moment in the film. In each case, Ford, representing a love bound by social limitations, foregrounds a woman's hand perching chastely on a man's shoulder, while the male figure's arm remains at his side. Like Angharad and Gruffydd, having finally overcome their emotional repression and expressed their feelings, Ma and Tom must now part. As Tom walks off toward the horizon, the score swells into "Remember the Red River Valley" once again. Thus, Ford pushes the Oedipal romance as far as it can go within the Classical Hollywood paradigm.

By remaining the principal object of Tom's love, Ma has helped prevent him from committing to a wife and children of his own. In a Freudian psychosexual sense, she has seriously stunted his growth into manhood. At the same time, though, Ma (together with seven years of prison) has endowed Tom with a protracted intellectual adolescence, allowing him to develop a political consciousness that supersedes the basic desire for genetic survival.

In addition to giving closure to Tom and Ma's sexually charged relationship, his big speech also completes the arc of the spiritual paternity plot involving ex-preacher and activist Jim Casy, reflecting Tom's conversion to the cause of working-class rebellion, as well as the further diminution of Pa Joad's authority as patriarch. As Tom explains to Ma, "I been thinkin' about ... Casy. About what he said, what he done. About how he died. And I remember all of it.... And I've been wondering [what might happen] if all our folks got together and yelled." Casy's mentorship and untimely death have led Tom to find a focus for his rage, and his last speech reveals his maturation into a

Top: Ma (Jane Darwell) and Tom (Henry Fonda) kiss good-bye in *The Grapes of Wrath* (20th Century–Fox, 1940, dir. John Ford). *Bottom:* Angharad (Maureen O'Hara) kisses Mr. Gruffydd (Walter Pidgeon) in *How Green Was My Valley* (20th Century–Fox, 1941, dir. John Ford).

man who has finally developed moral agency. As opposed to the young "Okie" farmer shown early in the film bulldozing Muley Graves' house — who justifies his actions by saying he needs the "three dollars a day" to feed his wife and children — Tom has resolved to follow Casy's example and sacrifice his own material well-being for the greater good.

Earlier, Casy finds his own moral center by becoming a union agitator, and he ultimately passes on his renewed spiritual calling to Tom. Having helped initiate a strike at a giant peach orchard, Casy tries to persuade his initially skeptical protégé, and in the process he expresses the core of his evolving philosophy:

> Tell them to come out with us, Tom. Them peaches is ripe. Two days out and they'll pay us [higher wages]. You'll have to take a beating before you'll know.... Tom, you've got to learn like I'm learning. I don't know it right yet myself, but I'm trying to find out. That's why I can't ever be a preacher again. A preacher's got to know. I don't know. I got to ask.

Throughout this lecture, Casy towers over Tom, who sits on the ground. He's shot from Tom's point of view at an extremely low angle, and near the end of his speech Casy crouches down over Tom for emphasis, creating a high-contrast close-up with his face glowing starkly in lantern light. Ford's use of lighting here both recalls the scene of Muley Graves telling his eviction story and anticipates the extended close-ups of Tom delivering his defining speech.[24]

One of the fundamental qualities that Casy models for Tom is this sense of ideological openness and defiance of easy certainties. As opposed to the powerful patriarchs — many of them played by John Wayne — in later Ford films, Casy is a father figure who eschews the pretension of absolute authority. He is a self-professed seeker who admits to not having all the answers. As he prepares to leave his mother and face an uncertain fate, Tom mirrors Casy's masculine ethos: "Maybe I can do something. Maybe I can just find out something. Just scrounge around and maybe find out what it is that's wrong. Then see if ain't something can be done about it. I ain't thought it all out clear, Ma. I — I can't, I don't know enough."

By the same token, Tom seems to be following Casy's lead by taking on a more placid demeanor and resisting the impulses to anger and aimless violent resistance that have caused him so much trouble to this point. Although he never expresses any regret for the two men he has killed — the first he drunkenly bludgeoned to death at a dancehall fight, which landed him in jail for manslaughter — Tom resolves to seek social justice, not personal vengeance. When Ma asks if he's "aiming to kill," he says, "No.... That ain't it."

In line with Ford's own ideological limitations, however, Casy's and Tom's progressive masculinity is somewhat muted by the fact that neither one of them evinces any desire to challenge the status quo with regard to women's place in society. While Tom declares to Casy in their initial conversation that, "I never let one get by me if I could catch her," he never interacts with women outside his family. Considering his unusually close tie to his mother, his statement indicates a fear of female sexuality, as well as an obvious desire to exert control over women.

As for Casy, he seems to fall on the opposite end of the misogynist spectrum: he idealizes and exploits women. Recounting his fall from grace as a preacher to Tom, Casy explains that his problem with sex is having too much of a good thing: "A girl was just a girl to you. To me they's holy vessels. I was saving their souls." Casy loves women as sexual objects, though not necessarily as individuals, but he also looks upon them as temptresses who have caused his disgrace: "I lost the spirit." As I've suggested, though, Tom and Casy's lack of maturity with respect to women seems to be inextricably related to their exceptionally progressive views of labor politics. In this narrative world, one can be a noble agitator or a solid family man; times are too hard for anyone to attempt both.

The film of *The Grapes of the Wrath* prescribes working-class politics and Oedipal love as cures for what ails the Depression-era United States. Ford shows the necessity for patriarchy to shift, change and persist, and he pays homage to the devoted mothers and radical father figures who helped mold and sustain heroic idealists for the generation to come. The film constantly looks backward to an ideal past when the patriarchal family was, in Ma's words, "whole and clear," while at the same time, Ford envisions a far more just American society — one in which people act on Casy's and Tom's idea that "A fella ain't got a soul of his own, just a little piece of one big soul."

Thus, to the extent that Steinbeck's book and Ford's film reflected a revolutionary impulse in the American mindset, World War II came at an opportune time for the political and economic elite in the U.S. Instead of, in Tom Joad's words, "One guy with a million acres" being the common enemy of "a hundred thousand [starving] farmers," the attention of the restless and downtrodden was directed abroad to the Japanese and the Germans. A year after making *The Grapes of Wrath*, and just two weeks after completing *How Green Was My Valley*, Ford himself joined the U.S. military, in which he would serve for over three years as a lieutenant colonel in charge of a Field Photographic Unit; his mission was "to record the history of the Navy in World War Two" (Eyman 251).

That war and the ensuing U.S.-Russian conflict served to temper Ford's left-leaning politics with a reverence for militarism, which in my view contributed to his increasingly less complex and more misogynistic portrayals of women. His misogyny and validation of patriarchal violence are most clearly evident in a number of his films starring John Wayne, and it's no accident that Ford's pre-war collaborations with Henry Fonda are some of his most progressive works in terms of gender.

Ford and Fonda: Interrogating Violent Masculinity

Throughout his career, Henry Fonda was extraordinarily adept at embodying alternative male heroism.[25] From 1939 to 1948 Ford and Fonda used their frequent collaborations (six fiction features in all), not only to create some of the best films of the period and of their careers, but also to ask some penetrating questions about the meaning of manhood and the nature of violence. In addition to his work with Ford in *Drums Along the Mohawk*, *The Grapes of Wrath* and *Fort Apache*, Fonda played the titular *Young Mr. Lincoln* (1939), the legendary Wyatt Earp in *My Darling Clementine* (1946), and an enigmatic priest in *The Fugitive* (1947).

In *Young Mr. Lincoln*, Ford and Fonda's first joint venture, the eponymous hero effectively uses the threat of violence to resolve conflicts peacefully. In one instance, Lincoln — a self-described "jack-leg lawyer" in the rural town of Springfield, Illinois— mediates a trivial property dispute between two obstinate old farmers. After the men refuse to accept the reasonable compromise proffered by Lincoln, he resorts to a veiled form of intimidation, calmly proposing the rhetorical question, "Gentlemen, did you ever hear about the time in the Blackhawk War when I butted two fellas' heads together, and busted both of them?" The two farmers get the message, and they immediately agree to the young lawyer's terms.

Later, during the film's crucial middle sequence, Lincoln again uses counterintuitive means to defuse a more volatile situation. In the wake of a murder the men of Springfield have formed a lynch mob, intending to impose swift justice on the two brothers charged with the crime. When the mob besieges the jailhouse and takes up a giant log to bust down the door, Lincoln intercedes. Standing on the steps of the jail and speaking down to the mob, he rolls up his sleeves and declares, "Now, gentlemen, I'm not up here to make any speeches. All I got to say is I can lick any man here, hands down." This challenge initially evokes laughter from the crowd, but when the biggest bully among them steps forward, Lincoln exhorts him to "come up and whet your horns," and the man backs down. Throughout the scene Ford uses point-of-view shots to heighten the tension and encourage viewer identification with Fonda's "Honest Abe," who even implores his audience at one point, "Let's look at this matter from my side."[26]

Lincoln effectively combines humor, menace and persuasive reasoning — a masculine formula crucial to his success as a frontier lawyer and, by implication, his political success later in life. After threatening the lynch mob to gain their respect and attention, he jokes with them for a few moments before turning serious: "Trouble is, when men start taking the law into their own hands ... they're just as apt to hang a man that's not a murderer as one who is.... We do things together that we'd be mighty ashamed to do by ourselves."[27] He then moves from this plain-spoken rhetoric to a quote from scripture: "Blessed are the merciful, for they shall obtain mercy." Appealing to the Christian virtues of "justice and tolerance"—those that Ford upheld most consistently in his work—Fonda's Lincoln also illustrates the director's belief, which became more explicit in his post–World War II films, that to achieve justice a man must be ready, willing and able to use force. The fact that Lincoln never has to resort to violence or brandish weapons to keep the peace, however, can be seen as a measure of Ford's pre–World War II openness to a mode of manliness that wasn't tied to violence. The parallel figures of Jim Casy (along with, ultimately, Tom Joad) and Mr. Gruffydd from Ford's films of this period represent his willingness to valorize unconventional—that is, non-military, non-official, non-phallic—forms of masculinity.

Twenty-three years and two American wars later Ford's faith in peaceful masculine practices seemed to have utterly vanished. 1962's *The Man Who Shot Liberty Valance* portrays Ransom Stoddard (James Stewart), another idealistic young frontier lawyer, as naively out of touch with the reality of being a man in a violent world. Nearly every element of the film — narrative structure, dialogue, characterization, and costume design, as Stoddard never wears a hat and frequently sports an apron—functions to emasculate the lawyer and draw an unfavorable comparison between him and the narrative's true hero, Tom Doniphon (John Wayne), the black hat-clad, macho gunslinger. The film's principal female character, Hallie (Vera Miles), who is courted by Doniphon but ultimately becomes Stoddard's wife, is revealed as a pitiable figure: the film implies that her tragedy is having chosen the fictitious killer over the real one.[28]

Only in the poignant schoolroom sequence near the midpoint of the film does Ford encourage viewer identification with Stewart's character and allow his narrative of clashing masculine codes to become fully dialectical. With the phrase "Education is the basis of law and order" scrawled on the blackboard behind him and featured prominently throughout the scene, Stoddard attempts to teach his motley group of salt-of-the-earth pupils about fundamental American principles. He tells them, "The governing power [of the American republic] rests with the electorate — now that means you ... the people," and explains the power of the press ("an honest newspaper") to illuminate issues and influence elections. Thus, he briefly models a masculine and democratic practice strongly opposed to Doniphon's vigilantism. Yet this lesson is cut short by the incursion of Doniphon, who declares that Stoddard's students are "wasting ... time" in light of the violence surrounding them: "Votes won't stand up against guns." Once his pupils have dispersed, Stoddard erases his mantra — "Education is the basis of law and order" — from the board and bitterly concedes to Hallie, "You heard what Tom said: when force threatens, talk's no good anymore." Then comes the revelation that Stoddard himself has been learning to shoot, further underscoring the primacy of Doniphon's masculine praxis.

Earlier, though, in his three complete post–World War II collaborations with Henry Fonda,[29] Ford offered muted critiques of the American cultural equation of masculinity with violence, even when the trajectory of his narrative clearly led toward deadly conflict, as in the case of 1946's *My Darling Clementine*. Perhaps due to its deceptive simplicity as a western narrative, as well as its remarkable subtlety and economy, this film stands apart as one of the finest of the Ford/Fonda films. The use of profound silences in the film allows Fonda to breathe life into the figure of Wyatt Earp and turn a mythic lawman into an extraordinarily compelling protagonist. Throughout the film, Earp avoids violent confrontation whenever possible, and his desire for peace is epitomized by his habitual refusal to wear a gun. Even in the final shootout sequence at the OK Corral, Ford and Fonda foreground Earp's reluctance to kill, as the sheriff holds his gun awkwardly in his hand rather than holstered on a gun belt like an archetypal quick-drawing sheriff.

Fonda's character is a formidable man, but also an easy-going and sensitive one. One of the most extraordinarily poignant moments in the movie occurs when Earp accompanies Clementine (Cathy Downs) to the dedication of the First Church of Tombstone. When the revelers begin dancing, after the presiding town elder makes it clear that this church will have nothing against the practice, Earp stands looking pensively from the dancers to Clementine standing beside him. Ford uses a low-angle medium shot to contrast Clementine's placidity with Earp's shyness, which Fonda expresses brilliantly.[30] After a few moments of nervous contemplation, Earp finally works himself up to asking Clementine to dance. As the two take part in the celebration, they enter into the fold of this fledging community as well. All the narrative and human complications that follow this scene serve to reinforce the fleeting beauty and vitality it represents.

Perhaps the major flaw of *Clementine* lies in its failure to extend — as it does so well in portraying its principal male figures — a full range of humanity to its female characters. Producing gender dynamics similar to many of the Oedipally charged *films noir* of this period, Ford uses narrative and stylistic elements to diametrically oppose Clementine, the idealized "good woman," to the film's *femme fatale*, Chihuahua, a barroom prostitute who leads Earp's troubled pal, Doc Holliday (Victor Mature), down a road of dissolution and vice and away from the wholesome, back–East goodness of Clementine. Chihuahua ends up completely ostracized and condemned when Billy Clanton, one of the film's gang of baddies, sleeps with her and later shoots her. Although Linda Darnell, who played Chihuahua, was the second billed actor in the film, her character dies off-screen after Holliday fails to save her life with surgery. The Anglo Clementine's fate falls on the opposite end of the traditional feminine spectrum from that of her half-breed Mexican prostitute counterpart:[31] she finally decides to stay in Tombstone and become the town schoolmarm.[32] Ford's employment of utterly conventional female types in *Clementine* epitomizes his movement away from complex representations of gender in his post-war films.[33]

Nonetheless, like *Young Mr. Lincoln*, in its representation of masculinity *My Darling Clementine* asks one of the most fundamental questions about patriarchy and society: Can men act assertively and do what is right without using violence? More specifically in the context of Ford's corpus of western films, can men promote justice and protect their families without harming others? Six years later, in *The Quiet Man*, the director asks a set of questions that are much less progressive: Can a man have a loving, functioning marriage without dominating his wife, and can he be accepted into a community if, when challenged, he refuses to employ violence to protect his property and reputation?

Ford's Good-bye to All That

Once again, of all Ford's heroes, it is *How Green Was My Valley*'s Mr. Gruffydd who most completely epitomizes the values of "justice and tolerance." Near the end of the picture — which would be Ford's last film before he entered military service in 1941 — Gruffydd preaches his final sermon to a faith community he now views as utterly corrupted by petty suspicion and "fear." Employing Phillip Dunne's beautiful prose and Walter Pidgeon's rich baritone voice, this speech is unparalleled in Ford's cinema.

Having honed his craft making silent films, Ford was notorious for pruning dialogue, which he looked upon as secondary and often unnecessary. In this climactic scene, however, he affords Gruffydd's lengthy monologue the full narrative weight it deserves. The sermon is precipitated by the actions of the hateful Mr. Parry and his many followers in the church, who have determined to hold a meeting to pass judgment on the strong-willed Angharad and possibly excommunicate her on the basis of her (falsely) alleged marital infidelity with Mr. Gruffydd.

Characteristic of his humble demeanor, the parson begins his homily by castigating himself along with his congregants: "You're cowards, too, as well as hypocrites. But I don't blame you. The fault is mine as much as yours. The idle tongues, the poverty of mind which you have shown, mean that I have failed to reach most of you with the lesson I was given to teach." Then Gruffydd moves to the back of the church, places his hand on young Huw's shoulder, and addresses his favorite pupil directly in a calm, resigned tone:

> Huw, I thought when I was a young man that I would conquer the world with truth. I thought I would lead an army greater than Alexander ever dreamed of. Not to conquer nations, but to liberate mankind. With truth, with the golden sound of the Word. But only a few of them heard, only a few of you understood.

After reflecting on his frustrated ambition and imparting his youthful ideals to Huw, he wheels around on the other worshippers, unleashing a scathing diatribe:

> The rest of you put on black and sat in chapel. Why do you come here? Why do you dress your hypocrisy in black and parade before your God on Sunday? From love? No. For you've shown that your hearts are too withered to receive the love of your divine Father. [Scoffs.] I know why you've come. I've seen it in your faces Sunday after Sunday as I've stood here before you. Fear has brought you here. Horrible, superstitious fear. Fear of divine retribution. A bolt of fire from the skies, the vengeance of the Lord and the justice of God. But you have forgotten the love of Jesus; you disregard his sacrifice. Death! Fear! Flames! Horror and black clothes! Hold your meeting, then. But know that if you do this in the name of God and in the house of God, you blaspheme against Him and His word.

With this clear-sighted affirmation of Christian love over base gossip- and fear-mongering, Gruffydd subverts religious and patriarchal tyranny. He passionately denounces the social pecking order enforced by pious intolerance and rejects the church leaders and their parishioners' amoral actions stemming from fear of a wrathful divine Father.

In Gruffydd's view, only through embracing and striving to emulate the compassion of Jesus—the son, both holy and human—can flawed people achieve grace and build a humane, enduring community, which he sees as the only force that can stand strong against the encroachment of capitalism upon the green valley. Gruffydd implores the parishioners to seek the peace which passeth all understanding, but they do not heed his words. They are corrupted by the pettiness and narrow-mindedness that preclude comprehension. Gruffydd cannot overcome the forces of greed and fear in the valley, but having molded the mind and spirit of Huw, the preacher's legacy of love and justice is assured.

In a time of countless human tragedies, one great artistic catastrophe was Ford's gradual shift away from the themes of compassion and community standing opposed to capitalism and modernity in his cinema. Having won consecutive Best Director Oscars (1940 and 1941) for *The Grapes of Wrath* and *How Green Was My Valley*, Ford was honored by the Academy as well for the war documentaries he made in 1942 and 1943, *The Battle of Midway* and

December 7. Like *How Green Was My Valley*, both of these films employ plaintive voiceover narration by the mellifluous Irving Pichel. As the adult Huw reflecting on a lost youth and community still "real in memory," Pichel declares, "How green was my valley then." In stark contrast, his main function in Ford's war propaganda films would be to demonize the Japanese and call for revenge against them. Repeatedly attesting to the "diabolical ... perfidy" of "the Japs," *December 7* closes with Pichel declaring, "Our faith tells us that to all this treachery [during the Pearl Harbor attack] there can be but one answer, a time-honored answer: 'For all they that take the sword shall perish with the sword.'" Brutally decontextualizing and distorting Jesus' invocation to Peter to put away his weapon and forego vengeance for his master's betrayal and arrest (Matthew 26: 47–56), this ending twists the Christian message of peace into a plank for propagating blind nationalism and bigotry.

In addition to Ford, a great number of Hollywood filmmakers put their art at the service of the Allied war effort by making propaganda pictures, including such liberal-minded *auteurs* as Frank Capra, George Stevens and William Wyler. Nonetheless, the dissonance between Ford's 1939–41 fiction films—amazingly progressive in terms of their portrayals of politics, gender and class relations—and his aggressively simplistic propaganda pieces is shocking testament to one of the many kinds of collateral damage sustained in wars: the loss of nuance and complexity, and therefore humanity, in art and mass media. Unfortunately, the ensuing Cold War, with its dire repercussions at home as well as abroad, pushed Ford yet further from his once-progressive views on men and women and their places in society.

CHAPTER 2

The Persistence of Patriarchy: Gender and Politics in John Ford's Later Films

> [T]here is an eerie fascination to the spectacle of Ford making movies in a way that unmade him. He destroyed his family in the process of creating stories to glorify the family. He dreamed up, out of his own lack of discipline, paeans to military and frontier disciplines. He made beauty out of ugly humiliation. His love scenes were hatefully confected. The happy endings were elaborated out of his own unhappiness, which he spread to others.— GARRY WILLS[1]
>
> When I direct a scene I always want to make the leading lady fall down on her derrière.— JOHN FORD, 1964[2]

Ford's post-war ideological shift toward aggressive militarism had enormous artistic and cultural impact.[3] The emerging reactionary bent in his films, particularly in his representations of gender, likely contributed to his success in weathering the political storm of the Hollywood blacklist years and the commercial challenges wrought by the advent of television. At the same time, though, Ford's changing worldview limited his vision and contributed to the unevenness of his later films. In addition, his shifting politics have, understandably, led to confusion about the director's legacy and the values—"justice and tolerance," above all—that he most consistently upheld, prompting even erudite critics such as Roger Ebert to conclude, mistakenly, that Ford was a lifelong conservative hard-liner. Ebert begins his 2002 "Great Movies" essay on *The Grapes of Wrath* by declaring, "John Ford's 'The Grapes of Wrath' is a left-wing parable, directed by a right-wing American director." That is an unfortunate misconception on the part of the great critic, but one that is in a sense legitimized by Ford's very real post-war tack to the right.

The years following World War II also marked the end, after 1947's *The*

Fugitive, of Ford's frequent collaborations with Henry Fonda as his principal star, and I believe this development moved the director further from the artistic pinnacle of his 1939–41 films. The humility and humanism Fonda brought to his heroic roles helped elevate Ford's work to a level of richness and compassionate insight that they would seldom reach again. These are films characterized by restrained beauty, muted triumph and abiding tragedy.

Like Walter Pidgeon's extraordinary turn as Mr. Gruffydd in *How Green Was My Valley*, Fonda's performances eschew the macho swagger and maudlin bonhomie typical of John Wayne's male figures. Scott Eyman remarks upon the contrasts in the masculine ethos of the two actors and their roles:

> Ford [used] Fonda in a very different way than he [did] John Wayne. Wayne's characters were earthy and warm, brawlers by temperament, capable of love and rage. Fonda's characters burned with a cold fire—they displayed strength, but a removed, abstracted, rather asexual strength, tempered by the actor's instinctive austerity [211].

Although I would cite Fonda's role of Gil Martin as evidence contradicting Eyman's suggestion that his characters were "asexual," the biographer effectively highlights some of the fundamental differences between the two stars.[4]

Wayne's star persona consistently exhibits a kind of domineering bravado that can seem like a grotesque caricature of manliness. Even in a more complex role, like that of aging cavalry officer Nathan Brittles in *She Wore a Yellow Ribbon*, the subtler elements of the performance tend to be overwhelmed by Wayne's trademark macho posturing. For instance, Brittles' frequent refrain to contrite subordinates is "Never apologize; it's a sign of weakness," a line which Wayne tears into with bombastic gusto.[5]

While Fonda usually played reserved characters, his performances evince far more emotional complexity than those of Wayne, who tends to alternate between fierce anger and cloying sentimentality. As discussed in Chapter 1, Fonda's semi-delirious speech recounting Gil Martin's experience of war in *Drums Along the Mohawk* simultaneously displays his character's anguish and pride over his actions in battle, as well as his deep vulnerability and need for his wife's sympathy and understanding. Wayne would never explore such deep ambivalence and emotional rawness in his film roles for Ford.

Ultimately, a crucial factor in the dissolution of Ford and Fonda's artistic partnership was their growing political differences. The star actor, who, like Ford, had served in the Navy during the war, later joined the Committee for the First Amendment, an organization founded to protest the House Un–American Activities Committee and the Hollywood communist blacklist.[6] Ford, on the other hand, served on the Tenney Committee and the Motion Picture Alliance for the Preservation of American Ideals, both of which actively supported the blacklist. As Joseph McBride states:

[Ford became implicated] more deeply in political tactics he would have found repugnant before the war and even as late as 1948. Influenced by the apocalyptic rhetoric of the cold war ... Ford, like many Americans, seemed increasingly willing to compromise basic civil liberties as a way of holding the line against the Soviet Union and protecting the United States from what they saw as the serious threat of internal subversion [472].

While Ford made political accommodations to ensure his continued success in Hollywood, Fonda gravitated away from film and toward the theater. After his work in *Fort Apache* in 1948, he did not play another major part in a motion picture until 1955's *Mister Roberts*, in which he reprised the title role he had made famous on Broadway. This film also marked Ford and Fonda's last project together, one that Ford would not complete. The two ended up coming to blows — Ford apparently struck first — during an artistic quarrel; Ford later became ill and had to be replaced as director.

Once close friends, the actor and director subsequently had a strained relationship, and they never collaborated on another film. Peter Fonda has suggested that the on-set fight between the two men was partially motivated by their increasingly disparate worldviews:

[Ford's] whole gang had gone way to the right ... and my father kept his head on his shoulders. He thought the House Un-American Activities Committee was terribly un–American. He was incensed by it; he walked across the street to shake hands with someone who was blacklisted. He and Ford and Wayne and [Ward] Bond had open disagreements, and then Bond suggested he was a pinko, and that was that [Eyman 436].

Although Ford did generally gravitate toward the Republican Party during this time and would "[end] his days supporting Barry Goldwater, Richard Nixon and the Vietnam War" (McBride 6), he never took such an extreme position as Wayne and Bond, both of whom were jingoistic anti-communists and supporters of Joseph McCarthy.[7] The director did, however, veer far enough to the right to make the documentary *This Is Korea!* (1951), a piece of pro-war, anti-communist propaganda that extols, among other weapons and tactics, the American military's use of napalm against their adversaries.

In his fiction films as well, Ford, who in the late 1930s had tried to develop a remake of Jean Renoir's anti-war masterpiece *Grand Illusion* (1937) (McBride 254), became more and more conventional in his valedictory portrayals of aggressive military men, many of them played by John Wayne. Ford also actively campaigned for the U.S. Navy to bestow more medals and honors upon him — to little effect. After serving additional time in the Navy to make *This Is Korea!*, though, he did manage to win the Navy's Air Medal and attain the rank of Admiral. Ford received official word about his promotion while on the set of *The Quiet Man*, and John Wayne supposedly reacted to the news by gleefully tossing the 57-year-old director into Galway Bay (McBride 510).

By 1950 Wayne had become the biggest box office attraction in the United States. Having "nimbly maneuvered to avoid volunteering or being drafted" during Word War II (Wills 65), Wayne nonetheless emerged as one of the most enduring images of the American soldier on the big screen, particularly through hit films like *Sands of Iwo Jima* (Allan Dwan, 1949). Subsequently, his personal politics increasingly came to reflect his star persona. According to Wayne's third wife, Pilar Pallette, "He would become a 'superpatriot,' for the rest of his life trying to atone for staying at home" (McBride 344). Despite the fact that Henry Fonda, who was two years older than Wayne, had volunteered to serve during the war and won the bronze star, his film career at this time was going in precisely the opposite direction of the Duke's.[8]

Thus, Ford's decision to embrace Wayne as his star of choice during the Hollywood blacklist years of 1948 through 1960 reflected not only the director's largely tacit support of right-wing politics during this time, but also his recognition of shifting market demands and public taste. Although Ford was privately contemptuous of Wayne for failing to enlist during World War II, he capitalized on the actor's growing stature during the early years of the Cold War.[9] Then as now, for ambitious filmmakers like Ford, Hollywood was a dirty game, but it was the only game in town.

Although Ford's films generally became less progressive in their take on gender relations as his career went forward and as Wayne became his regular collaborator, my contention is that his work continued to formulate cultural questions about gender, as well as questions about ethnicity and social class, even as he addressed those questions with less nuance and humanist compassion. In his seminal work on Ford's westerns, Charles Ramírez Berg explains how each of the director's movies in this genre functions to pose and answer a cultural question — usually about ethnicity and/or class— through the course of its narrative. For example, in *Drums Along the Mohawk* (which CRB classifies as a western) the "cultural dilemma" is "Can mainstream Lana learn to accept the margin?"; in *My Darling Clementine* the underlying question is "Can mainstream Clementine learn to accept the margin?" In both cases this cultural question is answered in the affirmative (145).

Along these lines, I would add that both of these works, as well as *Young Mr. Lincoln*, also ask cultural questions about masculinity and violence. In each case, Fonda's protagonist is a man who dislikes using force to solve problems, and the narrative dramatizes his dilemma of seeking peace despite violent discord in the world around him. In addition, *Drums* seems to pose yet another question about gender: namely, how do civilian women assert their agency in a time of war?

By the same token, the sensitive presence of Walter Pidgeon as Ford's leading man in *How Green Was My Valley* seems to ask: can a romance between an unconventional woman and man (Angharad and Mr. Gruffydd) flourish in a traditional, patriarchal community? The film's answer is clearly "No." Ford's investigation of that dilemma, however, may be one of his greatest and most humane achievements as a filmmaker. Ford brilliantly wraps the film's social and political critique in a deeply nostalgic family tale without ever diluting the subversive impact of his themes. Indeed, the tone of nostalgia tends to reinforce the anti-capitalist message. When the narrator finally declares, "How green was my valley then," his statement clearly reflects not just pining for his lost youth, but the deeper loss of a whole way of life to the avarice and recklessness of industrial profiteering enabled by the complicity of the Church.

The Quiet Man: The Assimilation of the Prodigal Son and the Fiery Spinster

Eleven years after *How Green Was My Valley*, Ford made another deeply nostalgic film — this one about his beloved Ireland — that, in addition to celebrating a marginal society, also articulates fundamental questions about heterosexual love in a patriarchal community. The film's response to those cultural queries, however, is a marked departure from the films Ford made just over a decade before. McCarthyist intolerance in the U.S., in its raging heyday in the early 1950s, likely made the director look to Ireland as an ideal antidote to the divisive and life-destroying clashes that were the order of the day in Hollywood. As biographer Joseph McBride describes Ford at the time, "His personal and professional allegiances thrown into turmoil by the cold war, he had lived for the past four years under the guilty shadow of ideological fratricide" (509). For nearly 20 years Ford had been planning to adapt Maurice Walsh's short story "The Quiet Man" for the cinema, and now he was finally getting his chance.

The resulting film, which has had a greater cultural impact than any other Irish or American film about the Emerald Isle, is a deeply troubling statement about patriarchy and Irish identity. Beginning by challenging traditional notions of gender, it finally gives emphatic validation to the male-dominated status quo. In addition, this is one of Ford's least subversive works in terms of representing social class, religion and politics, as the people of Inisfree seem to live remarkably free of ideological conflict despite the presence of autocratic landowners, the IRA, and the Catholic and Anglican churches in their midst. As McBride attests, "The breathtakingly beautiful Technicolor fantasy John Ford made in Ireland at the age of [fifty-seven] was not the fiercely political *Quiet Man* he would have made at forty" (509). In many ways, the film reflects Ford's yearning for a site of pre-industrial simplicity, a place where community and family life had somehow remained untainted by war and witch hunts, and where patriarchy was a benevolent force for the greater good.[10]

A number of contemporary Irish commentators, however, seek to defend the film as a subtle critique of stereotypical ideas about gender and the Irish. In the vanguard of this school of thought is the Irish scholar Luke Gibbons, who views Ford's picture as progressive in terms of its treatment of gender: "[M]ore astute critics see in the film a contestation of tradition, especially as it affects the subjugation of women." He points specifically to the film's final scene in which Mary Kate (Maureen O'Hara) tosses away Sean's (John Wayne) stick, a detail on which he relies heavily to support his view of the film's gender politics.[11] Gibbons' argument about the film needs to be quoted at length:

> If there is anything more stereotypical than the characters in *The Quiet Man*, it is the response of critics [and he goes on to cite Richard Schickel as one example] who take the film entirely at face value and see in it only the surface simplicity that Sean Thornton himself mistakes for the real Ireland....
>
> [A]lmost every aspect of the film ... is framed in such a way ... as to raise questions over what exactly it is we are seeing, and where reality ends and imagination begins. Ford's irony, humour and over-the-top treatment should be sufficient by itself to place much of what we see in *The Quiet Man* between the visual equivalent of inverted commas. The depiction of stereotypes, romantic escapism or nostalgic sentiment is not of itself an endorsement of them, any more than the portrayal of Ethan Edward's [sic] (John Wayne) Indian-hating pathology in *The Searchers* is an espousal of racism.... [M]uch of what passes for Ireland in *The Quiet Man* is filtered through Sean's nostalgic sensibility and the clash of viewpoints on Irish society with which he has to contend [18–20].

I take exception to Gibbons' reading of the film for three reasons. First of all, the tossing away of one stick does not in itself undo the film's overall narrative work of blatantly espousing male domination and female subjection to patriarchy, and though Ford has many merits as a director, a facility for "irony" is not one of them. Second, the "nostalgic sensibility" at work in the film belongs to the sentimentally Irish Ford himself, not just his protagonist. By the same token, because the film is ostensibly narrated by the town priest, Father Peter Lonergan (Ward Bond)—a device established by six instances of voiceover—explaining the narrative as a product of Sean Thornton's imagination is highly problematic.

Finally, Gibbons' invocation of *The Searchers* as a corollary to *The Quiet Man* makes very little sense. At the close of that film Ford indicates the social consequences of racial bigotry by isolating Ethan Edwards (Wayne) from his family and community. The end of *The Quiet Man*, on the other hand, depicts the utter necessity and desirability of patriarchal coercion and violence as a means of maintaining community. By abusing his wife in full view of a delighted public and using violence to settle accounts with her oafish brother (and then getting drunk with him), Sean Thornton ensures his acceptance into the fold by his wife and all the people of Inisfree. Thus, the protagonist is fully and finally rewarded for exhibiting exactly those Irish qualities that Gibbons deems stereotypical and that he claims Ford is ironically rebuking. Whereas the tragic figure Ethan Edwards must go into exile to pay the price for his and his community's intolerance, Sean Thornton gains happiness and validation as a result of his brutal conformity and chauvinism.

Furthermore, Gibbons fails to read Ford's depictions of "over-the-top" Irishness in the context of the director's portrayals of his favorite ethnicity in other works. Ford's cavalry films—including *Fort Apache*, in which the mostly Irish non-commissioned officers cannot resist drinking themselves into a stupor when they happen upon a barrel of rot-gut whiskey—as well as *The Long Gray Line* (1955), all three vignettes contained in *The Rising of the Moon* (1957), and his depiction of the *de facto* Irish Welsh people in *How Green Was My Valley*, all celebrate stereotypical aspects of Irishness: drinking, singing, dancing and brawling. In different combinations, these activities appear in nearly every Ford film from the late '30s onward, regardless of the ethnicity of his characters. This persistent showcasing of carnivalesque revelry reflects Ford's own ethnic identity and the way he viewed "his people," a category expansive enough to include any number of white ethnics outside the WASP mainstream, as well as the occasional Latino, Native American, and African-American.[12]

Therefore, by understanding that Ford is very much an ethnic filmmaker, we can view his rendering of Irish culture in *The Quiet Man* as a sincere, good-humored paean to this marginal, colonized society in all its aspects. It comes as no surprise, for instance, that Ford, who sometimes referred to himself as an "Irish rebel" and a "freedom fighter,"[13] romanticizes the IRA in the film, making it seem more like a gentleman's social club than an organization using sabotage and terrorism to achieve political ends. Ford has no problem playing up the "stage Irish" characteristics of his fellow ethnics. The figures in *The Quiet Man* may seem like caricatures, but they were likely as real to the director as any of his other movie characters.

Again, taken together with Ford's earlier work, the problem with *The Quiet Man* is not so much how it presents ethnicity as in what it says about gender. Addressing the cultural content of Ford's westerns, Charles Ramírez Berg creates five useful categories for conceptualizing the director's narratives: The Conversion-to-the-Margin Plot, The Assimilation-to-the-Mainstream Plot, The Cultural Balancing Act, The Contamination-of-the-Margin Plot, and The Cultural Redemption Plot (148–51). Retooling one of these terms just a bit, I will explain how *The Quiet Man* functions as an Assimilation-to-the-Marginal-Mainstream Plot. While Sean Thornton does successfully reconvert to the community values and lifestyle of Inisfree, where he was born before he and his mother emigrated, he is also compelled to become a coercive patriarch in his marriage, and in the end he publicly participates in the spectacle he had sworn off since leaving America: he puts up his fists and fights again.

Although Sean has retired from boxing, the plot of *The Quiet Man* hinges on his identity as a pugilist. The film begins with his coming to Ireland to escape the memory of death in the ring, and his reluctance to fight is the main cause of conflict in the latter half of the narrative. After he successfully pursues and weds Mary Kate, the quintessential wild Irish woman, her brother Will (Victor McLaglen), after having his marriage proposal rejected by the Widow Tillane, refuses to hand over Mary Kate's dowry money. Believing that Sean and the matchmaker Michaeleen Flynn (Barry Fitzgerald) have bamboozled him into surrendering his sister, Will goes into a rage and ends up punching out Sean; this blow triggers a flashback to Sean's last fight, in which his opponent ends up dead on the canvas. From this point on, viewers understand the reason behind the ex-pugilist's reluctant conversion to pacifism, while only one other character in the film has this knowledge: the Anglican vicar, the Reverend Playfair (Arthur Shields), who recognizes Sean as a famous boxer. By virtue of knowing this secret, Playfair ultimately becomes Sean's only confidant and counselor.

Much of the film enacts an emasculation drama. As Scott Eyman argues, "The plot is mostly about the way in which the town exerts social control of sex" (409). Only a man who has proven himself worthy can be a husband to one of Inisfree's own, even if Mary Kate is a "spinster," as the matchmaker Michaeleen Flynn calls her. Accordingly, Mary Kate, driven to honor tradition and live up to the standards of her town, acts as the chief agent of Sean's disgrace, as she insists that he force Will to cough up her dowry money. She backs up her demand by withholding sex, and later she calls Sean "a coward." Will, who tells his new brother-in-law that he won't hand over a penny without a fight, taunts Sean: "How would it be if I put one of my fists in my pocket, now? ... That's fair enough, isn't it?" Having killed his final opponent as a boxer, however, Sean wants no more of violence, but again and again he is pushed to abandon his pacifism. Thus, for John Wayne fans accustomed to seeing the movie icon punch, shoot and intimidate all comers, watching *The Quiet Man* may be an alienating and tedious ordeal, as the last half of Ford's film seems constantly to pose the question, what is he waiting for?

For Sean, though, the sport of boxing — and, by extension, any kind of fighting — is inextricably linked to capitalism in its most unbridled form: the ruthless, amoral pursuit of money. Ford emphasizes the venality of the sport at the end of the boxing flashback when he cuts from a high-angle view of the dead boxer's body to a series of shots of reporters snapping pictures of the corpse and of Sean. The scene ends with a close-up of Sean's stricken face as camera flashes assail his eyes. Clearly he will now become more famous for having killed a man in the ring.

After leaving both boxing and the U.S. behind, Sean remains bitter and regretful for having participated in this spectacle of carnage that brings in huge profits but frequently destroys people. This kind of soul-searching is a common trope of boxing films, a popular movie genre of the 1930s through the '50s that has had periodic resurgences in the last few decades.[14] Much of the drama in these films stems from the protagonist's struggle to deal with the corrosive influence of institutionalized brutality, and, in many cases, the money and fame the sport generates. *The Quiet Man* could be considered a post-boxing film, one in which the male protagonist has to wash himself clean of the sport and yet still learn to fight honorably outside the ring. Most of Sean's soul-searching occurs in the second half of the narrative, when he is compelled to overcome his well-grounded reservations about fighting and ostensibly redeem patriarchal violence from the corrupting influence of capitalism.

In contrast to the protagonists of other '40s and '50s boxing films, like *Body and Soul* (Robert Rossen, 1947), *The Ring* (Kurt Neumann, 1952) and *Requiem for a Heavyweight* (Ralph Nelson, 1956), in which men struggle to retain their humanity amidst the depraved environment of the fight game and escape it, Sean Thornton is finally persuaded to overcome his pangs of conscience and engage in violence once again. In addition to the emasculating taunts and insults that Will Danaher and Mary Kate direct against him, Sean is forced to endure the unspoken but clear condemnation of everyone in the town of Inisfree. Not a single person in the community seems to support Sean's determination to forego fisticuffs in his dealings with Will.

Fundamentally, then, *The Quiet Man* is a story of assimilation. In this regard, too, the film is in dialogue with the boxing genre, which consistently examines the central cultural dilemma of "selling out" (Ramírez Berg).[15] For male protagonists in boxing films the rise to fame and material success is frequently a downward spiral on a moral and spiritual level. Fighters "forget where they came from" and often end up alienating the friends, lovers and family members who helped them succeed in the first place. In many cases these men must either leave the game or be decimated by it. Sean's dilemma is different: instead of reclaiming the moral agency he has lost to fighting, he is being coerced into trading one sort of conformity for another. Whereas many boxing heroes face the choice between selling out and fighting, or walking away and retaining their human connections, Sean can keep his new wife and friends only by giving in and reestablishing his masculinity through violence.

In material terms, Sean has successfully reaped the fruits of his labor in a brutal sport, and unlike many fictional and actual boxers, he has apparently refrained from throwing his money away on a lavish lifestyle. He seems to have amassed plenty of wealth, which he uses to establish a new bourgeois life in Inisfree by dressing well, purchasing property and buying drinks for the men of the town at Cohan's Pub. In addition, he repeatedly tells Mary Kate that he has enough money for both of them and that she can forget about her dowry. In Ford's post–World War II cinematic world, though, wealth and reputation alone cannot constitute masculine authority. A "real man" must fight for what is his, including his wife. Sean's reluctance to meet Danaher's challenge affects the whole town; it undermines his marriage and depresses his friends. After Will offers to fight him one-handed and Sean refuses and leaves the pub, Ford shows Michaeleen Flynn standing apart, his face contorted in misery as he slumps dejectedly to the floor.

In the crucial scene that follows, Sean visits the Reverend Playfair (Arthur Shields), the only person in Inisfree who knows about his dark past in America, and Sean further explains the demons that haunt him and feed his aversion to violence. His choice of Shields to play the good Reverend is emblematic of Ford's soft-hearted portrayal of religious figures and institutions in the film. The figure of the Reverend Playfair is nearly the antithesis of Shields' earlier role in *How Green Was My Valley*: that of the rabidly puritanical and divisive Mr. Parry. As Sean's sole confidant, Playfair acts as a catalyst for the renewal of the ex-fighter's flagging machismo and his consequent redemption as a worthy patriarch in their rural community.

Once the reverend has shooed his wife to bed, treating her like an unruly child in the process, Sean explains the reason for his visit, "You're the only one I can level with. I've got to talk to somebody, or I'm going to blow my top." Playfair, a sports enthusiast, proceeds to open his scrapbook and read aloud a newspaper headline describing Sean's fatal bout: "Trooper Thorn Quits Ring," followed by the sub-head, "Heavyweight Challenger Hangs Up Gloves After Fatal Knockout Vows He Will Never Fight Again." While the vicar dismisses the tragic death as an "accident" and "just one of those things," Sean is not ready for absolution. On the contrary, in offering his account of the event, Sean indicts himself:

> Maybe it's just one of those things in the scrapbook, but not when you carry it around in here [points to heart]. Tony Godello was a good egg: nice little wife and home; couple of kids; clean fighter. But I didn't go in there to outbox him. I went in there to beat his brains out; to drive him into the canvas; to murder him. And that's what I did. For what? Purse? Piece of the gate? Lousy money.

Playfair responds to Sean's expression of guilt by acknowledging that "now money is behind your trouble with Danaher." When Sean complains about his wife's and friends' perception that he is "afraid to fight," however, the vicar abruptly shifts from being a sympathetic ear to acting as yet another agent of Sean's emasculation. He asks, "Well, aren't you [afraid] in a way?"

2. The Persistence of Patriarchy: Ford's Later Films 59

For the rest of the scene Playfair attempts to allay Sean's anxiety about capitalism and convince him of his obligation to fight Danaher — not for the money, but in order to properly assimilate into the community and save his marriage. The reverend argues that the dowry is "a good custom" and that "the fortune means more to [Mary Kate] than just the money," although he never elaborates upon those statements. He again hits Sean below the rhetorical belt by asking, "Is your wife's love worth fighting for?" Sean explains that for him to fight he has to be "mad enough to kill," and that if Mary Kate refuses to accept him until he fights, "Maybe she doesn't love me enough." This interchange represents one of the most unsettling and potentially subversive moments in the film, as the protagonist actually questions the fundamental hierarchical power dynamic of patriarchy.

Again, though, Ford exposes Sean's reluctance to conform as a flaw rather than a virtue, and the remainder of the narrative works to correct it. Playfair acts to expedite this process. He answers Sean's deep doubts by coyly rendering the judgment that "it's a difficult situation, but I think you'll find the right answer in God's good time." Then he immediately undercuts his professed impartiality by showing Sean pictures of himself as a young boxer and offering his advice on how to defeat Danaher and his "jaw of granite." Nonetheless, Sean's spirits appear to be lifting; sharing his troubles with Playfair seems to have been cathartic. Finally, though, the Reverend reminds Sean of his manly duty. He starts to offer Sean a drink before retracting the invitation and explaining, "Oh, no, no. You'll be in training now, of course." Hearing this, Sean avoids Playfair's gaze, and his smiling face falls. He sighs and grows sullen as the scene fades out. He again faces the prospect of isolation and ostracism unless he submits to the will of the community.

If Ford's view of masculinity seems bleak and reactionary in *The Quiet Man*, his representation of women is at least as regressive. Mary Kate is finally no less a conformist than her husband, and she ends up selling herself out in a much more literal sense. She is willing to buck certain aspects of tradition, but usually only in a manner that is in keeping with the archetype she represents — that of the wild Irish colleen. From her first appearance on screen, lasciviously meeting Sean's gaze while walking through a meadow, herding sheep, Mary Kate acts as the epitome of repressed sexuality seeking an outlet. Although she refuses to defy Will and pursue a marriage with Sean in the face of her brother's objections, once the matchmaker Michaeleen Flynn and other townspeople engineer a pairing for Will, he begrudgingly permits Sean and Mary Kate to enter into courtship. Subsequently, she submits to Sean's desire to expedite the seemingly interminable process, despite Michaeleen Flynn's protests, and before their marriage she consistently reciprocates Sean's physical advances.

Mary Kate is a complete conformist, however, when it comes to material things. Especially as compared to women in earlier Ford films, like Lana Martin and O'Hara's own Angharad Morgan, Mary Kate's fixation on money and possessions is startling, and at times it borders on the pathological.[16] Following the wedding and Will's unprovoked knockout of Sean, for instance, when the bride and groom are finally home alone together, Mary Kate's first words to Sean are a complaint about her lack of property: "Ever since I was a little girl I've dreamed of having my own things about me." Then she proceeds to give an inventory: "My spinet over there and a table here. And my own chairs to rest upon! And my dresser over there in that corner. And my own china and pewter shining about me!" She is practically inconsolable, and, given the circumstances, she strikes Sean (and likely many viewers) as solipsistic and ruthlessly unsympathetic.

Mary Kate then adds insult to injury, declaring a ban on conjugal relations pending receipt of her money and property. She reproaches Sean, "Don't touch me. You have no right.... I'll wear your ring, I'll cook, and I'll wash, and I'll keep the land, but that is all. Until I've got my dowry safe about me, I'm no married woman. I'm the servant I have always been, without anything of my own." That last line is crucial because, as it turns out later, Mary Kate has no objection to being a "servant"—in fact, she seems to enjoy domestic duties once her conditions are met. What she objects to is performing a servant's duties without being properly compensated by a *bona fide* patriarchal husband.

Mary Kate views her material possessions as integral to her identity as a woman and as a wife. She is so tied to her own bourgeois fantasy of married life that she cannot consent to sex without all her "things about" her. Thus, she is the very definition of a fetishist. As she finishes denouncing Sean for his failure as a husband, her fixation seems more petty and demented by the second:

> Haven't I been trying to tell you? That until you have my dowry, you haven't got any bit of me. Me, myself! I'll still be dreaming amongst the things that are my own, as if I had never met you. There's 300 years of happy dreaming in those things of mine, and I want them. I want my dream. I'll have it, and I know it. I'll say no other word to you.

She is obviously torn between her physical desire for sex and her determination to submit to her husband only under ideal material conditions.

The normally astute Garry Wills, who is keenly aware of Ford's tendency toward misogyny in his life and art, asserts that *The Quiet Man* is "definitely not" a film "that humiliates women," and that the character of Mary Kate is strong and independent in her own way (245). He explains her insistence on obtaining her full dowry as "a pledge of her separate dignity" and attempts to finesse the contradictions in her character: "In a world that treats women as property, having some property of her own makes a woman a disposer of commodities and not just a commodity herself. The place in society of the landholding widow (Mildred Natwick) indicates that" (243). The problem with this argument is that it conveniently ignores the fact that both Mary Kate and the Widow Tillane, by their very insistence on some form of autonomy, are threats to the patriarchal order that must be dealt with accordingly by the two strongest men in Inisfree, Sean and Will, who finally end up taming the two elusive shrews. Ford and his screenwriter Frank Nugent build up Mary Kate and the Widow Tillane to create conflict and challenge the authority of the principal male characters. Sean and Will both ultimately pass this test by proving their patriarchal credentials in a fight and thereby winning the hearts of their ladies. In Ford's post-war cinema, female empowerment is not something to be affirmed or celebrated, but a problem that needs fixing — even in his one "women's picture," *7 Women* (1966), which portrays feminism as a fatal disease.[17]

In the second half of *The Quiet Man*, Mary Kate places a series of obstacles between Sean and marital sex. The morning after their celibate wedding night, Mary Kate receives her furniture, but the fact that Will persists in withholding her dowry money of 350 pounds means that the marriage is still invalid — and therefore sexless— as far as she is concerned. Just when the couple appears to be approaching reconciliation, she spots her brother in town and demands that Sean confront him immediately. At this point, Mary Kate makes a very telling statement; when Sean says, "I don't give a hang about the money," she replies, "But [Will] does, and that's the whole point of it." She then expresses her rancor and anxiety over incurring the "shame" of the community by failing to obtain the dowry. Thus, her fetishism extends beyond the need for having her property "about" her; her libido is held in check just as effectively by her self-consciousness over perceived slights about her marriage from her brother and the rest of the town.[18]

Enraged by Sean's refusal to demand her money from Will, Mary Kate brandishes a riding crop, appearing to wind up to strike Sean, thus symbolically dominating him yet again. Instead of hitting him, though, she uses the whip to strike her horse, rushing off in the new buggy Sean has just given her and leaving him behind. This phallic motif is repeated moments later when Sean roams the countryside, fuming, then picks up a stick and breaks it over his leg. Shortly thereafter, Sean arrives home and Mary Kate immediately hands him the stick she's been using to stoke the fire. This gesture hardly seems organic to the scene but certainly works symbolically: Garry Wills explains Mary Kate's action here as an invitation for Sean "to beat her" as punishment for failing in her wifely duties, sexual and otherwise (244). Again, though, Sean refuses to wield the phallus; instead he tosses the stick into the fire.

Thus, given Ford's repeated use of phallic imagery, Mary Kate's stick toss at the close of the film could be read as a playfully mocking provocation of

Sean, but hardly a declaration of autonomy. Just before she tosses away the stick, Mary Kate whispers to her husband. According to Maureen O'Hara, what she actually said in John Wayne's ear, which was audible only to him and remains a mystery, is too racy ever to be repeated.[19] It's a stretch to read this gesture as any kind of feminist statement, however, since Mary Kate merely seems to be challenging Sean to do his husbandly duty. Yes, it's an invitation to sex, but Mary Kate's overt sensuality — again, a feature of the wild Irish colleen archetype — does not make her a progressive figure of femininity any more than the raw desire exhibited by *femme fatales* in *films noir* makes them into proto-feminist heroines. Mary Kate is a sexual creature, but for her the act of sex can exist only within the bounds of patriarchal marriage — and even then only after all the proper traditions and transactions have been honored. Viewed in this way, the character of Mary Kate is composed of two parts fantasy and one part anachronism, since "the real Irish culture of the time ... had a matriarchal counterforce to patriarchy" that Ford had no interest in exploring (Wills 241).

Throughout the film, Mary Kate uses sex as stock in trade. When she and Sean do reconcile just long enough to consummate their marriage, she immediately departs the ensuing morning, leaving behind Michaeleen Flynn to relay her statement of desperation: "I love him too much to go on living with a man I'm ashamed of." Their foregoing fireside reconciliation, however, is easily the most poignant and affecting scene in the film, as Sean and Mary Kate take a break from bickering, silently acknowledge their shared misery, and embrace each other. Both clearly believe that they have failed in the eyes of the community, and what makes this love scene so deeply felt, especially as opposed to Sean's brusque, stilted (but well-received) passes at Mary Kate during their courtship, is the sense that they are, for the moment, two lovers on equal terms stealing happiness in defiance of the outside world and all its onerous social strictures. In Ford's cinematic world — especially his imagined Ireland — this kind of love cannot last. Patriarchy is too vital to the community, the family unit, and finally, to Sean and Mary Kate themselves. She cannot permanently overcome her attachment to her dowry money unless Sean acts to defend her honor publicly, and he can never become assimilated, or complete his own redemption and that of patriarchal violence, until he does so.

Therefore, while in the first 106 minutes of *The Quiet Man* Ford conducts a somewhat critical, though clearly sexist, exploration of manhood, violence and traditional marriage, in the film's final 23 minutes he offers a practically unqualified vindication of male domination. In charting Ford's representations of gender over time, it's a telling sign that, while *Drums Along the Mohawk* begins with a husband's brutality against his wife, *The Quiet Man* ends with it.

Although the film is adapted from Maurice Walsh's 1933 short story, which does include a climactic fight, the first part of the donnybrook sequence in the film—featuring Sean pulling, pushing and dragging Mary Kate five miles over hill and dale and through sheep dung to toss her down at Will's feet—came straight from the minds of Ford and his screenwriter, Frank Nugent.[20] The film's literary source depicts not a single aggressive or abusive act occurring between the title character and his wife (named Shawn Kelvin and Ellen O'Grady in the story). Walsh's Shawn, while at home, asks his wife to go with him when he finally decides to settle accounts with her brother, and once she reluctantly consents, the two make the journey by cart and horse. Again, there is no hint of coercion.

Several factors apparently contributed to Ford's determination to enact the subjugation and debasement of Mary Kate so emphatically on screen. First, the fact that he changed the lead female character's name from Ellen to Mary Kate may seem innocuous enough, but a cursory look into Ford's personal life shows that this choice had great significance for him. As both Peter Bogdanovich and Joseph McBride point out, Mary Kate is named after the "two great loves of Ford's life": his wife, Mary, and "Kate" Hepburn. In a sense, Mary Kate's personality reflects the two women as well; she is a free spirit (Hepburn) who is firmly tied to Irish-Catholic tradition (Mary Ford). Throughout his life, Ford was notorious for enacting Oscar Wilde's maxim, "Yet each man kills the thing he loves." His friends, family and frequent collaborators most often bore the brunt of his colossal, alcohol-fueled mood swings and mostly verbal bullying. That he should create a character based on the two women he loved most and then have her literally dragged through shit was perfectly in keeping with his temperament.[21]

Secondly, Ford himself probably had romantic designs on Maureen O'Hara throughout the making of *The Quiet Man*. While McBride merely states that Ford and his leading lady were "feuding" during the shoot (516), Eyman speculates about the likely reasons behind their spat—he quotes Andrew McLaglen, Victor's son and the film's assistant director, who said, "I think it was an affair" (400). According to the younger McLaglen, Ford aroused suspicions when he took over the rooming assignments for the cast and crew, making sure O'Hara stayed next door to him. Furthermore, when Ford went into a funk in the middle of the shoot and suddenly took a day off, McLaglen again suspected lovesickness as the culprit: "We knew why he was under the weather. I think Maureen had turned him down the night before" (Eyman 405). Eyman also suggests that Ford's characteristic professional efficiency (he often did only one or two takes of a given scene) was temporarily mitigated by his wish to live vicariously through John Wayne/Sean Thornton: "For the rain-drenched love scene between Wayne and O'Hara, Ford demanded an unusually high number of takes,[22] as he told the actors to make their kisses more passionate, their embraces tighter. 'Ford just had me do all the things he wanted to do himself,' Wayne told his wife" (401). Thus, Ford's portrayal of Mary Kate and his direction of O'Hara likely reflected his desire simultaneously to revere and debase both the character and the actress playing her.

In the donnybrook sequence, which takes place the day after Sean and Mary Kate's brief reconciliation and marital consummation, Ford plays spousal abuse for laughs. Sean shoves, throws, drags and kicks Mary Kate for five miles, as townspeople follow along behind, delighting in the spectacle. Now, finally, Sean shows his readiness to take up the phallus. When an old woman hands him a rod, declaring, "Sir, here's a good stick to beat the lovely lady," Sean accepts it and says, "Thanks!"

Although Maureen O'Hara later called *The Quiet Man* her favorite film, her participation in the project took a considerable toll on her body; the battery that she had to undergo as Mary Kate was very real for her. In a scene where Wayne blocks a punch she throws at him, she broke her wrist and had to go to the hospital. According to O'Hara, Ford and Wayne took fiendish pleasure in her pain: "Of course, [they] loved it. They thought it was funny" (Eyman 408). During the shooting of the donnybrook, O'Hara suffered another major injury. At the point in the film when she tumbles down a hill and Wayne picks her up at the bottom and drags her, O'Hara seriously hurt her back; she later had to have it remedied with surgery. Although in her DVD commentary O'Hara tells tale after tale of Ford's capricious abuse of actors, she invariably excuses his conduct by extolling his incomparable brilliance.

Like many who knew Ford well, O'Hara characterizes the director as volatile and Janus-faced. In a 1996 interview for Bogdanovich's documentary, she says of Ford, "He could be kind, gracious and gentle, with a wonderful sense of humor; but he could also be vindictive and mean. All one can do with John Ford is accept him with all of his faults and virtues, and love him." Regardless of just how intimate her relationship with the director may have been, O'Hara clearly speaks from experience, having seen Ford as benevolent dictator as well as ruthless tyrant.

In many ways Sean Thornton aptly represents both extremes of Ford's personality, and the end of *The Quiet Man* enacts the protagonist's passage into proper patriarchal manhood, a state of being in which he must — for the good of all — be willing to fight and to put his wife in her place when necessary. While in Walsh's story Shawn Kelvin is finally motivated to fight more by sorrow than anger, Ford and Wayne's Sean Thornton acts as a surly manchild bent on revenge. He unleashes most of his rage on Mary Kate, as he prods and tosses her around for all to see and finally throws her down viciously in front of her brother. Once Sean threatens to nullify the marriage unless Will produces the 350 pounds he owes Mary Kate, Will relents and gives over the cash. Sean, showing that he is motivated not by greed but solely by his

2. The Persistence of Patriarchy: Ford's Later Films 65

Sean (John Wayne) prepares to hurtle Mary Kate (Maureen O'Hara) forward, as members of the community look on approvingly in *The Quiet Man* (Artisan/Republic Pictures, 1952, dir. John Ford).

need to prove himself to Mary Kate and the people of Inisfree, then burns the money, his wife assisting him by opening the furnace door. Once Sean lands his first punch on Will's jaw, he finally dispels all doubts about his fitness as a patriarch. What follows is a quick descent into carnivalesque comedy and a fight scene whose reputation has been much inflated over the years. Often dubbed the "longest brawl ever filmed,"[23] it actually contains several extended interruptions, though from first punch to last it does have a total duration of 9 minutes, 18 seconds. The donnybrook is a sequence that has many parallels in Ford's body of work, including very similar brawls in *She Wore a Yellow Ribbon* and *The Searchers*, and it's thematically in keeping with Ford's characteristically perverse acknowledgment of the paramount importance of community. Sean fights and later gets drunk, and therefore he belongs.

Likewise, the completion of Mary Kate's character arc marks her total assimilation. The climax and resolution of her marital feud with Sean is not so much "concocted by her" (McBride 515) as demanded by the community itself. Events may have indeed unfolded to her liking, but what's most important to her is the validation of the townspeople, who witness Sean's capitulation to tradition and her consequent justification as a wife and vindication as a former "spinster." After Sean compels Will to hand over her money and punches out her brother, Mary Kate announces, "I'll be going on home now. I'll have the supper ready for you." Then she flashes a proud look at the assembled villagers, walks through the crowd, and commences her passage into proper bourgeois married life.

None of the film's main characters finally retains moral agency. Like so many figures in Ford's work, Sean and Mary Kate are compelled to change themselves in order to conform to the community. Whereas some of Ford's earlier films, such as *Young Mr. Lincoln* and *How Green Was My Valley*, address the consequences of individual decisions to submit to the communal will, Ford's post–World War II films, particularly *Fort Apache*, *Rio Grande*, *The Quiet Man* and *Donovan's Reef*, tend to gloss over the personal costs of assimilation. In *The Quiet Man*, Sean's blood money is finally redeemed — though he refuses Will's money, he keeps all the wealth from his boxing career — and even the ruthless capitalist Danaher, the much-maligned landowning miser, gains acceptance in the community, as well as a rich fiancée in the Widow Tillane, after he brawls with Sean.

In the penultimate scene, Sean and Will cap their drunken revelry by going home together for dinner at the Thornton cottage. Visually referencing the earlier scene of Mary Kate's rejection of Sean, Ford frames her in the cottage doorway beaming as she watches her husband and brother stumble in drunkenly. At last she is free to be the happy servant, and though she chastens her brother, she accepts orders from Sean. When he commands her to "Hurry it up" and serve dinner, she bristles — her hot temper and old habits getting the better of her for only an instant — but then controls herself and does as she is told.

As the scene ends and she serves the food, Mary Kate is in the center of the frame between Will and Sean, but as a woman in this patriarchal community, she is more marginalized than ever. As Ford cuts to the final farewell scene, in which the (predominantly Catholic) townspeople turn out to show their appreciation for the Reverend and Mrs. Playfair, and "cheer like Protestants," the director crafts one of his most affirmative endings — one unmitigated by unresolved social conflict. Now that their errant son has returned, regained his capacity for violence and tamed his shrewish wife, all is well in Inisfree.

The Rugged Individualist Embracing the Status Quo: John Wayne's Star Image

John Wayne, with his exceptional physical stature and utterly conventional mannerisms and personal politics, performed a vitally important function in

Ford's post-war cinema. In contrast to many Hollywood protagonists before and since, Wayne's characters could perform the great trick of surrendering to authority without appearing weak. As Ramírez Berg argues, "Character agency (the degree of a protagonist's self-determination, from passive victim to active hero) is equated with action in the movies" ("Gendered Actions..." 2). Many of Wayne's characters in Ford films, however, proceed from agency to passivity. The particular dynamics of his star persona made it possible for him to embody individuals who, rather than moving in the course of the narrative from acceptance of the status quo to finding the strength to change it, move in exactly the opposite direction. Thus, Wayne represented the rugged individualist who becomes a complete conformist. Like Sean Thornton in *The Quiet Man*, Wayne's characters in Ford's *They Were Expendable* and *Fort Apache* initially defy what they view as an unacceptable state of affairs — essentially, military superiors forcing men to follow orders contrary to their moral sense and better judgment — only to end up selling out and giving in.

In his seminal book *Stars* Richard Dyer explains how movie icons function to embody and reconcile such ideological contradictions: "The relation [of a star's image to contradictory ideologies] may be one of displacement ... or of the suppression of one half of the contradiction and the foregrounding of the other ... or else it may be that the star effects a 'magic' reconciliation of the apparently incompatible terms" (30). Wayne as the strong but passive conformist in Ford movies seems to accomplish precisely such a magical synthesis of seemingly incompatible ideas within the Hollywood paradigm. The political consequences of Wayne's star persona should not be underestimated. As Dyer points out:

> [I]t is probably true to say that [movie stars] are widely believed to be politically insignificant and unimportant, and that the only "real" politics, it is widely held, is decision-making within the institutions of society. Because of this belief, the ideological significance of stars is masked or discounted. One might then suggest that just because it is so masked its real political power is all the greater for being less easily resisted [7–8].

The allure of Wayne's persona endures to this day, I believe, because he's widely viewed as an essentially *apolitical* figure. Nothing could be further from the truth, of course, given his outspoken support of American wars — in Korea and Vietnam — and his participation in glorifying them on screen.

The fact that Wayne tended to align himself, in his film roles and public statements, with the political and societal status quo, however, serves to make him seem like a timeless patriotic figure, creating the illusion that he put his country first and stood above any kind of petty partisan arguments. Again, this perception is nonsensical: Wayne avoided national service in the '40s to advance his budding film career and later co-directed and starred in a film, *The Green Berets* (1968), which was his cinematic vindication of the American military occupation of Vietnam. Furthermore, at times Wayne himself contributed to the historical amnesia regarding his political commitments:

> Although he served four terms as president of the MPA [Motion Picture Alliance for the Preservation of American Ideals], Wayne said in his 1971 *Playboy* interview, "Our organization was just a group of motion picture people on the right side, not leftist and not Commies.... There was no blacklist at the time, as some people said. That was a lot of horseshit" [McBride 475].

Thus, one of the overriding consequences of Wayne's persona has been to help perpetuate the dangerous myths that nationalism is not a political stance (and so incurs no individual responsibility for its repercussions) and that dissent is inherently unpatriotic — that in times of war, the United States, no matter its policies and actions, requires the full, unwavering devotion of its people.

On August 30, 1952, just 16 days after *The Quiet Man* hit U.S. theaters, John Wayne's only other 1952 picture, *Big Jim McLain* (Dir. Edward Ludwig), was released. Produced by Wayne's own company, Batjac, and co-written by his good friend and scribe of choice, James Edward Grant, the latter film makes explicit, and attempts to justify, the morally perverse mentality of the Blacklist era, indicating the degree to which Wayne's rugged conformist persona could be employed to support a deeply reactionary and unconstitutional agenda. *Big Jim McLain* features the Duke in the title role as a tough, no-nonsense investigator for the notorious House Un-American Activities Committee.

Although the filmmakers take great care to heap praise on HUAC at both the beginning and end of the picture,[24] Wayne's character ultimately contends that the committee fails to go far enough and that the Fifth Amendment is an impediment to bringing "commies" to proper justice. In one of the film's final scenes, McLain tells a police chief (played by actual Honolulu Police Chief Dan Liu), "There are a lot of wonderful things written into our Constitution that were meant for honest, decent citizens. I resent the fact that it can be used and abused by the very people that want to destroy it." If the film put forth even a cursory legal formula for establishing which folks are "decent" and which are legitimate threats to national security, it might be dismissed as merely misguided and an unfortunate product of what Lillian Hellman has called "Scoundrel Time."

As is so often the case with Wayne's protagonists, however, McLain actively promotes a quasi-religious, fanatical devotion to his country. Near the middle of the film he drives his love interest, Nancy (Nancy Olson), to a scenic mountain overlook. When she begins musing about why her boss may have become a communist, McLain interrupts to set her straight:

> Look, baby. I don't know the why. I've heard all the jive: this one's a commie because momma won't tuck him in at night, that one because girls wouldn't welcome him with open arms. I don't know the why. The what I do know. It's

2. The Persistence of Patriarchy: Ford's Later Films 69

John Wayne as Jim McLain, the happy anti-communist warrior, in *Big Jim McLain* (Warner Bros., 1952, dir. Edward Ludwig).

like when I was wearing a uniform. I shot at the guy on the other side of the perimeter because he was the enemy. [Smiles big.] Hey, we better get out of here, or I'll start talking politics.

Once again, Wayne's persona works its magic. He conceals his aggressively political embrace of the status quo beneath hard-core patriotism. McLain wouldn't be so pretentious as to engage in "talking politics"; he's just telling it like it is. This kind of simple-minded, un-nuanced view of the Cold War pervades the film, and it makes no distinction between suspected U.S. Communist Party members and North Koreans fighting American forces across the Pacific. "These people" are one and the same, as far as McLain is concerned, and he lumps them all into one giant international conspiracy, thus justifying his desire to circumvent the Constitution — only out of deep love for his country, of course.

Meaningful debates regarding the dark period of HUAC, the Hollywood Blacklist, and Joseph McCarthy still occur. Legitimate questions remain, such as was Alger Hiss really a Soviet spy? How many active Communist Party members were in the U.S. during this time, and what (undoubtedly small) proportion of them was engaged in dangerously unlawful, as opposed to "Un-

American," activities? Which of the artists and others denounced by McCarthy and/or HUAC and their friendly witnesses were guilty as charged, and which were suspected erroneously or were merely guilty by association? Historians have had substantive disagreements regarding these questions. As president of the *uber*-vigilant MPA, and star and producer of the extreme right-wing propaganda film *Big Jim McLain*, however, John Wayne did his part to poison legitimate political discourse and err grievously on the side of virulent, anti-intellectual nationalism. To say that Wayne's star persona helped promote the mantra of "America, right or wrong" would be inaccurate; his public and private conviction was more along the lines of "America: never, ever wrong."

As critics and historians have pointed out, Wayne's anti-communist stance represented the antithesis of bravery in the late '40s and '50s. Although late in life he would claim that he "was never much of a joiner" because he felt "capable" of doing his own "thinking" (Levy 225), Wayne was more sheep than shepherd during the Blacklist era. The historian Garry Wills, an avowed admirer of the Duke in many respects, explains how Wayne refrained from taking any overt position on communism until the time was propitious for joining the witch hunt:

> In that whole period, from 1939 to 1947, Wayne's name does not appear on any side of the struggle [over communism]. A noncombatant during the physical shooting of World War II, he was also a noncombatant in the ideological war. The same careerism that kept him from wearing a uniform kept him from taking a stand. His role, finally, was to emerge after the battle and shoot the wounded. He became "outspoken" only after … the [film] industry was voicing *only* one side…. To step in then [as President of the MPA] was joining a bully, not an underdog…. Despite Wayne's image as a nonconformist, one who goes his own way for his own reasons, nothing was more conformist in the Hollywood of the 1950s than to berate Communists and to call oneself brave for doing so. Wayne, after all, could not take credit for his one truly nonconformist act in the 1940s—his defiance of all the pressures to join the military…. Wayne the late-arriving anti–Communist cut no profile in courage [197–9].

Despite the glaring contradictions between his conduct and avowed "American Ideals," Wayne remains the most enduring screen icon of all time. A 2011 Harris poll found that Americans ranked him as their fifth-favorite movie star, past or present—and for over a decade he has been the only deceased actor to make the Harris list of top ten stars—illustrating Wayne's unique appeal as a man who is at once boldly individualistic and dangerously conventional.

Ford's Cold War Concessions

Whatever his personal doubts about Wayne, John Ford's use of the actor as star of eleven of his post-war films carried a great deal of ideological freight, as Ford surely knew. After his most unsuccessful collaboration with Henry Fonda, *The Fugitive*, which was a huge commercial failure, the director "would increasingly rely on Westerns as a means of ensuring a healthy career" (Eyman 344–5). As long as he was playing it safe, what better way to stay above suspicion in a city and country torn apart by loyalty oaths and blacklists than to hitch his wagon to John Wayne's ultra-conservative star? In addition to Wayne, Ford worked closely with two other ardent anti-communists during the late '40s and early '50s: his producer and partner, Merian Cooper, and the renowned character actor Ward Bond, one of the original founders of the MPA (Eyman 386–7). While Ford served on the executive board of the MPA and gradually moved to the right politically during this time, he seems to have avoided openly political activities.

Ford did, however, help salvage the Screen Directors Guild in 1950 by successfully mediating a dispute between Joseph L. Mankiewicz and Cecil B. DeMille over control of the Guild. This battle was brought to a head by DeMille's insistence on enforcing an oath of loyalty to the U.S. government upon Hollywood directors. Ironically, though, all the filmmakers who protested DeMille's hyper-patriotic edicts were required to sign the very loyalty oath they disdained in order to remain Guild members in good standing and subsequently retain the power to oppose DeMille. Although Ford was not in the vanguard of the anti–DeMille faction of the Guild, as were other great directors, such as Mankiewicz, William Wyler and George Stevens, he finally lent crucial support to their side after Mankiewicz insisted, "John Ford has to be heard." This pronouncement prompted Ford's famous assertion, which he used by way of dramatic (but quite unnecessary) introduction: "I am a director of Westerns." As an elder statesman of the Guild, he acted as a voice of reason, effectively but carefully admonishing DeMille and tipping the balance against him without further dividing the directors' union (Eyman 381–5).

Undoubtedly, Ford was deeply ambivalent about the personal and professional compromises he made to continue his prolific movie career, particularly with regard to Hollywood's biggest star. According to Maureen O'Hara, during every shoot, Ford would constantly scapegoat someone — put one actor "in the barrel"— and very often his object of derision was John Wayne (DVD commentary, *The Quiet Man*). In most cases, Wayne obediently endured the director's abuse: "His docility with Ford was almost childlike" (Wills 199). As late as the early '60s, Ford continued to ridicule the Duke for his failure to join in the Allied war effort, and this was still a sore spot for Wayne. Garry Wills describes how during the making of *The Man Who Shot Liberty Valance*, Ford deliberately pitted Wayne against Woody Strode, the actor playing the Duke's most loyal friend in the film:

> Ford ... took this opportunity to renew his sardonic references to Wayne's lack of military service, contrasting his record with that of his new star, Woody

Strode.... The riding of Wayne rubbed his nerves so raw that he started a fight with Strode — which Ford had to end with hasty pleas to Strode not to hurt the older, weaker man because "We need him" [264].

Like a son vying for the favor of an autocratic father, the 50-something Hollywood legend lashed out at Strode rather than the sadistic man who measured him against his costar. This incident both exemplifies Ford's capriciousness and offers insight into the personal conflict Wayne likely experienced attempting to reconcile the fantasy of his warrior/westerner image with the reality of his actions during wartime.

To a certain extent *The Searchers* (1956), which many critics consider John Ford's supreme masterpiece, can be read as a repudiation of the persona and politics that John Wayne had so carefully cultivated since World War II. The film tells the story of a man who has been so corrupted by intolerance and hubris that he is willing to destroy anyone who presents a challenge to his Manichean worldview — even his niece, whom he disowns after she has been abducted by Comanches and lived for years with her captors. Yet Ethan Edwards (Wayne) ultimately stops himself from committing the act that would utterly blacken his soul. As Garry Wills points out, although Ethan is a "hateful hater" and the most merciless of all the characters Wayne played in Ford films, Ford "makes him relent in the end, surrendering his hate" (185). In my view the final narrative turn of *The Searchers*— just as much as it functions as a qualified affirmation of racial tolerance — works to promote American Exceptionalism: the idea that although the U.S. engages in aggressive actions, our moral character remains so unimpeachable that we would never be guilty of the kinds of gruesome, genocidal atrocities that other races and nations have perpetrated.

The crux of the film's endorsement of American Exceptionalism is in the relationship between Ethan Edwards and Scar (Henry Brandon), the Comanche chief and villain of the story. Scar is Ethan's doppelganger: "When he at last confronts Scar, [Ethan] is looking in a mirror, though he will not admit it" (Wills 258). Scar is the man responsible for the murder of Ethan's brother and beloved sister-in-law, and the abduction and captivity of Ethan's niece, Debbie (Natalie Wood), whom Scar keeps as one of his harem. Like Ethan, though, Scar has seen family members—his two sons—slaughtered by the people he views as his mortal enemy: in his case, white Texan settlers. In Ethan's presence Scar declares his desire to avenge "each son" by taking "many scalps." Beyond this revelation and the one instance in which Scar shows a flash of wit by trading insults with Ethan over their respective commands of language, however, Ford makes no attempt whatsoever to humanize his villain.

Ethan is really no less ruthless in his quest for revenge. Early in the film he commits the cardinal sin (in Ford's cinematic world) of cutting short a

2. The Persistence of Patriarchy: Ford's Later Films

In *The Searchers* (Warner Bros., 1956, dir. John Ford), Ethan (John Wayne), with Scar's scalp in hand, has finally sated his bloodlust.

funeral, that of his brother and sister-in-law, in order to set off quickly in pursuit of their killers, failing to heed the sage advice of an old woman present at the service: "If the girls are dead, don't let the boys [Ethan's nephews] waste their lives in vengeance." Later on, he shoots his enemies, Anglo as well as Native American, in the back and defaces a Comanche's dead body by shooting out his eyes so that, as Ethan explains, "he can't enter the spirit world."

Nonetheless, the narrative moves inexorably toward revealing the complexity of Ethan's motivation, racist though it may be, and validating his revenge against Scar. Although Ford conveniently avoids a bloody confrontation between his hero and the Comanche chief, which might have further humanized Scar, he does show Ethan preparing to scalp Scar's dead body (whom Ethan's partner, Martin, has killed in self-defense) and later emerging with his bloody trophy in hand. The close-up of Wayne's face registering his reaction to this deed is mesmerizing; Garry Wills aptly describes Wayne's expression as one of "post-orgasmic blurriness" (259). Ford perfectly crafted this sequence of images to inspire ambivalence toward Ethan, but he never allows his audience to see Ethan's enemy as a conflicted figure as well.

Scar is consistently portrayed, and referred to by the white characters of the film, as a figure of menacing violence and sexuality. This is a far cry from Ford's one exceptionally dignified rendering of a Native American antagonist, that of Cochise in the earlier *Fort Apache*, a man who speaks eloquently and is photographed throughout the film, particularly in low-angle close-ups, in a way that morally equates him with his Anglo adversaries. By contrast, Scar barely talks or changes expression during the little time he is on screen, and he is afforded close-ups only when he is engaged in terrorizing white people.

Ethan finally solidifies his status as a tragic figure by briefly becoming what he has despised — by adopting Scar's own brutal methods against him. In scalping his adversary, Ethan passes beyond the pale and enters a realm from which there is no return in white American society. As an Anglo, Ethan is justified in his revenge, whereas Scar's revenge is symptomatic of a savage degenerate. Ford clearly implies that Ethan is fearsome and pitiable because he has allowed his quest to corrupt him to the point where he is momentarily almost indistinguishable from his and American society's enemy.

Almost indistinguishable, but not really. Ethan remains redeemable because he finally accepts Debbie as his niece once again, just as he had earlier begrudgingly embraced the part–Cherokee Martin (Jeffrey Hunter) by naming him the sole heir of the Edwards family fortune. Ford implies that, as opposed to the Comanche and their lack of civilized restraint, white men — even the cold-blooded Ethan — resolutely refuse to cross certain moral lines. Ethan himself indicates the distinction between humans (read, white people) and the Comanche earlier in the film: "A human rides a horse until it dies, then he goes on afoot. Comanche comes along, gets that horse up, rides him 20 more miles. Then eats him." Ultimately, Ethan, as a representative of white America, ends the cycle of revenge through violence, which in his case is acceptable, even though his methods must be condemned, resembling as they do those of the savage Other.

Although he cannot return to his family and civilization, Ethan successfully reunites what remains of his clan and community, and in the final analysis he has the decency to leave them all alone. The amazingly dense economy of the film's final scene is a Fordian *tour de force*. Echoing the first images of the movie, Ford frames his final shot from within a shadowy doorway, capturing Ethan handing off Debbie to Mrs. Jorgensen (Olive Carey) before he steps back to allow Martin and Laurie (Vera Miles) to enter the home that is now completely alien to him. After peering into the house, Ethan turns and stalks off into the bright light of the desert as the door closes on him. Even as Ethan's character arc adds remarkable complexity to the figure of the westerner, existing as he does "on the periphery of both the [civilized] community and the wilderness" (Schatz 51), in the end he is romanticized for completing his quest, turning his back on domestic stability and heading off into the great unknown.

In this way Ethan is ultimately much less a pariah than a kind of tarnished Christ figure. He redeems the racism of his frontier community — and thus affirms the dictates of Manifest Destiny — by going into exile to atone for the sins of white America. He is far from the only intolerant figure in the film, and thus reading *The Searchers* as a cogent denunciation of racism is difficult to do. The half-mad sidekick Mose (Hank Worden) repeatedly dances and chants in grotesque imitation of the Comanche, and when he does so the film's score employs jaunty music to cue laughter; while late in the film the avuncular Samuel Clayton (Ward Bond) announces to a young cavalryman, "I'm the hard case out here, not them childish savages." By the same token, the other major secondary characters, Laurie and Charlie (Ken Curtis), repeatedly and contemptuously taunt Martin for having unwittingly taken possession of a "squaw bride" while trading goods with the Comanche, another episode that is played for laughs.

Even Martin, the man with Cherokee blood who frequently acts as the voice of tolerance in the film and tempers Ethan's ruthlessness with pleas for mercy, treats his "squaw" companion, Look (Beulah Archuletta), with vicious disregard. After she fails to understand Martin's numerous entreaties to return to her tribe, Look crawls in bed with him; but Martin administers a mule kick to force her out, sending her rolling and flailing down a rocky slope. Ethan watches in rapt amusement and jokingly chides Martin, "You know, that's grounds for dee-vorce in Texas. You're really rough!" One could perhaps attribute Martin's behavior in this instance to Ford's sadistic delight in sexist humor more than his frequently patronizing treatment of Native Americans. In any case, the film consistently treats both women and Indians with contempt, rendering it in this respect merely typical Hollywood fare of the 1950s.[25] Thus, Ethan's racism doesn't exist in a vacuum of tolerance, and *The Searchers* is problematic as an anti-racist statement. The scholar Douglas Pye, while acknowledging the film's troubling but conventional representations of race and gender, ultimately concludes that the "incoherence" of *The Searchers* "is an essential aspect of its greatness" because Ford "achieves" so much within the "context" and "traditions" of the western genre. As stated above, however, Ford had earlier proven himself capable of portraying both Native Americans and women — the former in *Fort Apache*, the latter in his films of 1939–41— with far more nuance and coherence.

The narrative of *The Searchers* clearly establishes that Ethan comes by his malicious hatred of the Comanche honestly: in addition to being motivated by his personal enmity, Ethan's bigoted ideas (though not his Comanche-like methods) are essentially endorsed by everyone in his community save Martin. In a sense, by riding away, Ethan is taking one for the team and establishing the accepted limits of white imperialist intolerance. Blatant racism cannot be tolerated, whereas bigotry within reason is tenable. Tellingly, the only character in the picture who stands for "justice and tolerance" with any consistency is Martin, who embodies the racial divide as a man of mixed heritage. It seems nearly impossible to expect any full-blooded Anglo to be unprejudiced in the world of *The Searchers*.

Furthermore, the film never refutes Ethan's statement in reference to Debbie that "Living with Comanches ain't being alive." Ford distinguishes his hero from his native adversaries by showing him capable of transcending his hatreds in the best interest of his people. Ethan's final act is to restore his niece to life as an Anglo, rather than following through on his previously expressed intention of killing her simply because he cannot abide her living on as a devalued piece of sexual property, one irrevocably contaminated by seven years of captivity with the Comanches. The fact that the Wayne persona could bear the weight of *The Searchers*' thematic ambivalence seems incredible in some respects, but in the end Ethan does what Wayne's characters almost always do: he holds his renegade impulses in check for the greater purpose of upholding order and civilization. And Ford romanticizes him for doing so.

Five years later, in *Two Rode Together* (1961), Ford crafted a strikingly similar tale about the redemption of another racist Texan — this time, Sheriff Guthrie McCabe, played by James Stewart. McCabe despises Comanches just as fiercely as Ethan, but he likewise ends up having a slight change of heart and warms to a woman (Elena, a Latina played by Linda Cristal) who, like Debbie, had been for years the sexual property of a Comanche "buck." *Two Rode Together* even goes one better than *The Searchers* in terms of redeeming a bigot. McCabe finally follows his heart and leaves his cushy job as a corrupt backwater sheriff to ride off with the ex-captive Elena, as his cavalryman buddy Jim (Richard Widmark) quips, "Well, I guess old Guth finally found something he wanted more than 10 percent of." This scene comes moments after McCabe's old flame, the brothel madam Belle, confronts and insults Elena for her Comanche-tainted past, prompting McCabe to threaten, "Belle, I'm going to beat hell out of you!"

In much the same vein, *The Searchers* features several uncomplicated, caricatured women, one of the hallmarks of Ford's cinema in its final phases. The most interesting female character in the film by far is Martha Edwards (Dorothy Jordan), Ethan's sister-in-law and forbidden love, but Scar's raiders murder her before the end of the film's first act. Although Natalie Wood makes the most of what little screen time she has and plays her role with earnest conviction, the character of Debbie Edwards is little more than a plot device — a piece of bait that drives the narrative and provokes Ethan's rage. Ford never explores the trauma she endures as a captive, and Debbie's quick reconversion from loyal defender of "my [Comanche] people" to happy Anglo sister/niece/daughter is unconvincing in the extreme. Debbie is a woefully underwritten and underdeveloped character.

Though they are accorded more screen time and more lines, Mrs. Jorgensen and her daughter Laurie represent unimaginative variations on two common Fordian types: the durable, desensualized, idealized frontier mother, and the randy, hot-tempered maiden in need of a disciplinarian husband. Mrs. Jorgensen offers the film's most unvarnished validation of Manifest Destiny, speaking of her people's patient suffering and determination to tame the West: "We be Texicans. A Texican is nothing but a human man way out on a limb — this year and next, and maybe for a hundred more. But I don't think it'll be forever. Some day this country's going to be a fine, good place to be. Maybe it needs our bones in the ground before that time can come." As Ford's Abe Lincoln would say, Mrs. Jorgensen is the kind of woman that "ask[s] for nothing, and give[s] everything."

Laurie Jorgensen is a different kind of male fantasy figure: a younger, lustier version of Mary Kate Danaher, minus many of the traditionalist inhibitions. She first appears in the film already intent on marrying Martin: she greets him with a kiss on the mouth, and moments later she purposely walks in on him bathing. When he protests, she replies, "Now, looky here, Martin Pawley, I'm a woman. We women wash and mend your dirty clothes all your lives. When you're little, we even wash you! How you can ever make out to be bashful, I'll never know." Those words make Laurie sound like a walking, talking resolution to any lingering Oedipal issues Martin might have: she actually wants to be both mother and wife to her prospective husband.

In keeping with her hot-tempered "feminine" frailty, though, Laurie predictably settles on another beau when Martin frustrates her designs by continuing in his and Ethan's search quest for another five years. Considering these romantic complications, Ford could have easily portrayed Laurie sympathetically by focusing on her very warranted frustration, but instead he emphasizes only her tempestuous, inconstant nature. Martin receives much better treatment: clearly he does love Laurie in his awkward way, but he must have the manly wisdom to do what's best for all by striving to keep Ethan's desire for vengeance in check, despite Laurie's pouty, selfish pleas for him to remain with her. When Martin and Ethan return to the Jorgensens' after their first encounter with Scar and the now-tainted Debbie, they find a celebration in progress: Laurie is about to marry Charlie, who is seemingly the only other eligible bachelor for miles around. After Martin takes the bride-to-be aside and declares his love for her, she quickly forgives and embraces him; but this reconciliation creates conflict between Martin and the spurned Charlie. The two men argue and start to brawl, and as Ethan, Laurie and the other revelers look on, the two suitors duke it out.

During this sequence Ford creates one of the most misogynistic images in his whole body of work. While Martin and Charlie go at each other, Laurie first pleads with Ethan to "make them stop." Ethan responds dismissively, "Why? You started it." Then he guides Mrs. Jorgensen (Laurie's mother) indoors, chiding her, "You're a lady, remember." Ford's camera then pans quickly and seamlessly from a medium shot of Ethan to a close-up of Laurie's face,

Ford zeroes in on Laurie (Vera Miles), as she gleefully watches two men fighting over her in *The Searchers* (Warner Bros., 1956).

which is contorted in an expression of joy that she simply cannot hide. Although she holds a handkerchief to her mouth to feign consternation, her eyes betray her completely. Witnessing the battle between Martin and Charlie for the privilege of marrying her, Laurie experiences a paroxysm of delight. Much as he portrays Mary Kate in *The Quiet Man*, Ford shows Laurie beaming with pride as she sees men fight over her and gauges the consequent rise in her value as sexual property. The difference is that Mary Kate left the scene of the brawl after the first punch, thereby retaining some degree of dignity, whereas Laurie keeps staring at the macho spectacle in rapt amazement. She is a deeply discomfiting illustration of Ford's most chauvinistic ideas and impulses.

As is the case with many of Ford's later films—but not the well paced and compelling, if deeply cynical, *The Man Who Shot Liberty Valance*—the sum of the brilliant parts of *The Searchers* is greater than the movie as a whole. Particularly in the final act, when Ford interrupts the rising action to insert the sequence featuring the aborted wedding and brawl, the film evinces a tonal schizophrenia that seriously detracts from the gravity of its themes. Similarly, after Ethan relents in his homicidal pursuit of his niece and tells her, "Let's go home, Debbie," Ford cuts to a brief scene of Samuel Clayton tending a minor wound on his posterior before proceeding to the bravura last scene.

The Searchers is ultimately a film that pulls as many punches as it lands. Had Ford been willing to risk alienating his audience by having Ethan Edwards die as a result of his seemingly insatiable thirst for vengeance, he might have made a movie that actually deserves the vaunted reputation it enjoys today. As Garry Wills contends, "the story *demands* that he [Ethan] die" (251). Instead, Ford tinkered with the John Wayne persona in compelling fashion, but he ultimately lent more credence to the idea that America needs tough and uncompromising vigilantes to ensure its safety and survival. Wayne himself apparently had few qualms about the implications of his role in *The Searchers*, subsequently naming one of his sons Ethan (b. 1962) after his character in the film.

Rather than being a magnificent aberration, *The Searchers*, though frequently brilliant artistically, continues Ford's post-war pattern of endorsing social and political stasis, including imperialist violence and the marginalization of women and minorities. Many admirers of Ford point to *Cheyenne Autumn* (1964), the director's penultimate fiction film, as a remarkable expression of remorse and a love letter to the Native Americans he and other Hollywood filmmakers had so often caricatured and denigrated in their films. Seeing the film as some meaningful blanket apology to all native tribes is wishful thinking, however, given that Ford had most often stereotyped native peoples from tribes other than the Cheyenne. His most frequent screen monsters were the Apache and the Comanche, and he made no films centering on their suffering and displacement.

Furthermore, immediately preceding and following *Cheyenne Autumn*, Ford made *Donovan's Reef* and *7 Women*, two films that portray Asians in a patently racist manner. Following his and other American filmmakers' concerted efforts to demonize the Japanese in propaganda films during World War II — and Ford's Oscar-winning documentary *December 7* is appallingly racist, even for 1943 — portraying Asians as sneaky, conniving grotesques was an affirmation of some of the most widely held prejudices in the United States. Ford seems to have shared these bigoted views of Asians, and thus it's no great surprise that one of his final film projects, on which he served as executive producer, was the documentary *Vietnam! Vietnam!* (1971), yet another piece of pro-war, Asian-patronizing, paternalistic propaganda.

That World War II and the Cold War altered Ford's views on politics and society so drastically is, I think, tragic, but in hindsight it is unsurprising, considering that Ford's very Catholic worldview was always inflected by conservative as well as liberal ideas. As Joseph McBride puts it, "No doubt Ford would not have remained commercially viable for so long had he not been simultaneously reactionary and progressive" (420). By the same token, those who knew him well attest that Ford had a personality that was at once tyrannically patriarchal and endearingly maudlin; he acted tough professionally to compensate for a deeply sympathetic disposition. The actor Lee Marvin said of him: "Ford was probably the most liberal man I ever met. Yet he didn't act it" (Eyman 362).

Like so many Americans after the atrocious but ultimately successful Allied effort in World War II, Ford believed that an aggressive foreign policy was the only way to ensure U.S. national security — that the best defense was a great offense. This view of the world was not only shortsighted and morally flawed, but ultimately it has had far-reaching geopolitical repercussions that continue to be felt today. According to the pacifist A.J. Muste, "The problem after a war is with the victor. He thinks he has just proved that war and violence pay" (qtd. in Zinn 424).

At his best, though, Ford questioned the rationality of interpersonal and military violence. During his peak period of 1939–41 the director combined his love of the carnivalesque and his disdain for pious hypocrisy and upper-crust pretension with an appreciation for peaceful male figures and heroines who exhibit courage and independence, as well as family loyalty. The cinematic world Ford created in those years parallels the kind of society envisioned by another great American humanist, Bruce Springsteen;[26] as the chorus to his anthemic "Land of Hope and Dreams" declares,

> This train
> Carries saints and sinners
> This train
> Carries losers and winners
> This Train
> Carries whores and gamblers
> This Train
> Carries lost souls
> This Train
> Dreams will not be thwarted
> This Train
> Faith will be rewarded
> ....
> This Train
> All aboard

Ford's increasingly conservative views, however, along with the toxic political and professional climate in Hollywood during the blacklist years, would lead him to largely abandon this kind of idealistic, nostalgic vision of America.

In many post-war Ford films, the ideal social unit is not the working-class nuclear family but the military squad, whether it's comprised of cavalrymen (in his famous 1948–50 trilogy), PT boat crewmen (in *They Were Expendable*), pilots (in *The Wings of Eagles*), or old Navy buddies who still drive around in jeeps and salute their captain (in *Donovan's Reef*).[27] In these hyper-macho environments, Ford frequently portrays his major female characters as threatening interlopers and agents of distraction who must be marginalized, tamed and/or converted to the military way of life, as occurs in *The Wings of Eagles* (1957), as well as *Rio Grande* and *Donovan's Reef*. Tellingly, the last scene in *The Wings of Eagles* features a long, tearful good-bye between old Navy buddies Frank "Spig" Wead and "Jughead" Carson (John Wayne and Dan Dailey), not, as one is led to expect, any kind of resolution to the tortuous relationship between Wead and Min, his estranged wife (Maureen O'Hara).

Ford's final fiction film, *7 Women* (1966), apart from being one of his most openly racist works—it portrays Chinese people in 1935 as medieval, Orientalized savages—is such a muddled thematic and narrative mess that it makes female empowerment look about as attractive and fulfilling as life on a chain gang. Feminism is a dark road with a dead end in this film. In her showcase speech near the middle of the narrative, Anne Bancroft's doctor protagonist declares:

> Normal—what the hell is so normal about my life? It took me eight years to become a doctor. I gave everything up so I could study. And for what? Anything I could get. There are no top jobs for women doctors. I couldn't even open a decent office—had to sweat it out in the worst hospitals. And when I finally gave myself a little time for a little love, I wound up picking the wrong guy. What do you think of that...? Oh, well, it was nice while it lasted. But for keeps he preferred his wife. So what's normal about that?

To complete her self-loathing diatribe, the doctor tells her young friend, one of many nuns at the convent in which the entire film is set, "You know, Emma, you're the only one that still has a chance. There's a real world outside. Get out of this rat race—go and find it." Thus, Bancroft's embittered heroine presents her own autobiography as a cautionary tale. Accordingly, then, in the film's final scene, clearly keeping in mind the scant value of her wasted life, she immolates herself by poison after dispatching the Genghis Khan-ish villain, whose concubine she has become to bargain for the lives of her fellow white captives. This final act is unprecedented in Ford's cinema. It is practically impossible to imagine him conceiving a male protagonist as such a ruthlessly cynical, spiritually bereft—and ultimately suicidal—loner. Ethan Edwards, deeply wrathful and compromised though he is, receives much better treatment from Ford in *The Searchers*.

Many critics, including Luke Gibbons and Joseph McBride, defend Ford against accusations of misogyny, in light of Richard Schickel's essentially true charge that the director "was as patronizing and fearful of them [women] as he was of Indians." I would qualify that statement only by saying that Ford's work was not always thus—at least not from 1939 to 1941. I see very little to be accomplished by engaging in a quixotic defense of pictures like *The Quiet Man*, which Schickel correctly points out as particularly "witless and vulgar" in its sexism.[28] As a productive alternative, I suggest that those interested in discovering Ford's cinema, as well as representations of exceptionally complex gender identities from the Classical Hollywood period, seek out the films he made with a young Henry Fonda, along with the director's mid-career masterpiece, *How Green Was My Valley*. These works show Ford at his most sympathetic, mature, and subversive.

Although he is now most often discussed in conjunction with John Wayne, Ford had done a whole career's worth of films prior to directing the Duke in *The Searchers*, *The Quiet Man* and a string of cavalry movies; and in some ways Wayne did Ford more harm than good, both professionally and personally. In a 1951 puff piece, Ford claimed that his star had "something intangible that no director can impart or create: the ability to be a real man" ("John Wayne — My Pal" 273). Never, though, has a figure of American masculinity — behind a façade of unalloyed confidence and corniness — been more artificial, hollow, and morally bankrupt. As screenwriter James Edward Grant, Wayne's frequent collaborator, put it plainly: "All you gotta have in a John Wayne picture is a hoity-toity dame with big tits that Duke can throw over his knee and spank, and a collection of jerks he can smash in the face every five minutes" (McBride 639). Ford and Wayne's final film together, *Donovan's Reef*, sticks to Grant's formula almost precisely,[29] with barroom brawler Donovan (Wayne) finally getting the best of his initially self-assured young love interest, declaring, "Amelia, you have a mean Irish temper, but I love it. From now on, I wear the pants in this family." Then he proceeds to manhandle and place her over his knee, spank her repeatedly, and kiss her, as Amelia first struggles against him but finally submits.

Before the nadir of *Donovan's Reef*, Ford often pushed the limits of the Wayne formula, but the star's typical, calculated two-note performances, along with Ford's persistent marginalization of women in his later cinema, severely limit the appeal and impact of many of these films today. Nonetheless, prior to fully embracing the paper tiger that is Wayne, John Ford's art effectively challenged patriarchal power structures and the American addiction to violence. In a sense, the thematic shift in his post–1941 work serves to underscore the brilliance of what he achieved in the years just before he was seduced — paradoxically — by war and the commercial appeal of John Wayne.

CHAPTER 3

Assimilation, Integration, Continuity and Critique: Gender and Genre in the Hollywood Irish Cinemas of John Ford and Jim Sheridan

> [W]hat we do as men in baptism with every child ... is to rechristen it into the male world. Because we know the power of the female. — JIM SHERIDAN[1]

In the previous chapters I have mainly discussed John Ford's treatment of gender, but in the process I have also tried to illuminate the Irish as well as American cultural and political content of his films. Indeed, his cinema is an inescapable landmark for filmmakers on both sides of the Atlantic. Ford has certainly had a tremendous impact on the American *auteurs* who have gained prominence since his death in 1973, most notably Peter Bogdanovich, Steven Spielberg and Clint Eastwood. Stylistically and thematically, their films clearly reveal this influence, for better and for worse, and all three have talked openly about their enormous debt to Ford.

Yet it is perhaps Martin Scorsese, another great admirer of the director, who has best adapted the Fordian ambivalence about American history and ideals in his own work, while making of it something provocative, challenging, and original. In *Taxi Driver* (1976), *Raging Bull* (1980), *Goodfellas* (1990), and *The Departed* (2006) Scorsese has used typically white ethnic anti-heroic male figures to push the limits of genre conventions and interrogate notions of violence, the kind of cultural commentary that Ford made meaningful but oblique gestures toward in *The Searchers* and *The Man Who Shot Liberty Valance*. Much like Ford, Scorsese, particularly in the later (current) phase of his career, evinces a remarkable aversion to narratives set outside male-dominated environments. In contrast to Ford's work, though, Scorsese's films are frequently concerned with spectacular familial disintegration.

It is Irish filmmakers who have, for the most part, carried on the artistic legacy of Ford's obsession with the family and its survival—dramatized most effectively in his 1939–41 period. In particular, the Irish films of Jim Sheridan—*My Left Foot* (1989), *The Field* (1990), *In the Name of the Father* (1993), *The Boxer* (1997), and *In America* (2002)—all more or less directly engage Ford's work, along with questions of gender, politics, and ethnic identity in both Irish and American contexts. Ruth Barton, in her cogent overview, *Irish National Cinema*, defines her country's film canon according to recurring "images, themes and characters":

> Alongside this repository of [rural and urban Irish] images is a range of themes that recur within these films—of rebellion and sacrifice, of departure and return, of spiritual voyages, and these in turn are animated by a panoply of characters, many of them borrowed from the repertoire of early stage and vaudeville representations—the fighting Irishman, the buffoon, the long-suffering mother, the feisty colleen, the rebel son [7].

These tropes and types form the "foundation of an Irish cinema and have become, for each new generation of filmmakers, a way of defining their work, whether they choose to reject them, incorporate them or rework them" (7). Ford, having been well acquainted with Ireland and its literature, and having begun his career in the pre-sound Hollywood film industry, took his storytelling cues directly from the stage traditions that Barton describes. In many ways his work bridges the silent and modern film industries, as well as the Irish and American cinemas.

Therefore, the first part of this chapter will offer a typology of male and female characters in Ford's films, establishing the breadth and limits of the Irish-American director's representations of masculinity and femininity, and briefly touching on other important Ford films not covered in Chapters 1 and 2. Although I have identified these types independently, they are all clearly variations on those that Barton has categorized previously. I will then proceed to show how Sheridan essentially picks up where Ford left off in terms of gender and genre, employing archetypes with increasing complexity and opening up the possibility of progressive, non-patriarchal power dynamics within the Irish family.

Archetypes of Manhood in the Films of John Ford

1. The Bumbling Oaf

In Ford films this figure is often played by the strapping actor Ward Bond. His roles as Adam in *Drums Along the Mohawk*, Cass in *Young Mr. Lin-*

coln, Lov Bensey in *Tobacco Road* and Boats Mulcahy in *They Were Expendable* are prime examples. Others include Dai Bando (Rhys Williams) in *How Green Was My Valley* and Ole Olsen (John Wayne) in *The Long Voyage Home*. This character has a capacity for violence and may lack moral clarity. He needs a good leader to keep him on the right path and channel his aggression toward a socially sanctioned goal like war, boxing, or physical labor. Lacking guidance, he may engage in criminal behavior, as Cass does. John Wayne's portrayal of Ole Olsen is a variation on this type and a huge departure from the typical Wayne screen persona. Ole is a Swedish farm boy without an aggressive bone in his body. When one of his friends punches him to keep him from drinking and missing his ship home, Ole accepts the blow with a smile. In fact, he is almost always smiling and affable, a trait that marks him as distinct from most other Wayne characters.

2. The Dissolute Man

This character is often Irish and a projection of Ford's own Jekyll and Hyde personality. He is a drunk who is prone to fail himself and everyone around him. In Ford's world, though, such figures are usually redeemable. Victor McLaglen's Gypo Nolan, the protagonist of *The Informer*, betrays his best friend to British agents and blows the reward money on a night of boozing, but he ultimately receives forgiveness from God and man. McLaglen's roles, including Gypo Nolan, the avuncular drunkard sergeants in each entry of the cavalry trilogy, and Will Danaher (in *The Quiet Man*), are dissolute/oafish hybrids very much in line with the long-established "stage Irishman" figure.

Poetic drunks also pop up in a number of Ford films. *The Long Voyage Home* features both the doomed English sailor and alcoholic, Smitty (Ian Hunter), and Driscoll (Thomas Mitchell), the Irish sailor, singer and drinker who, near the film's climax, cries out, "Is there to be no more light in the world? Is there no place in this dark land where a man who's drunk can find a decent bit of fun?" Mitchell also plays a good-hearted, drunken doctor in both *The Hurricane* (1937) and *Stagecoach* (1939). Three of the most memorable dissolute men from later Ford films are poetic drunks as well: the ultimately courageous theater troupe leader Dr. Hall (Alan Mowbray) in *Wagon Master*, *The Quiet Man*'s matchmaker, Michaeleen Flynn (played by the incomparable Barry Fitzgerald), and the brilliant boozehound newspaperman in *The Man Who Shot Liberty Valance*, Edmund O'Brien's Dutton Peabody, who incurs the wrath of outlaw gunslingers and survives to oversee the political birth pangs of his frontier town. Additionally, in *The Sun Shines Bright* (1953) the eloquent and merciful Judge Priest rationalizes his drinking at all hours by declaring, "I need to get my heart started!"

3. The Loose Cannon

Elements of the loose cannon may overlap with characteristics from any of the other categories. The distinguishing factor is that these men exhibit intelligence and moral agency; the problem, however, is that they are hot heads who get themselves into trouble and require the tempering influence of a community and/or other strong men to keep them focused on honorable goals. John Wayne's Rusty Ryan (also a troubled son) in *They Were Expendable* and Ethan Edwards (also a distant father figure) in *The Searchers* are figures in this mode. So are Ben Johnson's Tyree (another young man in need of guidance) in *Rio Grande*, Ashby Corwin (John Russell) in *The Sun Shines Bright*, and Victor Mature's (grotesquely dissolute) Doc Holliday in *My Darling Clementine*.

The outright villains in Ford's films tend to be morally depraved loose cannons, such as Caldwell in *Drums Along the Mohawk*, Scar in *The Searchers*, and Lee Marvin's horrifying Liberty Valance. Ford often validates not one particular mode of masculinity but rather one side of a racial, class and/or political divide; thus, Valance might be considered good if only he were in with the right crowd. Gilhooley, Marvin's character in *Donovan's Reef*, seems to have a lot in common with Valance, the character he played a year earlier. This unrepentant brawler and chauvinist, however, happens to be the right-hand man of John Wayne's Donovan, and this association validates Gilhooley's behavior.

4. The Strong, Distant Father

Such a figure is practically ubiquitous in Ford films. In some instances he is villainous, like the nearly identical Old Man Clanton (Walter Brennan) in *My Darling Clementine* and Uncle Shiloh Clegg (Charles Kemper) in *Wagon Master*, as well as, to a great extent, Lieutenant Colonel Thursday in *Fort Apache*. Generally, though, military commanders, particularly in Ford's postwar films, are morally upright practitioners of paternal tough love: Lieutenant John Brickley (Robert Montgomery) in *They Were Expendable*, as well as John Wayne's characters from the latter two entries in the cavalry trilogy — Nathan Brittles in *She Wore a Yellow Ribbon* and Kirby Yorke in *Rio Grande*. These officers love and discipline their men like sons, but their allegiance to their country and mission trumps affection and camaraderie. For example, John Brickley finally leaves his men behind on the island of Corregidor to face imprisonment or death at the hands of the Japanese, explaining to the reluctant Rusty Ryan, "Look, son, we're going home to do a job, and that job is to get ready to come back," as they depart on the last plane escaping the island.

This pattern of sage authority figures guiding younger men via enlightened paternalism through militaristic rites of passage continues in Ford's later work. The Reverend Playfair plays strong surrogate father to Sean Thornton's wayward pacifist son in *The Quiet Man*, and Martin Maher, Sr. (Donald Crisp, who had played the much more kindly patriarch in *Valley*) keeps his namesake (Tyrone Power), whom he refers to as "my eejit son," from wavering in his military duties at West Point. Similarly, Tom Doniphon dispenses pragmatic paternal advice to the idealistic lawyer Ransom Stoddard in *Liberty Valance*: "I know those law books mean a lot to you. But not out here. Out here a man settles his own problems [with a gun]." Wayne's Ethan Edwards is a father figure to Jeffrey Hunter's Martin Pawley in *The Searchers*, but Martin has some success in tempering Ethan's ruthlessness with his own sense of justice, although, as I argue in Chapter 2, the elder man's transformation rings false as, at best, a concession to Hollywood commercial practice and, at worst, a naïve endorsement of American Exceptionalism (or maybe a combination of both). *The Last Hurrah*'s Frank Skeffington (Spencer Tracy) is a more tender patriarch, at least in his relationship with his nephew Adam, whom he has anointed as his heir apparent, while he has essentially given up on his actual son, Frank, Jr., who is a dissolute fop. Similarly, Judge Priest (Charles Winninger) of *The Sun Shines Bright*— a film Ford allegedly held dear as one of his favorites— practices a reactionary but gentle form of enlightened paternalism as he upholds the values and rigid social hierarchy of the Southern Confederacy. At the same time, Priest advocates a measure of tolerance as the arbiter of the law in his Kentucky community and as matchmaker to two troubled young people.

In sharp contrast, Ford's earlier films *The Grapes of Wrath* and *How Green Was My Valley* feature exceptionally nurturant and progressive father figures: Jim Casy in the former work and Mr. Gruffydd in the latter. Both of these men lead gently by example, not by using emasculation or coercion, patiently guiding their protégés toward justice and tolerance. In *How Green Was My Valley* the young protagonist Huw has the benefit of two kind father figures in his life, with Mr. Morgan (Huw's natural father) acting as the reserved but benevolent working-class patriarch, and Mr. Gruffydd providing intellectual and spiritual edification.

5. The Troubled Son

As indicated above, this archetype usually appears as the counterpart to an aloof patriarch. In both *Expendable* and *Fort Apache* John Wayne's character (Rusty Ryan; Captain York) struggles to reconcile a superior officer's orders with his own conscience, but he ultimately bows to military/patriarchal authority. Other examples of sons who finally reconcile themselves to the dictates of autocratic father figures include Jeff Yorke in *Rio Grande*, Sean Thornton in *The Quiet Man*, and Ransom Stoddard in *Liberty Valance*. *The Last Hurrah* is an interesting case in which the troubled son, Frank, Jr., is practically unredeemable, and the good surrogate son/nephew, Adam (Jeffrey Hunter), has a fairly uncomplicated, affectionate relationship with his uncle/father figure, Mayor Frank Skeffington. Adam needs little guidance to be set on the right path by Frank, which is one reason why the middle of the film is devoid of interesting conflict.

In *The Grapes of Wrath*, on the other hand, the narrative builds toward the rebellious Tom Joad's climactic acceptance of Jim Casy's spiritual legacy of humane egalitarianism. In a slightly different vein, the final act of *How Green Was My Valley* chronicles the expulsion of Mr. Gruffydd, along with the mining accident that claims the life of Mr. Morgan. The film's last images depict Huw's memories of the two father figures he has lost, as his adult self intones in voiceover, "Men like my father cannot die. They are with me still — real in memory as they were in flesh. Loving and beloved forever. How green was my valley then." These words recall Mr. Gruffydd's farewell to Huw, "We will live in the minds of each other," and suggest a form of paternal transcendence predicated on genuine love and compassion, as opposed to the atrocious falsehoods and distortions that underpin the martial transcendence propagated by Captain York at the close of *Fort Apache*. Speaking of his needlessly sacrificed comrades, York declares: "They aren't forgotten because they haven't died. They're living. Right out there.... Faces may change — and names — but they're there.... They're better men than they used to be. Thursday did that. He made it a command to be proud of."

6. (Blessed Is) the Peacemaker

Across Ford's body of work, the peacemaker has varying degrees of success upholding order through nonviolent means. One of the most successful by far is Abe Lincoln, who manages to stop a lynching and stand for justice through a combination of wit, charm and exclusively verbal intimidation. In a bizarre echo of *Young Mr. Lincoln*, the comically nostalgic *The Sun Shines Bright* features Judge Priest casually stepping in to prevent the lynching of a black man wrongly accused of raping a white woman. Later in the film, members of the lynch mob campaign for the Judge's reelection, bearing a sign proclaiming, "HE SAVED US FROM OURSELVES." Rather than illuminating the endemic racism behind this abortive act of vigilantism, however, the film highlights the Judge's essential function in maintaining the benevolent white-dominated status quo of his "old Kentucky home."

In *My Darling Clementine* Sheriff Wyatt Earp frequently goes about his business without a gun and tries to prevent conflict from escalating, but in the end he reluctantly takes up a pistol to battle the sociopathic Clanton gang alongside the impetuous Doc Holliday. By the same token, for much of the duration of *Fort Apache* Captain York attempts to broker peace with Cochise and his tribe, yet, bound by duty and patriotism, he must follow in Thursday's footsteps and lead a genocidal campaign against the U.S. Army's newest enemy. In *She Wore a Yellow Ribbon*, Ford's next cavalry movie, Nathan Brittles keeps the peace by staging a bloodless cavalry charge — an oxymoron if there ever was one — through an Indian camp, having declared to his barely articulate, drunken Indian chief counterpart: "Yes, we are too old for war. But old men should stop wars." The disembodied voiceover at the film's muddled conclusion then declares of the cavalry: "Wherever they rode, and whatever they fought for, that place became the United States." In this way, the film promotes a notion perhaps best described as "Manifest Destiny lite."

Conversely, in some of Ford's pre-war films, peacemaking goes hand in hand with the idea of social justice. In addition to Abe Lincoln, both Jim Casy, who believes in "one big soul that belongs to everybody," and Mr. Gruffydd, who preaches "justice," "truth," and "love" while railing against "hypocrisy" and "fear," embody the "peace which passeth understanding." Each man imparts this ethos to his surrogate son, even as he himself is ultimately rejected by society at large. In my view, Ford's rendering of his protagonists as "victorious in defeat"[2] — an oft-repeated trope in his work — is never more sublime and affecting than in these films.

Ford's later cinema, reflecting the lessons he took from World War II, often depicts peacemaking as a fool's errand. *The Man Who Shot Liberty Valance* dramatizes the harsh rites of passage endured by the idealistic lawyer, Ransom Stoddard; this character starkly contrasts with the hero of *Young Mr. Lincoln*. Whereas Lincoln threatens violence in order to avert conflict, Stoddard begins as a pacifist and is forced to confront his own naïveté and accept the validity of violence in the figure of John Wayne's gun-slinging Tom Doniphon, who ultimately paves the way for Stoddard's successful political career.

The final scene of *Valance* is one of emasculation. After Ranse has confessed to reporters that it was not him but Tom who really killed the titular villain, he asks the train conductor to make an unscheduled stop to let him and his wife, Hallie, off at the next town. The conductor responds, "Nothing's too good for the man who shot Liberty Valance," unintentionally cutting Ranse to the quick. The film ends with discomfiting silence, as the politician and his wife sit looking straight ahead, avoiding each other's gaze. The implication is that not only has Ranse's career been predicated on a lie, but so has his marriage. Hallie had agreed to marry him only in the wake of his shootout with Valance, and she had always carried a torch for Tom, as evidenced by her tears at his funeral and her gesture of planting the cactus rose, the same gift that Tom had given her before she chose Ranse. Thus,

Ford's last great film attests to his increasingly bleak view of peaceful conflict resolution.

Female Archetypes in Ford Films

1. The Whore with a Heart of Gold

This common Hollywood figure features prominently in two early Ford films, *The Informer* (1935) and *Stagecoach* (1939), which both take some pains to humanize their fallen women, Katie Madden (Margot Grahame) and Dallas (Claire Trevor). In Ford's post-war *Wagon Master* (1950), the saucy prostitute Denver (Joanne Dru) eventually and implausibly becomes monogamous with a noble horse-trader (Ben Johnson's Travis Blue) and gains acceptance from a westward-driving Mormon community. Later, in *The Sun Shines Bright,* Ford uses the occasion of a prostitute's funeral to create one of his trademark parade-of-the-common-folk community-building sequences, with Judge Priest offering a poignant eulogy and appealing to his constituents' most merciful impulses. In the cases of Dallas and Denver, the whore with a heart of gold reforms and converts completely to the family-oriented values of her community. Significantly, one fallen women who fails to conform and become monogamous, *My Darling Clementine*'s Chihuahua, is finally shot dead.

2. The Strong but Obedient, Durable, Desensualized, Working-Class Mother

This exceedingly common type in Irish drama and film ranges, in Ford's work, from a cardboard cutout such as Abigail Clay (Alice Brady) in *Young Mr. Lincoln*, Mary O'Donnell (Maureen O'Hara), the idealized surrogate military mom in *The Long Gray Line*, and Mrs. Jorgensen (Olive Carey) in *The Searchers* to the much more active matriarchs featured in several of the director's pre-war movies, including Ma Joad in *The Grapes of Wrath* and Mrs. Morgan in *How Green Was My Valley*. In the latter film, the adult Huw describes his father as the "head" and his mother as the "heart" of the household, and in the domestic sphere she wields as much power as Mr. Morgan. For her part, Ma Joad steadily eclipses her husband in authority, leading to Pa's resigned admission in the film's final scene: "You're the one that keeps us goin', Ma. I ain't no good no more, and I know it." In addition, Ada Lester (Elizabeth Patterson) of *Tobacco Road* (1941) stoically holds her remaining family members together, despite the abject failures of her lay-about husband, Jeeter.

3. The Wild, Headstrong Lady

This mode of femininity is prevalent throughout Ford's cinema as well. Such a character can be sympathetic and fairly complex, like *How Green Was My Valley*'s Angharad and the wonderful Mrs. McKlennar from *Drums Along the Mohawk*, as well as, to a lesser extent, *Young Mr. Lincoln*'s Ann Rutledge and Sandy (Donna Reed) in *They Were Expendable*. Among women in later Ford films, Hallie in *Liberty Valance* is perhaps the most complex — although she regrets not marrying a swaggering gunslinger, she is still portrayed as having strong, conflicting emotions.

On the opposite end of the spectrum are Ford's "feisty colleens," who are often little more than caricatured narrative devices. Examples of these include Kathleen Yorke (Maureen O'Hara in *Rio Grande*), Mary Kate (*The Quiet Man*), Laurie (*The Searchers*), and Marty (Shirley Jones in *Two Rode Together*). The most transparently malicious representation of this type is the brash, self-loathing and fatalistic feminist Dr. Cartwright from the woeful *7 Women*.[3] Again, most of these uncomplicated, often desperate women appear in Ford's later films, whereas far more active female characters show up in his work from 1939 to 1941. A great example is *Drums Along the Mohawk*'s Mrs. McKlennar, the exceptional Fordian — and Hollywood — female who is at once maternal and unabashedly sensual and tough.

4. The WASP Outsider

This figure accords with mainstream bourgeois American culture and is, therefore, marginal in Ford's world. In many cases, she is redeemable, as is the case with Lana Martin (*Drums*), Clementine, Philadelphia Thursday (*Fort Apache*), Eloise Kelly (Ava Gardner in *Mogambo*), and Amelia Dedham (*Donovan's Reef*). As WASP-ish women with a wild streak in post-war Ford films, however, both Kelly and Dunham must be humiliated and tamed as part of the price of their redemption. Alternatively, the WASP woman can be little more than a villainous impediment, like Mave, Adam Caulfield's snob of a wife in *The Last Hurrah*, and the even more execrable figures of Agatha Andrews and Florrie Pether in *7 Women*. Somewhere between these two extremes is the character of Mary Todd from *Young Mr. Lincoln*, who is spunky and charming, but also threatening in the sense that she is determined to propel her future husband into the realm of upper-class decadence and pretension. WASP outsiders may also be male in Ford's cinema, like Lt. Col. Thursday and Horace K. Maydew, Judge Priest's political rival in *The Sun Shines Bright*, but generally they are women.

Ford and Sheridan:
Dramas of Assimilation and Integration

Establishing working definitions of Ford's gender types is crucial to charting the trajectory of Irish cinema in general and the work of Jim Sheridan in particular. In *My Left Foot* (1989) and *In America* (2002), the first and most recent of Sheridan's Irish films, he is in dialogue with *The Grapes of Wrath* and *How Green Was My Valley* specifically. Sheridan makes a direct visual acknowledgment of the former film's profound influence by showing Sarah Sullivan, a principal character of *In America*, watching the final scene of *The Grapes of Wrath* on television. The rest of this chapter will focus on *My Left Foot* and *In America*, the director's most ostensibly depoliticized films, detailing the way that Sheridan constructs these pictures in terms of gender and genre, as well as the way in which both act as cinematic responses to Ford's pre–World War II movies. Chapter 4 will explore Sheridan's representations of gender in his more overtly ideological works, considering how he consciously constructs his family narratives with the goal of filling thematic gaps in the Irish film canon, cleverly manipulating Hollywood genre conventions in the process.

Sheridan's Irish films are all centrally concerned with parent-child relations. *My Left Foot* depicts a young man resisting an alternately tyrannical and tender father while being sustained emotionally and intellectually by a strong, compassionate mother. *The Field* shows a son's difficulty in rejecting his emasculating, psychologically warped father when his mother is silent and emotionally absent. Both *In the Name of the Father* and *The Boxer* portray rebellious sons accepting good fathers, while the latter film also depicts a young man taking on the role of affirmative paternal figure. By the same token, as Sheridan himself puts it, "[T]he mothers in all the films I have done have been amazingly strong" (Barton 154). With the exception of *In the Name of the Father*, in which the protagonist is imprisoned and thereby involuntarily estranged from his mother,[4] Sheridan's Irish films all feature complex maternal figures who challenge and subvert patriarchal authority with mostly productive results.

Through his close attention to family dynamics and their cultural implications, Sheridan has created complex narratives of "social integration," to borrow Thomas Schatz's term. Schatz defines Hollywood film genres according to their value-laden storytelling patterns:

> Ultimately, genres of indeterminate, civilized space (musical, screwball comedy, social melodrama) and genres of determinate, contested space (Western, gangster, detective) might be distinguished according to their differing ritual functions. The former tend to celebrate the values of *social integration*, whereas the latter uphold the values of *social order*. The former tend to cast an attitudinally

unstable couple or family unit into some representative microcosm of American society, so that their emotional and/or romantic "coupling" reflects their integration into a stable environment. The latter tend to cast an individual, violent, attitudinally static male into a familiar, predetermined milieu to examine the opposing forces vying for control [29].

Schatz goes on to characterize the "thematics" of these two genre categories: he describes genres of order as principally concerned with "mediation — redemption," a "macho code," "isolated self-reliance," and "utopia-as-promise"; whereas genres of integration focus on "integration — domestication," a "maternal-familial code," "community cooperation," and "utopia-as-reality" (35). This theoretical model provides a productive analytical approach to both Ford and Sheridan, since the sociocultural content of the former's films tends to engage questions of "integration" as well as "order," while in the latter's work, "social integration" is always the central focus, even within the context of ostensibly "macho" genres like prison and boxing films.

Although Ford was famous for making westerns, most of his films are mixed-genre family melodramas in which, as Charles Ramírez Berg has indicated, the main characters often end up either falling in line with community-sanctioned values, negotiating between conflicting values, or defining themselves in opposition to the prevailing social order. I would argue that, while Ford's post–World War II films, with their repeated pattern of vexed father-son relations, tend to raise issues of social integration, in most cases they work out their narrative/cultural problems through the assimilation of their protagonists, thereby reaffirming social order. When the community is a military regiment, the protagonist (usually John Wayne) has little choice but to conform, finally staying true to a pro-status quo macho code.

Ford's pre-war films, on the other hand, frequently feature communities integrating, if only temporarily, and protagonists resisting assimilation. In *Young Mr. Lincoln*, for example, Abe brings order to a frontier community by persuasively impressing his sense of justice upon others without resorting to violence. In *How Green Was My Valley*, both Angharad and Mr. Gruffydd attempt to advance tolerance and find love on their own terms, and their failure to reach their goals is emblematic of the community's decline; thus, the film depicts a tragic lack of social integration. In *The Grapes of Wrath*, Tom Joad becomes Jim Casy's disciple in promoting the concept of the universal human family, even as he is finally resigned to a rootless, lonely life on the run. The ending of *Drums Along the Mohawk* features one of Ford's most unequivocal celebrations of community integration, with Lana and Gil having achieved a marriage of relative equality in the midst of a multi-ethnic farming community at the dawn of American nationhood. A negotiation process occurs in these films, indicating community formation predicated on the integration of different backgrounds and values, rather than the rejection of one set of values in favor of another — what I view as the process of assimilation dramatized in Ford films like *They Were Expendable, Fort Apache, The Quiet Man, The Man Who Shot Liberty Valance,* and *Donovan's Reef.*

The narratives of Sheridan's films, however, are all concerned with the balancing of individual and community identities. They almost invariably place young people within repressive social milieus, whether this is the patriarchal family unit itself (*My Left Foot, The Field*), a prison (*In the Name of the Father*), or a community polarized by sectarian conflict (*The Boxer*). The repressive force in *In America* seems to be the emotional baggage of Irish history and colonial patriarchy, which cannot be mitigated by time and distance alone. The troubled sons (and sometimes daughters) in Sheridan's films recognize the dehumanizing aspects of their environments and resist assimilation, maturing by negotiating conflicting values and, with the tragic exception of Tadgh in *The Field*, learning from good parental figures. The two Sheridan films that most clearly depict successful social integration, however, are *My Left Foot* and *In America.*

My Left Foot: Mother Love and the Dark Side of the Working-Class Patriarch

Near the beginning of the Dublin-set *My Left Foot*, the characteristically self-critical protagonist, Christy Brown (Daniel Day-Lewis), issues a warning about his just-published autobiography, which is the source material for the film itself: "It's a bit sentimental," he tells his nurse, Mary. This statement could well serve as a disclaimer for all of Jim Sheridan's work. Just as Mary eventually becomes enamored of Christy, however, audiences in Ireland and the U.S. have often been won over by Sheridan's deft synthesis of Irish nostalgia, Hollywood artifice, and grim social realism.[5] The sentimentality in his narratives derives from both the Irish literary tradition and Hollywood filmmaking practice, and in that respect his most obvious influence is the famously maudlin John Ford. Viewed in conjunction with Ford's work, however, Sheridan displays significant restraint in his emotionally charged family dramas.

In *My Left Foot* Sheridan explodes the working-class family model that Ford elegized in *How Green Was My Valley*. He reveals the tension between an autocratic, alcoholic father and his family, while shifting the narrative focus to a mother-son relationship. In the first half of *Valley*, Ford explores the bond between Huw and Mrs. Morgan, particularly in the sequence when they both fall ill and convalesce together, but once Huw begins to navigate male rites of passage, Mrs. Morgan becomes more of a secondary character.

Mr. Morgan and the spiritual mentor Mr. Gruffydd are ultimately the main subjects of nostalgia in *Valley*, which ends with the adult Huw's elegy of "men like my father."[6] In *My Left Foot* these narrative developments are reversed: once the incredibly ambivalent relationship between Christy and his father has been established, Paddy Brown (Ray McAnally) recedes into the background, and the love between Bridget Brown (Brenda Fricker) and Christy becomes the emotional center of the film. Appropriately enough, in one of the picture's most sentimental moments, she tells her son, "You have my heart broken, Christy Brown. Sometimes I think you are my heart." The obviously Oedipal overtones of this relationship recall the intimate bond between Tom and Ma Joad in *The Grapes of Wrath*.

While Sheridan seems keen to debunk some of the romantic notions of working-class family life that Ford often conjured up, his first film is careful to dramatize the dark side of patriarchy without making the father into a cartoon villain. While I would agree with Ruth Barton that "ambivalence about modernity lies at the heart of *My Left Foot*'s narrative" (*Jim Sheridan: Framing the Nation* 16), I would add that the film is equally concerned with ambivalence about patriarchy. Paddy Brown is terrible at times, and he certainly inspires deep resentment in his son Christy. Yet Paddy is the same man who, after his infant son is diagnosed with cerebral palsy, resolves to keep Christy with the family: "I'll go in a coffin before any son of mine will go in a home." Later, Paddy praises the boy when he shows the family that he can write by scrawling "MOTHER" on the floor with chalk. Capping one of the film's most emotional sequences, Paddy triumphantly carries Christy on his shoulders into the local pub, announcing, "This is Christy Brown, my son, genius."

Then again, Paddy is the unreliable hothead who loses his job and endangers the family's welfare over a minor dispute with his foreman. Most repugnantly, he is the brutal tyrant who calls Sheila (Alison Whelan), his teenage daughter, "a dirty bitch" when she reveals she is pregnant, and threatens to "break every bone in her fucking body." As Christy listens to his father's rampage from upstairs, he seethes and wails, "I'll fucking kill him!" This episode crystallizes Christy's close relationship with Sheila, whom he loves but cannot protect from either their father or the perils of adulthood. In an earlier scene Christy watches apprehensively through his window as Sheila kisses a young man, signaling her budding sexuality, which will lead to a quick, difficult passage into marriage and parenthood due to the dictates of their religion and community.

By the same token, Sheridan explores Christy's anxiety over his mother's sexuality. One night, lying in his cramped bed among his brothers, Christy tosses and turns in agony listening to his father's coital grunts and moans in the next room. Although Sheridan omits the undoubtedly harrowing experience of child mortality endured by the actual Brown family—in reality, Bridget gave birth to 22 children, only 13 of whom lived to adulthood[7]—the film clearly suggests that Paddy acted recklessly in satiating his appetite for sex as well as booze (Donnelly). During his horribly derisive rant in the wake of Sheila's pregnancy, Paddy callously declares: "That's a lovely picture. The old woman that lives in the shoe and the daughter who couldn't keep her knickers on." Nonetheless, he prides himself on his virility, violently confronting a fellow pub-goer who mockingly suggests that Paddy "tie a knot in it" after Bridget gives birth to Christy.

Throughout most of the film, Christy's ambivalent negotiation of rites of passage into patriarchal masculinity is a process of assimilation as well as integration. Sheridan frequently alternates between dramatizing spaces and activities in which Christy is successful, accepted and therefore masculinized, and exploring sites of his emasculation. When Christy is home alone writing or painting, spending time with his mother, playing with his siblings in the streets, making a joke at his father's expense, flirting with a woman one-on-one, and finally, reluctantly being feted by socialites and artists, his cerebral palsy does not prevent him from fully thriving within his environment. When he is twice rejected by women he pines for, when he rages impotently against his father's excesses and abuses, and when he is viewed superficially by others as a mere "cripple," however, Christy is unmanned, depressed, and at one point suicidal.[8] Fittingly, Sheridan employs a point-of-view shot through the curtains of Christy's upstairs window to reveal the last image the young artist sees before his botched suicide attempt: his father caressing his mother's face as they stand in the street below.

That Christy successfully clings to his artistic identity is a triumph in itself, and he does so despite his father's nearly total lack of interest in or recognition of his talents—with the notable exception of the early scene in which Paddy parades his son before the other pub revelers. Yet until the final 17 minutes of *My Left Foot*, Christy remains beholden to the conventional patriarchal social order: in order to prove his masculinity, he plays sports, drinks hard, sings rebel songs, and starts a barroom brawl. His main sources of love and acceptance, though, are his mother, sister, a female teacher, and, later, his nurse and future wife, Mary, all of whom appreciate his intellect and poetic sensitivity while essentially dismissing his macho swagger as a façade. As Bridget lectures Christy after he has descended into a funk: "You get more like your father every day. All hard on the outside and putty on the inside. It's in *here* [points to her heart] battles are won. Not in the pub, pretending to be a big fella in front of the lads." Thus, she cogently exposes the fictions and contradictions crucial to patriarchal manhood.

Nonetheless, Bridget is able to recognize and appreciate her husband's periodic expressions of affection. Shortly before his death, responding to his wife's suggestion, Paddy determines to build Christy his own room and workspace, and he challenges his sons to a sort of brick-laying race. Bridget then surreptitiously implores her sons, "Lads, let your father win. He needs it." After her sons follow her directive, Paddy, having clearly overexerted himself, declares, "They've a long way to go to be a better man than their father." Bridget then turns to Christy and says succinctly, "[T]hat's the nearest he'll ever come to saying he loves you." Thus, Sheridan reveals a complex relationship between Bridget and Paddy: she endures his rage, resists his authority when she needs to, yet she also knows how to bring out the good in him; and despite his glaring faults, Paddy exhibits a deep sense of loyalty to his family.

Although Bridget's remarkable forbearance accords with that of other archetypal Irish mother figures, at times she exhibits remarkable agency by, for example, covertly hoarding the money necessary to buy Christy a wheelchair. Had she not hatched this scheme behind her husband's back, Sheridan clearly implies, Paddy might well have blown the cash at the pub. Furthermore, Bridget confronts her husband after he loses his job and demands an explanation, eliciting an indignant, dismissive response from him: "Don't you question me in front of the children." Paddy goes on to concoct a story casting himself as a proud rebel standing up to his tyrannical boss: "A brick hit the foreman accidentally on purpose." This romantic blarney makes his older sons laugh, but Bridget, Sheila and Christy are not amused. Christy responds by uttering an insult, which Paddy fails to decipher, a pattern repeated later when Christy cracks wise about the porridge the family has subsisted on ever since Paddy was fired. In the latter scene, the whole family laughs at Paddy's expense. When he demands to know what Christy has said, Bridget replies, "He just says the porridge is lovely." As often occurs, she and Christy are partners in subverting the authority of the tyrannical patriarch.

In keeping with *My Left Foot*'s Oedipal drama, one of Christy's most intimate moments with his father comes when Paddy is dying. Arriving home from errands, Bridget and Christy discover Paddy collapsed and wedged up against the kitchen door. When Bridget and Christy manage to push the door open, he tumbles onto the floor next to his expiring father, their two heads falling together — an image Sheridan captures in close-up. This incidental contact is as close as Christy ever comes as a grown man to embracing Paddy. Charting the narrative's classical Hollywood three-act structure, the father's demise occurs almost exactly 80 minutes into the 100-minute running time of the film. This clearly marks plot point 2, or the narrative's lowest point for the protagonist, who, one might argue, may now have even greater difficulty identifying with and making peace with his father, the main rival for his mother's affections. The final act lifts Christy up in every sense, however, dramatizing his artistic triumph and the full resolution of his Oedipal dilemma, two developments which are inextricably linked.

In *My Left Foot* (Miramax, 1989, dir. Jim Sheridan), Father (Ray McAnally) and son (Daniel Day-Lewis) share a rare peaceful moment.

From the image of Christy lying with his dying father, Sheridan cuts directly not to a church funeral scene, but to a pub memorial for Paddy, a scene that epitomizes the Brown family's conflicting emotions about their *paterfamilias*. The first shots of this sequence are of the proprietor checking his ledger and Bridget paying her husband's bar tab, the tidy sum of "7 pounds, five shillings and sixpence," according to the publican. As usual, Bridget is left to deal with the damage wrought by Paddy. Her face is resolute, her sorrow attenuated by relief.

What follows this unceremonious transaction, however, is an homage to Paddy that would have made John Ford proud. Attempting to break through the solemn cast of the occasion, Bridget tells Christy to sing "Paddy's favorite," and her son obliges, leading the mourners in the rebel anthem "The Foggy Dew," which commemorates the martyrs of the Easter 1916 Rising and is the only indication of Paddy's—or anyone's—political inclinations during the film. As Christy begins singing alone, a surly man sitting at the bar insults him, which inspires the other pub revelers to join in with Christy, their voices rising to belt out the song's refrain. This show of solidarity only irks the resident bully further, and he proceeds to up the ante by insulting the man of the hour: "His father was nothing but a mouth. Like all the Browns." As tempers flare, Christy keeps order momentarily and faces the bully, who says, "I don't fight cripples." Christy responds by kicking the man's pint from his hand, setting off a full-fledged brawl. In the ensuing moments, carnivalesque anarchy reigns, as everyone in the pub, save Bridget, gets their licks in, even

Sheila. The revelers smash the bar and requisition all the cash in the till, as Christy declares, "Drinks are on the house!"

As Ford often did, Sheridan makes this donnybrook a celebration of community. Although he was clearly no saint, the Browns and their neighbors will not abide any affront to Paddy in the wake of his death. He may have been terrible at times, but he was one of their own, and they treat him accordingly. As in most of Ford's fight scenes, the violence Sheridan stages here is highly stylized, quite silly, and completely harmless. The important distinction between the brawl in *My Left Foot* and those in Ford's films is that this contest is not a strictly hyper-masculine confrontation, with women and older men cheering from the sidelines; Sheridan has all sorts of women and men, including the physically limited Christy, enter the fray. It is an inclusive, delirious moment of catharsis for the Browns and their community.

From this point forward, though, Christy leaves conventional patriarchal masculinity behind, succeeding artistically and thereby replacing his father as the breadwinner of the family. With the help of his brother Benny, Christy completes his "own story"—the book *My Left Foot*, first published in 1954— which brings him recognition as an author and, just as crucially, generates financial comfort for the Browns. When Christy receives an 800-pound advance for the book, he and Benny stash it away in Bridget's money tin. The following scene, in which Bridget discovers the money as her children sit expectantly at the dinner table, is a poignant, and very Fordian, affirmation of family. Everyone cheers as Bridget stares in awestruck wonder at the bankroll. Alone with Christy later, she declares: "That's more money than your poor father ever earned in a whole year." Christy responds by playing up the father-son comparison even further: "Da was a bricklayer, Ma, and I'm a writer. I know it's mad money. I want you to have it." Christy thus shares his triumph; his success is aligned with that of his whole family in a way they never could have imagined while at the mercy of Paddy.

Christy's full passage into manhood occurs only after his father dies, he completes his memoir (and grows a beard in the process), meets his future wife, and is able to tell his mother, near the end of the film, "Go on, I'm all right ... I'm fine," as he prepares for his first date with Mary. After spending much of the film struggling with his Oedipal baggage, as well as his physical handicaps, he has finally found the love and acceptance that can—in some respects, at least—supplant the sustaining force of his mother's devotion. Christy had earlier lashed out at his teacher and love object, Dr. Cole, for her perceived condescension, telling her, "You're not my mother. Never forget that." As he has matured into the post–Paddy and post-book publication present, however, Christy can joke with Mary about his hang-ups. When he asks her for a match and Mary warns him, "Don't think I'm your mother just because I'm looking after you for the evening," Christy offers the rejoinder: "I don't need a fucking psychology lesson, I just need a fucking light."

Sheridan consistently emphasizes Christy's irreverent, self-deprecating sense of humor, which effectively mitigates many of the narrative's deeply sentimental elements.[9] Referring to himself derisively as a "cripple" and "mental defective," Christy makes it easier for audiences to root for him; as he resists being commodified as fodder for just another sappy inspirational story, he makes a strong case for himself as the subject of a genuinely powerful overcoming-the-odds tale. As Sheridan himself puts it, "I love Christy Brown. In some way, you are allowed [to] tell the Christy Brown story because he's so crippled. The audience will allow you [to] tell that story out of their culture because of his unique physical condition that somehow mirrors an interior emotional condition" (Barton 149).

In the process of reading his memoir, Mary, the audience surrogate, has fallen in love with Christy, and their budding romance emerges as the focus of the film's final scenes, which take place in and around the idyllic estate of Lord Castlewelland. When Mary wheels him out for his appearance as the guest of honor at a cerebral palsy foundation benefit, she parks Christy in front of a French door, outside of which is Dr. Cole, who turns to observe the two but cannot hear them. Dr. Cole watches from outside the glass (at the right of the frame) as Christy asks Mary on a date and she tentatively accepts. Sheridan thus manipulates the mise-en-scène to take the full measure of Christy's progress from the failed infatuation of his youth to the mature, mutual attraction of his adulthood. Furthermore, the director's visual language here shows a clear debt to Ford, the master of using windows and doorways as frames with frames to add depth and evoke nostalgia for happy reunions, sad partings and lost time.

My Left Foot's penultimate scene incorporates two Ford-inflected tropes to dramatize the completion of Christy's social integration. First, Sheridan stages a "farewell to the players," similar to the roll call Ford often employed to close his films — such as in *Fort Apache* and *The Quiet Man*. Christy's brothers and sisters bid him good-bye in turn and then pile into chauffeured Rolls Royces, as their hero and benefactor waits for his date. Christy appears happy and serene but remains irascible, telling one of his older brothers, "You're not me Da," and warning one of his younger brothers to "Get in the car before I kick your ass." As Sheila and Bridget prepare to go, they look at Christy anxiously; they clearly worry that he may have his heart broken again. This is the moment when Christy assures his mother that he can now take care of himself emotionally, letting her know, "I'm all right ... I'm fine." He is no longer a child, and she can let him go.

Ford's influence on the narrative once again becomes apparent after Christy's family departs. The celebrated author stays behind, consorting with

3. The Hollywood Irish Cinemas of Ford and Sheridan

Christy (Daniel Day-Lewis) and his once and future loves, Dr. Cole (Fiona Shaw, right) and Mary (Ruth McCabe) in *My Left Foot* (Miramax, 1989, dir. Jim Sheridan).

the rich host of the foregoing benefit, Lord Castlewelland, played by the elder statesman of Irish film, Cyril Cusack. Christy, who has expressed contempt for social elites at several points in the film, is at ease with the unpretentious Lord, who kindly fetches Christy some champagne for his rendezvous with Mary. Christy then tells him, "I hope to see you again," and Castlewelland replies, "Yes, I hope to see you again, Christy ... before closing time." Here, as in Ford's cinema, the surest way for a wealthy outsider to gain acceptance from fun-loving working class ethnics is to show fondness for drinking. This is yet another significant moment of integration: Christy is welcomed into high society, and the rich gentleman enters the inner circle of good folk based on his appreciation of our hero as well as a little boozing.[10]

The dramatic payoff of Christy and Mary's romance is a brief but powerful final scene that marks the protagonist's full maturation into adulthood and his entry into the canon of Irish authors. Mary takes him to a hilltop promontory, where they can look down upon all of Dublin, and Christy picks out literary landmarks: "You can just see Joyce's tower down there. And that's where J.M. Synge was born, at the foot of the mountains." Thus, he places himself in the context of great figures of Irish letters—his artistic fathers—and, by extension, Sheridan is doing the same.[11]

The allusion to Synge (1871–1909), whose short but influential career as a resident writer for Dublin's Abbey Theatre spanned the first decade of the twentieth century, is particularly apt. Synge's affinity for poets, tramps, cripples and outcasts is one of the most prominent features of his plays and prose. In one of his many essays on rural Irish life, "The Vagrants of Wicklow" (1901), Synge makes his sympathies clear: "In the middle classes the gifted son of a family is always the poorest — usually a writer or artist with no sense of speculation — and in a family of peasants, where the average comfort is just over penury, the gifted son sinks also, and is soon a tramp on the roadside" (169). In *My Left Foot*, Bridget Brown upsets this repressive patriarchal pattern by sustaining her gifted son, giving Christy the support he needs to establish a creative identity and career.

As opposed to the nostalgic yearning for youth, pre-industrial simplicity, and a lost working-class patriarch in the closing sequence of *How Green Was My Valley*, the finale of *My Left Foot* leaves little doubt that the Browns are ultimately far better off without Paddy and his excesses. They have rallied around Christy, who has propelled his family to prosperity and stability before finding a love and a life of his own. The narrative ends not with nostalgia, but by looking ahead. After Mary says a toast to Dublin, Sheridan captures the couple in a final freeze frame overlaid with a title that states, "Christy Brown married Mary Carr on the 5th October, 1972." The trajectory of their lives is set, and once again a woman's love is the key to Christy's growth as a human being and his integration into a functional family unit. Thus, Sheridan completes the narrative of Christy's passage into manhood, one that first stands in ambivalent relation to patriarchy before renouncing it in favor of progressive masculinity.

In America: Embracing Matriarchy, Androgyny and the Magical

In Sheridan's cinematic world, patriarchy, which in Ireland has historically been inextricably tied to colonialism, is completely retooled or else rejected altogether. The subjects of the next chapter, the three films Sheridan made in the 1990s subsequent to *My Left Foot—The Field*, *In the Name of the Father*, and *The Boxer*—can all be viewed as attempts to diagnose problems with patriarchy in general, and colonial patriarchy in particular. Additionally, the latter two films radically alter father-son dynamics, positing peaceful modes of masculinity as alternatives to violent extremism in the midst of the Troubles, the conflict that largely defined late twentieth-century Irish and British politics.

Sheridan's most recent Irish film, however, is, like *My Left Foot*, more concerned with heterosocial relationships, as the family it portrays, the Sullivans, includes a mother, a father, and two young daughters, ages 5 and 10. *In America* (2002) is a narrative of complete familial and social integration predicated on a repudiation of the patriarchal model and all its attendant denials, fictions, and dysfunctions. It is a story about emigration, the loss of a son, and the process of grieving that each family member must undertake in order to ensure their collective survival.

In many respects an autobiographical piece, *In America* reflects Sheridan's own experience of emigrating (while in his early 30s) with his wife and two daughters from Ireland to New York City in the early 1980s. On his DVD commentary, the filmmaker expounds the actual events that inform much of the film's first act, which deals with the family's illegal immigration to New York via Canada and their acclimation to a new city space, specifically the multicultural Hell's Kitchen section of Queens. In order to raise the dramatic stakes and add layers of cultural meaning to the narrative, however, Sheridan interposes a tragic event from his youth: the 1967 death of his younger brother, Frankie, at the age of 11— when Sheridan was 18 (Barton, *Jim Sheridan* ... xi).[12] Thus, at the beginning of *In America* the Sullivan family (the fictional Sheridans) has lost their son and brother so recently that the father, Johnny, tells a customs agent at the Canadian-U.S. border that he has three children, and his wife, Sarah, has to correct him. This initial scene clearly establishes Johnny's failure to mourn his son, leading him to a state of emotional isolation that endangers the welfare of the family.

Combining two family histories, that of Sheridan's original nuclear family, along with the one he shares with his wife and children, the film establishes a kind of double consciousness: a narrative center that is shared by the father, Johnny (Paddy Considine), and his older daughter, Christy (Sarah Bolger). This is not to say that the two other main characters, Sarah (Samantha Morton) and the younger daughter, Ariel (Emma Bolger), are tangential to the plot (more on that below), but the main narrative problem rests with Johnny, the flawed, goal-oriented protagonist seeking integration and professional success, and Christy, a redeemer and young artist figure. Viewing the film in terms of Thomas Schatz's generic categories is illuminating, then, because the main male character is a variation on a classically feminine archetype, a confused and frustrated figure in need of community acceptance, commonly seen in social melodramas (one of Schatz's "genres of integration"), while his ten-year-old daughter takes on the traditionally masculine role of family/social savior, a lynchpin of macho "genres of order." Therefore, while Johnny changes most in the course of the narrative (a clear marker of his status as protagonist), Christy has the most power to influence events by helping to restore her family's cohesiveness, specifically through her relationship with Johnny.

The film is structured by reference to Christy in two ways. First, her voiceover narration and her practice of recording events with her video camera — some of her footage doubles as the film narrative — mark her as an author surrogate and thus possibly a co-protagonist. As Sheridan attests, "The camcorder is there because in a way the little girl represents me because it wasn't my son who died, obviously, it was my brother. And so the emotions of the film are hers, and the perspective is hers, which is also kind of mine. And in that way [Johnny] becomes like my father" (*In America* Director's Commentary). At the same time, though, Sheridan dramatizes many of his own past struggles as a husband, father and thespian through the character of Johnny.

Second, Christy is the focal point of the film's magical tropes. The "three wishes" bequeathed to her by Frankie initiate and resolve conflict during the first and third acts of the film: her first wish sets the emigration narrative's chain of events in motion; her last facilitates her father's psychic recovery. By the same token, Christy's wishes function as a thematic device: she must, with the help of her mother, sister, and their shaman-like neighbor Mateo, compel her father to believe in magic, re-learn how to pretend at home and on the stage, and regain the faith he lost when Frankie died. This family-oriented process of mourning and renewal is part of Sheridan's overall cultural critique in the film:

> This is about the fact that the Irish can overcome death, or leave it behind, or a husband and wife can leave it behind. I thought of the [Long Kesh] hunger strikers and we being the only Western society that could have that — ten men dying one after each other [in 1981] — and I thought ... we've got to leave this suicide culture behind [*In America* Director's Commentary].

Such an engagement with Ireland's turbulent recent history reveals itself obliquely in the course of Sheridan's intermittently light-hearted social melodrama. Viewing Johnny's stunted passage through grief on a metaphorical level, however, puts this cultural message in perspective: as in all of Sheridan's first five films, the main male character of *In America* becomes emblematic of Irish Catholic masculinity broadly defined. It is Sheridan's deft manipulation of established Hollywood genre conventions, the narrative text of the films, that endows ethnically specific works like *My Left Foot* and *In America* with mass appeal, while creating a space for effective sociopolitical commentary, the films' subtext.

In America's cinematic allusions add more layers of cultural meaning to the narrative. As Ruth Barton argues, "the film is held together through its referencing of *E.T.*" (*Irish National Cinema* 189). Early on, the Sullivans go to see the 1982 Steven Spielberg film to escape the New York summer heat; soon after, Johnny stakes and almost blows all the family's savings to win Ariel a stuffed E.T. in a carnival game. Later, the family's African neighbor, Mateo (Djimon Hounsou), who is dying of AIDS, compares himself to the eponymous character to help Ariel make sense of his disease and eventual passing: "I'm an alien, like E.T.— from a different planet. My skin is too sensitive for this Earth, right? The air is too hard for me."[13] Finally, Johnny picks up on this comparison to comfort Ariel in the wake of Mateo's death, thus signaling the return of his sense of magic — what Sheridan calls "the invisible" substance of the film — and his alignment with Mateo's androgynous, spiritual-seeker masculine ethos.

The film's other main cinematic point of reference, John Ford's *The Grapes of Wrath*, resonates just as deeply, as it indicates a rich thematic continuity between Ford's pre–World War II works and Sheridan's films in three important respects. First, both narratives reflect the Irish experience of famine and emigration. Ford said of *Wrath* that "the story was similar to the Famine in Ireland" in terms of the displacement and suffering of a whole class of people (Cowie 8), while Sheridan connects his narrative to Irish historical trauma more indirectly: "This is based on the myth of the Irish coming to America after death on a mythological level, which ... the Irish did after the Famine" (*In America* Director's Commentary). In both films the story of one family's bereavement and migration becomes representative of an entire people in transition.

By the same token, both films posit a shift toward matriarchy as a necessary and productive adjustment that enables the struggling family to endure emotional as well as material privation. The moment when Sheridan literally alludes to Ford occurs about midway through *In America*: he shows Sarah Sullivan, who has recently learned she is pregnant, lying in bed watching the final scene of *Wrath* on television. Sheridan zeroes in on the screen as Ma Joad declares, "They can't wipe us out, they can't lick us. We'll go on forever, Pa, 'cause we're the people." Then the camera pans to reveal Sarah's reaction: she is engrossed by the film, and, as *Wrath*'s score swells to usher in the end credits, her face flashes an appreciative smile. Having finished the movie, she calls Johnny to bed, and when he remarks upon her "happy" demeanor, she assures him that, as Mateo has told her, "Everything's gonna be all right" and that "the baby will bring its own luck." Characteristically, though, Johnny seems slightly gloomy and incredulous.

Like Ma Joad, Sarah evinces an unwavering commitment to sustaining and protecting her family. Throughout most of the narrative she is emotionally stronger and more pragmatic than her husband. Shortly after the bedroom scene, she confronts Johnny about his inability to engage with their daughters, and he accuses her of having "gotten over" Frankie. Without raising her voice, Sarah responds resolutely: "I had to get over him, Johnny, for the sake of the kids." She implores him to follow her lead, mourn their loss, and become emotionally available to her and their daughters once again.

Undeniably, some fundamental aspects of Sarah's character track with the long-suffering mother archetype of Irish stage and film. She puts her career as a teacher on hold to work in an ice cream shop, while Johnny continues to pursue acting, and she puts the lives and happiness of her daughters, as well as her unborn child, ahead of her own. When she is told that her pregnancy is a danger to her life, she resolves to keep the baby and expresses absolute faith that she can endure whatever happens. Johnny has serious doubts about her decision, but she insists that she is protecting all her children by going through with the dangerous birth: "I don't care what they [the doctors] say. What do they know about us? And my baby?" Sarah's power is fundamentally tied to her role as wife and mother.

Nonetheless, Sarah is a dynamic matriarch, and she represents a sharp departure from the hardy Irish mother archetype in one essential respect: her sexual agency. Sarah's playful seduction of Johnny caps the film's first act and moves the narrative forward, as their sex results in her pregnancy. This love scene is the only semi-explicit one in all of Sheridan's Irish-themed work, and it's all the more striking for the fact that the sexual encounter involves a married couple and is initiated by a woman. In this way, Samantha Morton's Sarah could hardly be more unlike Jane Darwell's Ma Joad, a figure Ford represents as formidable but incapable of love beyond the bounds of maternity.[14] Sarah is sexually assertive as well as stoic in the face of tragedy.

Crucially, though, Sheridan further humanizes Sarah by showing her disorientation and vulnerability in the wake of the traumatic premature birth of her third daughter. This is the only time she breaks down emotionally during the course of the narrative, as she conflates the precarious health of her newborn daughter with that of her late son, recalling Frankie's tragedy and accusing Johnny of negligence: "You should have taken the gate down. It's your fault [Frankie fell down the stairs]." This scene ends with Sarah instructing her husband, "If the baby dies, just don't wake me up," the one instance of her resolve wavering and her stoicism giving way to despondency. Thus, Sarah is not simply an unflaggingly loyal glutton for punishment, as sometimes seems to be the case with Irish mother figures from Sean O'Casey's dramas to Ford's later films; she is a fighter who periodically loses heart but manages to summon up the courage to continue. Sheridan endows Sarah with a full range of emotions and a complex psyche, thus representing an important and necessary critique of, and progression in, the cinematic portrayal of Irish womanhood.

The third thematic connection between *The Grapes of Wrath* and *In America* hinges on the male spiritual guide figure common to both films. In the earlier work the pacifist ex-preacher Jim Casy acts as a surrogate father to Tom Joad, whose biological father has declined in authority throughout the family's arduous journey. Likewise, *In America* features a nurturant outsider who helps reorient a confused and alienated male protagonist. In this case, though, the spiritual guide, Mateo, is a black African whose own tribal religious and cultural heritage parallels that of the pagan Celtic Irish. Like Jim Casy, Mateo at times displays an otherworldly serenity, despite suffering

In the film *In America* (20th Century–Fox, 2002), Sheridan foregrounds Sarah (Samantha Morton) as she composes herself before responding to Johnny's (Paddy Considine) accusation that she has "gotten over" their dead son.

complications from full-blown AIDS. Additionally, although his sexual orientation is never made explicit, Mateo could be viewed as a figure of queer masculinity, as Sheridan himself cites the bisexual artist Jean-Michel Basquiat as an inspiration for the character (DVD Director's Commentary). Whatever the case, Djimon Hounsou's alternately booming and gentle voice, his muscular, statuesque physique, and the deep spirituality and sensitivity he brings to the role all mark Mateo as an extraordinarily androgynous figure. Thus, he can help teach Johnny to move between death and life, isolation and integration, anger and compassion. Once Mateo meets the Sullivans, his rage at his own approaching death subsides, as he determines that his life's legacy is now bound up in their survival and happiness. When Johnny angrily confronts him about endangering Sarah by supporting her decision to go through with her pregnancy, Mateo remains calm and still as Johnny verbally assails him.

At the same time, Mateo seems to have instant access to his deepest emotions. When he first meets Christy and Ariel, and they freely recount the events of Frankie's accident, illness and death, he immediately empathizes with their brother's condition and breaks into tears. In this way, Mateo is the antithesis of Johnny, whom Sarah and his daughters recognize as unfeeling and spiritually bankrupt long before he is able to acknowledge his condition. When he finally does so, he makes his enraged confession to Mateo (in the course of his vain attempt to intimidate him): "I asked [God] to take me instead of [Frankie]. And He took the both of us.... I'm a fucking ghost. I don't exist. I can't think, I can't laugh, I can't cry." Johnny then asks Mateo if he would rather be in his place, and Mateo gently scoffs at Johnny's ignorance: "I wish." At this moment Johnny finally abandons his suspicious posture toward Mateo and recognizes the other man's suffering: "You're dying, I'm sorry." This concludes the first of three conversations about Frankie that Johnny has with Mateo; thus, the latter fulfills the vital function of grief counselor, as Johnny cannot discuss his feelings about his dead son — or even speak Frankie's name — in the presence of his wife and daughters prior to the film's cathartic penultimate scene.

Mateo is also able to engage freely with Christy and Ariel, as he shares their belief in magical forces and can play and pretend, even in the face of his own mortality. When he feels ill and Ariel gives him lemon drops, which she thinks have healing powers, he smiles and plays along. Mateo succinctly diagnoses Johnny's principal affliction: "You don't believe," describing the psychological hang-up that prevents him from surrendering to his childish impulses as well as the state of his soul. For much of the film Mateo effectively stands in for Johnny as a father figure to his daughters, nurturing and protecting them emotionally, while Johnny remains at a distance, caught in a cycle of anxiety, depression, and self-loathing.

The film is remarkable for the way Sheridan refuses to infantilize Christy and Ariel, as they, too, develop an understanding of Johnny's malaise and help compel him to seek a life after Frankie. Early in the film, five-year-old Ariel clearly apprehends some of the dysfunctions that are addling her family; she complains that Christy pays more attention to her camcorder than to her, and she tells Johnny, "You don't play with us ... like you used to." Later on, while in a semi-delirious, somnambulant state, Ariel approaches Johnny and cannot recognize him, declaring, "You're not my dad. I want my real dad." Her half-groggy, half-perceptive outburst stems from Johnny's refusal to kneel and say bedtime prayers with his daughters, which clearly upsets Ariel, again marking his refusal to play along with his daughters, even at the cost of their peace of mind.

Like Ariel, Christy protests her father's emotional absence, but as the older sister, she is more active, taking measures to protect her family and facilitate Johnny's recovery. When her parents argue at night, Christy wraps her arms around Ariel and rocks her maternally. When her newborn sister needs a transfusion, Christy volunteers her own blood, which leads to one of the film's most poignant moments. Johnny, trying to allay her anxiety over the procedure, puts his hand on her head and asks, "Are you OK, little girl?" She chafes at his touch and forcefully rebuffs his condescension: "Don't 'little girl' me. I've been carrying this family on my back for over a year, ever since Frankie died. He was my brother, too. It's not my fault that he's dead. It's not

At a playground, Mateo (Djimon Hounsou) talks to Johnny (Paddy Considine) about his late son in Sheridan's *In America* (20th Century–Fox, 2002, dir. Jim Sheridan).

my fault that I'm still alive." Thus, she ultimately confronts her father about his isolation and lack of empathy for her own grief and suffering, which is in many ways just as profound as his own.

Furthermore, it is Christy who pushes Johnny to begin fully mourning Frankie and to speak his son's name. When Johnny asks Ariel to look up in the sky and imagine Mateo flying past the moon with E.T., Ariel waves and says, "Bye, Mateo.... Look after Frankie." Christy takes this opportunity to use her third and final wish. She tells her father to "Say good-bye to Frankie," and then repeats her command. Johnny stares at her, looking stricken, but then obeys and speaks the words, which have a powerful, healing effect on him: he is finally able to cry for his son. Thus, Christy's last wish works its magic, and in the scene that follows and punctuates the film, she decides to take another step in her own mourning process by no longer dwelling on the suffering that Frankie endured. She turns off the video of her ill, bald-headed but beaming brother, her voiceover declaring, "It's not the way I want to see Frankie anymore."

Ultimately, Johnny has to follow the lead of Sarah, Christy and Ariel by bonding with Mateo, accepting his wisdom, and understanding that the ability to express faith in the invisible and the magical constitutes a form of mental strength and an affirmation of life over death. As Sarah tells Johnny, "Sometimes I think our entire lives are make-believe." Sheridan is finally more optimistic about the condition of the emigrant ethnic family than Ford. As opposed to the fading patriarch in *The Grapes of Wrath*, Johnny is a salvageable paternal figure, and by virtue of deferring to the women and androgynous surrogate father in his life, he finally can be integrated into the matriarchy as an equal partner, rather than marginalized as a relic due to his ineffectuality, like Pa Joad.

Ford and Sheridan: Mirror Opposites

The shift toward matriarchy that Sheridan depicts in *In America* is both more traditional and more radical than what Ford suggests in *The Grapes of Wrath*. In Ford's film he essentially dramatizes the need for the patriarch to either lead, follow, or stand aside; more centrally, he shows the shifts and accommodations necessary to fill the resultant power void. At his mother's urging, Tom briefly becomes the head of the Joad clan, but when he is compelled to leave the family to escape the police and pursue a greater calling, Ma herself becomes their *de facto* leader. Sheridan, on the other hand, portrays the Sullivans' embrace of matriarchy as an almost unconditionally affirmative development, with Johnny ultimately becoming a more active, nurturant, and androgynous father, the antithesis of a traditional patriarch judged principally by his aloof strength and ability to provide for his dependents. To this end, Johnny's professional success at the film's close — he finally lands a part in a play — is tied directly to his recovered ability to play and "make-believe" with his children.

Sheridan finally upholds the primacy of the traditional two-parent nuclear family, while showing that an egalitarian family model that eschews patriarchy and emotional repression is possible and practicable, even in the midst of destabilizing tragedy and transition. As he says of the narrative's cultural implications:

> [W]e're so used to the warrior god story of the male who goes out and challenges the world and is part of a patriarchy. And this is more of a matriarchy — a man surrounded by women. The woman takes the active role in the procreation of life and sex and everything. And that freaks certain people out, and I say, "To hell with them.... That's what I intended" [DVD Commentary].

As Ruth Barton notes, however, the film's progressive-traditionalist themes run counter to the prevailing pattern of contemporary Irish cinema:

> Ultimately, *In America* is a celebration of the Irish-American encounter and the strength of the family unit. Where so many Irish films of the 1970s onwards ended with the disintegration of the family, Sheridan argues for its durability, a prognosis aided rather than defeated by modernity [*Irish National Cinema* 190].

Sheridan's Irish films seem to become increasingly hopeful about the prospects of the nuclear family and increasingly open to active matriarchs and alternative modes of fatherhood. One can observe this development simply by charting a progression from Christy Brown's torturous Oedipal dilemma in *My Left Foot*— which begins to be resolved only after his father's death — to Johnny Sullivan's successful psychic recovery and maturation toward androgynous, engaged fatherhood. By the same token, although Bridget Brown and Sarah Sullivan share in common a profound determination to preserve the wellbeing of their respective families, Sarah's overt sexual agency in her marriage is a marked departure from Bridget's implicit sexual servitude to Paddy.

By contrast, Ford's body of work moves in precisely the opposite direction over time, as his fathers become more militaristic and autocratic, and his mother figures less dynamic and more submissive and marginal. Female characters like Lana Martin, Mrs. McKlennar, Mrs. Morgan and Ma Joad are absent from Ford's later films. Much like his friend John Wayne, Ford knew little of domestic happiness and often viewed his film shoots and frequent trips on his boat, the *Araner*, as welcome escapes from quotidian family life. Garry Wills likened Ford to Wayne in calling the director a "truant from his own home" (42). Wills also describes the "Ford film set" as "war on a minor scale" and asserts that Ford "was afraid of his own tenderness," which fueled his misogyny: "Women were especially resented as potential underminers of his manliness. He reduced them to tears, all but the tough ones," such as Katharine Hepburn and Maureen O'Hara (72–3). As I've argued earlier, Ford's post–World War II films become increasingly regressive and backward-looking, his worldview more and more wedded to patriarchy, an accurate reflection of which is the crude statement (quoted at the outset of Chapter 3) he made in 1964: "When I direct a scene I always want to make the leading lady fall down on her derrière" (McBride 641).

Sheridan, on the other hand, tends to portray women leading families in an overwhelmingly positive light, particularly in *In America*. He made the film in part to honor his own wife and three daughters: "*In America* is really about how great my wife was, and my kids, and ... it's really a love poem to them" (DVD Commentary).[15] When Sarah has her baby near the end of the film, the infant is given the name Sarah Mateo Sullivan, incorporating the monikers of her mother and father, as well as the androgynous man who helped guide the family through their process of mourning, adaptation, and integration. Thus, Sarah Mateo's name affirms matriarchy as well as alternative masculinities.[16]

Taken together, the cinemas of Ford and Sheridan display a productive distinction between regressive and progressive idealism. As Schatz makes clear in his work on Hollywood genres, films are not mere entertainments; they trade in rituals and myths and generally function to uphold the status quo by telling Western audiences exactly what they want to hear and believe about themselves. They almost invariably raise vexing sociopolitical questions about family, love, work and war in order to offer affirmative, reassuring but invariably incomplete resolutions to these dilemmas. Ford's films frequently challenge the status quo, but they usually evoke what he views as the glorious American past to find answers, inspiration, and heroes (and the occasional heroine) embodying time-tested, fundamental values. According to Martin Scorsese, Ford attempted through his art to cling to the ideal of the "nineteenth-century family" (*Directed by John Ford*). This is the impetus behind his dramas of assimilation in which old ways of thinking tend to trump more modern ideas, and patriarchy ultimately offers the most practicable organizing structure for families, communities and societies. This view is the heart of Ford's regressive idealist cultural critique, particularly in his post–World War II films.

In contrast, Sheridan's work addresses history and employs myths in order to imagine a more peaceful, egalitarian future. Speaking of the cultural commentary in his cinema, he declares:

> The idea that you can get over [the] death, as a couple, of a child is probably pretty far-fetched except in extreme situations. So I think films in some way are about necessary lies.... *In the Name of the Father* was about the idea that a nonviolent father could be at the center of Irish society, and the zeitgeist was such that in a few years it became a reality.... So necessary lies are very important to me because they seem to be what civilization is about [*In America* DVD Commentary].

Where the finales of Ford films often reveal a deep sense of nostalgia and an obsession with transcendence, Sheridan is bold enough to critique the cultural legacy of pivotal Irish historical traumas, ranging from the Great Famine to the Troubles, and envision new ways of thinking and acting. Both *My Left Foot* and *In America* dramatize a rejection of patriarchy and the kind of complete, progressive familial and social integration that is possible through the revaluation of womanhood and the emergence of female agency. Additionally, *In America* depicts the formation of a community that integrates cross-cultural, androgynous figures of masculinity as well as powerful, dynamic women. There are considerable merits to both filmmakers' engagement with Irish and American cultures and generic narrative forms. In the final analysis, though, Ford depicts the family as he imagines it was or would have liked it to be, while Sheridan shows the family as he believes it should and could yet be.

CHAPTER 4

Jim Sheridan: Reconstructing the Family, Redefining the Nation[1]

> Pray for the dead, and fight like hell for the living.— MARY "MOTHER" JONES[2]

Jim Sheridan posits a Freudian sense of lack in Irish literature and culture: "In *My Left Foot* I was always thinking of the Oedipal bit, and in *In the Name of the Father* I was thinking of the Good Father.... I had to think when was the Oedipal story ever told, when was the Good Father [story] ever told in Ireland?" (Barton, *Jim Sheridan* ... 144). Sheridan also suggests that his last Troubles film, *The Boxer*, fills a crucial void as an "Irish love story": "There's no love stories in Irish literature.... In repressed ... broken cultures love stories have not much prominence.... It's very difficult to do" (Director's Commentary, *The Boxer* DVD). Sheridan's films attempt to reconstitute affirmative figures of masculinity in a post-colonial culture. As Declan Kiberd writes:

> Critics ... might argue that a fiercely patriarchal system, such as colonialism, could hardly have left men feeling useless in their domestic spheres; and there is ample evidence to show that the head of the Irish household was often just as autocratic as his British counterpart.... But the evidence of Irish texts and case-histories would confirm the suspicion that the autocratic father is often the weakest male of all, concealing that weakness under the protective coverage of the prevailing system.... Patriarchal values exist in societies where men, lacking true authority, settle for mere power [Kiberd 390–91].[3]

Taking up this theme, Sheridan suggests that colonialism functions to undermine the familial structure of its subjects, declaring:

> [The British] want to split the family. [They] want to split the authority of the father and son because that's the basic way to destroy a society. Most of my films are about that point, about the son not being able to look up to the father and the father not being an authority figure. They're deeply responsible films. They're not about getting at the Brits [Crowdus and Leary 5].

In his three 1990s films, *The Field*, *In the Name of the Father* and *The Boxer*, Sheridan illustrates the effects of colonialism on the Irish family unit. Ultimately, he traces a path away from patriarchal tyranny, bitterness and dissolution, and envisions family and community life characterized by peaceful, active freedom, with women integrated as equal partners in family and social life.[4] Furthermore, in *The Boxer* Sheridan distinguishes sport-mediated aggression from paramilitary violence, and considers the implications of both Irish institutions for notions of masculinity in families and communities. We must bear in mind that the stereotype of the "fighting Irish" did not always carry the negative baggage it does today; originally it was embodied by the figure of the "hardman"— a bare-knuckle fighter who competed according to rules of sport — not that of the "gunman" and his unbridled violence (Feldman 46). In seeking to reclaim Irish masculinity from a heritage of patriarchal violence, Sheridan uses widely appealing story structures such as the coming-of-age tale, the prodigal son, and the star-crossed lovers,[5] successfully reconstructing masculinity in widely resonant terms, not merely European or Irish ones.

Employing the terminology of Louis Althusser, I would argue that patriarchy acts as an Ideological State Apparatus that serves colonialism and capitalism.[6] Both of these latter institutions employ ideologies based on a fundamental contradiction in which the exploited believe they are free: "The individual *is interpellated as a (free) subject ... in order that he shall (freely) accept his subjection*, i.e., in order that he shall make the gestures and actions of his subjection 'all by himself'" (Althusser 101–2). In her illuminating study, *Male Subjectivity at the Margins*, Kaja Silverman establishes the vital connection between Althusser's Marxist political theory and the formation of masculinity. She argues that "conventional masculinity" (i.e., patriarchal masculinity) operates through belief in a "dominant fiction," which "depends upon a kind of collective make-believe in the commensurability of penis and phallus" (Silverman 15). A representation of male power, the phallus is purely imaginary, though it may be projected upon real objects (buildings, motor vehicles, the male member itself). Yet patriarchy functions through its subjects' belief in just such an illusion. As Althusser says, "... [I]n ideology men represent their real conditions of existence to themselves in imaginary form" (87).

If we combine Marxist with psychoanalytic theory and take patriarchal masculinity to be founded on the positive Oedipus complex, as Silverman suggests, we see the fundamental contradiction upon which this ideology rests: men, "always-already" castrated, live in utter denial of their lack.[7] Kiberd suggests this contradiction when he describes patriarchy as "the tyranny wrought by weak men" who "settle for mere power" (391). Thus, a man disavowing lack may possess "power" but not necessarily authority.

All of Sheridan's Irish films cogently address male lack. As discussed earlier, *My Left Foot* deals with the phallic implications of physical disability and the Oedipal dilemma, and *In America* puts its male protagonist through a process of mourning and maturation that compels him to renounce egocentric patriarchal masculinity and follow the nurturant lead of his wife, daughters, and androgynous male mentor. Sheridan's second film, *The Field* (1990), focuses on patriarchal emasculation from its opening scene, as elderly Bull McCabe demonstrates his superior ability to haul baskets of seaweed, while his son Tadgh struggles to keep up. Gerry Conlon, protagonist of *In the Name of the Father* (1993), must face the potentially castrating effects of physical confinement and a pacifist father. In *The Boxer* (1997), a hardman, Danny Flynn, struggles to set a peaceful example for his deeply divided community by confining his aggression within the ring, leaving himself vulnerable to Harry, an IRA gunman, who threatens to destroy the boxer to maintain the violent patriarchal order. Thus, Sheridan repeatedly challenges and subverts traditional ideologies of masculinity in Irish culture.

Sheridan also portrays patriarchy as effecting a destructive deferral of life in the present in favor of a privileging of the past. In the three films I'm about to analyze, this deferral finds its embodiment in a powerful agent of dissolution: Bull (*The Field*), Joe McAndrew (*In the Name of the Father*), and Harry (*The Boxer*). Each of these men constantly looks backward to justify ruthless acts of violence in the present. In each case Sheridan works dramatically toward a dismissal of such figures. In his words:

> The past is only useful insofar as it dictates how you act in the future, and when you look at the past as if there's some trauma back there that explains in a bitter, twisted way why you have to be bitter and twisted, that's when you get fucked up, and it requires a psychic adjustment [Crowdus and Leary 3].

As Rita Felski writes, "Being oppressed is no guarantee of clarity of vision or possession of truth" (40). Sheridan upsets the operation of patriarchy by depriveleging the "vision" that uses past trauma to invalidate the future. The experience of colonial oppression informs all three films discussed below; the experience of prison life is essential to both *In the Name of the Father* and *The Boxer*. This last film alone offers a vision of the future: only in *The Boxer* does a functioning, subversive masculine practice evolve within a living community.

Revision, Myth and Ill-Fated Coming-of-Age in *The Field*

As discussed in Chapter 2, John Ford offered an oblique but abortive critique of patriarchal masculinity with *The Quiet Man* (1952). Sean Thornton initially resists the one-dimensional conception of Irish masculinity espoused by his adopted community but is ultimately subsumed by it and reindoctrinated into violent, patriarchal manhood. A former boxer who has suffered the trauma of an opponent's death in the ring, Thornton refuses to fight, even when provoked by his brother-in-law; but his community, including its religious figures and his own wife, shuns him until he takes up violence once again. After the climactic fistfight, everyone — even his antagonistic brother-in-law — embraces him as part of the community, and his wife, reassured by his success at violence, accepts a subservient domestic role. Though male lack is initially privileged in *The Quiet Man*, it is finally disavowed in the interest of patriarchy.

In *The Field*, Sheridan changes the perspective and seizes on the tragic undertones of *The Quiet Man*'s Yankee-fighter-returns-to-his-roots narrative, while ostensibly adapting John B. Keane's classic Irish play (also entitled *The Field*). In this case, the identity of a young rural Irishman (not an Irish-American) hangs in the balance, as Tadgh McCabe (Sean Bean) seeks an alternative to his father Bull's (Richard Harris) tyrannical, primordial attachment to land and honor. By focusing on Tadgh, as opposed to the more obviously central figure of Bull, one may view *The Field* as a tragically stunted *Bildungsroman*. Tadgh initially seems destined to live under the oppressive aegis of his father and the code passed down from Bull's "father's father's father's father." Though the film is set in the 1930s, Bull's repeated polemics about the potato famine and the British "echo a narrow, nationalist interpretation of history" (Barton 48) that is related to the hard-line Republicanism characteristic of the IRA.[8] As Ruth Barton observes, "The film sees history not as linear, but as circular and repetitive ... both older and younger generations are trapped in time and in a cycle of violence" (47). Throughout the film, however, Tadgh gradually forges the will to resist Bull, and in the end he nearly cuts his ties with his father and the land. His final annihilation only serves to condemn his community as a place with no affirmative models of masculinity because manhood here remains shackled to self-destruction.

The Field concentrates primarily on the spiritual crisis in the life of Bull McCabe. In her penetrating study of the film, Cheryl Herr discusses the concept of "habitus" as the dominating force in Bull's life. By "habitus" she means ingrained and unexamined behaviors, such as Bull's working practices with the field and his macho displays to men in the local pub, that influence an individual's actions so that they work constantly toward maintaining these reflexive habits.[9] Thus, "The habitus ... offers resistance to outright changes in collective practices; it is essentially conservative" (Herr 32). It is so powerful an agent for Bull that "his everyday rituals are not choices for him, and he is a tragic figure only insofar as he shows himself unable to make strategic accommodations to an emergent cultural paradigm" (Herr 36). Furthermore,

"The film of *The Field* ... shows us the Bull's coming to consciousness of his habitus — all that he has taken for granted and left relatively unanalyzed" (Herr 33). Bull's son Tadgh proceeds to his own "coming to consciousness" within the film, as he moves from diffident acceptance of his father's dictates to open resistance in his final confrontation with Bull, threatening his father's life and denying his heritage and inheritance: "I don't care about the land. I never cared about the land." Tadgh's emerging voice within the film has been little discussed in criticism, though it invites analysis given that Sheridan heightens the father-son conflict in his adaptation of Keane's play; in the dramatic text Tadgh never dares question his father and functions as little more than Bull's lackey.

Tadgh barely speaks throughout the film's first hour, even during the six-minute American wake sequence in which he is a central figure. When he does open his mouth, it is upon Bull's prompting. Tadgh begins to talk only as he and his father set out to give the Yank (Tom Berenger) "a fright." He tells Bull that they had best heed the bad weather and forget about the Yank, and after his first tentative resistance is brushed aside, Tadgh begins to ask questions about his family, possibly for the first time in his life. He asks about his mother and about his brother, Sheamie. Tadgh begins to find his voice as he attempts to recover something of his lost brother.

In a sense, Bull and Sheamie offer Tadgh different models of masculinity from which to compose his own character, although this formula is obviously problematic. Since Sheamie lived to be only "13 years, 6 months," and Tadgh has no personal memories of his brother, it is hard to trace an influence, though Bull suggests that both his sons have the same "bad strain" in them. Sheamie's self-immolating guilt, probably as much a residual effect of the Great Famine as of his father's ruthlessness, may be a more humane sort of example for Tadgh, but it is no more affirmative a model than Bull's, as it leads only to suicide. The Yank, who had emigrated and escaped the narrow confines of Carraigthormond, could be viewed as a positive alternative model for Tadgh if not for the fact that his hunger for land and power is even more destructive than Bull's: with his plan to cover the eponymous field in concrete, he seeks to ravage the land and leave it barren, while Bull's life's work has been to protect it and keep it fertile.

Tadgh's stunted growth as a man proceeds precisely from this lack of a positive figure of masculinity in his family and community at large. For even as he throws off the yoke of his father, he appropriates Bull's violence against the Yank for his own in wooing Katie (Jenny Conroy), the "Tinker's daughter," and he bolsters his pride by threatening the lives of her father as well as his own. Since, aside from Bull, the only other prominent male figures in the film are a bumbling cowardly mooch (Bird O'Donnell, played by John Hurt), the coldly calculating Yank, and a priest who becomes the exploitative outsider's dupe, Tadgh has slim pickings for role models. As Kerstin Ketteman states, "Beyond the murdered Irish-American there are no local Irish characters to counterbalance or to mitigate the powerfully evil figure of the Bull, and the pathetic figures of his followers" (159).

At the same time, Tadgh's mother remains emotionally distant and completely mute for most of the narrative, leaving him with little counterbalancing maternal influence in his life. Having played tough but big-hearted Bridget Brown in *My Left Foot*, Brenda Fricker's performance as vengeful Maggie McCabe adds painful irony to the narrative. While Maggie has taken up her vow of silence to punish Bull for what she perceives as his culpability for Sheamie's death, Tadgh's painfully confused identity is clearly the collateral damage of this parental dysfunction.

Ultimately, Tadgh fails to escape his father, as his final attempt to temper the increasingly volatile Bull's rage and self-destruction precipitates his own demise. Tadgh's death serves as the final indictment of a community devoid of any positive masculine presence. Indeed, manhood here seems an exercise in futility and impotence, as we last see Bull furiously striving to beat back the encroaching tide. Here Bull plays out the tragedy of the Cuchulain myth, which inverts and predominates over that of Oedipus in Irish culture, as the patriarch unwittingly destroys the last of his line.[10] In the world of *The Field*, the past consumes the future, and the sins of the father are visited on his sons and finally obliterate the younger generation. Sheridan has never shied away from dark subject matter, but this is the only one of his Irish films that ends in tragedy, leaving his viewers resigned to a despondent, fatalistic sense that patriarchal hubris and destruction are virtually inevitable in such a context — a place still defined by the legacy of colonialism.

In the Name of the Father: Weighing Terrorism, Pacifism and Justice

Sheridan's subsequent films, *In the Name of the Father* and *The Boxer*, both follow a similar pattern of constructing masculinity; but in each case the *Bildungsroman* element is fully realized, and a positive male figure plays an essential role in establishing the character of the protagonist. *In the Name of the Father* pits the deadly slick IRA man Joe McAndrew (Don Baker) against gentle consumptive Giuseppe Conlon (Pete Postlethwaite) in a battle for control over Giuseppe's son, Gerry (Daniel Day-Lewis), the quintessential angry young misfit. Because Gerry in his youth has felt intense shame about his father's physical decrepitude — "Why'd you have to be sick all your life?" — he also assumes that his father is weak and irresolute in spirit. When father and son are confined to the same prison cell, they revert to their previous relationship on the outside, as Gerry continues to defy his father, refusing to become an embodiment of compliance and respectability in the face of adversity. Thus, in this early stage, Gerry is acutely vulnerable to the charms of militant ideology.

Though Martin McLoone argues otherwise, Sheridan's handling of the IRA man Joe McAndrew, who is a pure narrative invention in a film that is substantially faithful to Gerry Conlon's own memoir, represents a pointed political statement.[11] While McLoone contends that Jim Sheridan "is not a political filmmaker and *In the Name of the Father* is not a political film" (73), one might counter by citing Sheridan's clearly anti-extremist stance, as evidenced in his portrayal of Gerry's relationship with McAndrew. Because Sheridan cleverly sets up both Gerry and his audience to embrace McAndrew initially, however, he has drawn criticism from those who construe the film as an endorsement of the IRA.

Indeed, McAndrew at first seems like an honorable man: his carriage is composed and resolute in the scenes in which he orchestrates the Guildford Pub bombings. Moreover, when he confesses to those bombings (for which he has not been charged), he challenges British authority, declaring, "You've got innocent people in jail for that." In a film that hinges on the exposure of gross injustice, drawn from a memoir called *Proved Innocent*, McAndrew's words sound like music to our outraged ears. When he first appears in prison he impresses Gerry by offering bold resistance to the bigotry of English prisoners in the cafeteria, compelling the young man to fight alongside him. In resisting the hierarchical restrictions placed upon them by English prisoners as well as wardens, McAndrew brings about a carnivalesque release of tension for Gerry. Thus, Sheridan leads his audience, along with his protagonist, to a perilous momentary allegiance with this bold and charismatic figure.

After McAndrew's brutal attack on the prison warden, however, Sheridan compels viewers, as well as Gerry, to dismiss the paramilitary leader and all the reactionary ideological baggage he carries with him: "Violence is the only thing they [the Brits] understand," he maintains. In all three films discussed in this chapter, violent masculinity functions, in Kiberd's terms, as a show of "power" that ultimately has no "authority." In *In the Name of the Father*, McAndrew proves effective at maiming and killing, but he finally lacks ideological and moral potency in Gerry's eyes; he lacks the authority to influence the young man's actions because his rhetoric makes reference only to the past, and in the end Gerry sees no future in vengeance.[12] His final statement in the film, "I will fight on, in the name of my father, and of the truth," is a promise of affirmation: he will assert his father's authority and recuperate his wounded name. He will not seek revenge through violence, which would go against his father's fundamental belief that all people — Irish, British, Catholic, Protestant — are "children of God." Thus, Sheridan's film comes out strongly against

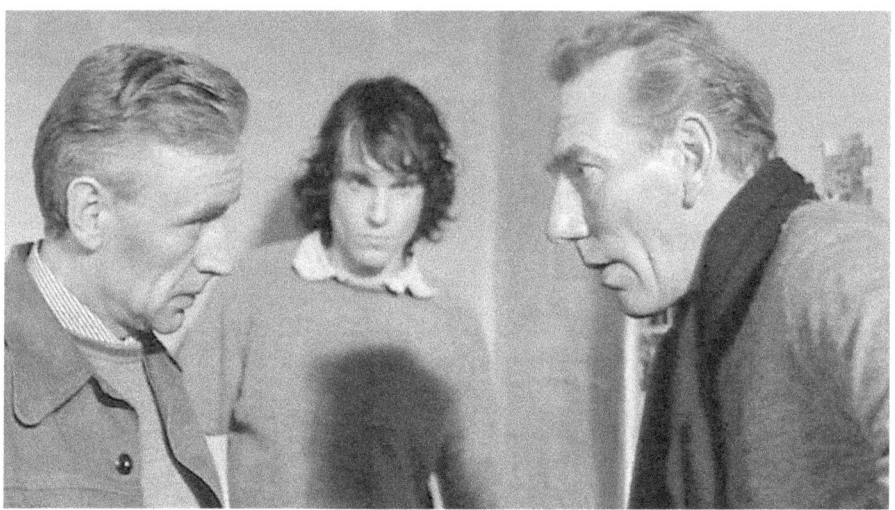

As Gerry (Daniel Day-Lewis) looks on, Joe McAndrew (Don Baker) offers friendship and protection to Giuseppe (Pete Postlethwaite), which the latter staunchly refuses in Sheridan's *In the Name of the Father* (Universal, 1993).

extremism, while acknowledging its attractiveness, especially to an oppressed young individual such as Gerry.

Sheridan's sympathetic treatment of McAndrew's Republican ideals, which contrasts with his views on the IRA's practical program of violence, has nonetheless led some critics to claim that Sheridan finally wishes to drum up support for extremists and their brutal methods.[13] As Lance Pettitt argues:

> A common ploy to attack *In the Name of the Father* in both Britain and the USA was to smear it by association as "pro–IRA," a gross distortion of the screenplay that carefully distanced Giuseppe and Gerry from the republican movement in Belfast and from the sadistic IRA prisoner ... in prison itself [260].

Like a prodigal son, Gerry eventually embraces the father he had shunned, as Sheridan's narrative clearly sets Giuseppe apart as the most influential paternal figure and primary role model for the young man. Giuseppe emerges as the "Good Father."

To be adequately understood, Gerry's resistance to Giuseppe must be framed within the context of colonialism. As Declan Kiberd suggests, colonized countries like Ireland and Northern Ireland often generate "weak fathers" who rely on patriarchal modes to emphasize their potency as men; such men may have power but little authority, according to Kiberd. Consequently, "When ... fatherly authority is not asserted, the child may become a self-indulgent subversive with no respect for the configurations of the larger community ... in other words, a rebel" (Kiberd 381–91). Gerry's fundamental error is to mistake Giuseppe for such a "weak father," when in fact he is neither weak in spirit nor regressively patriarchal — he is a loving husband and a gentle but determined father.

By contrast, Gerry initially lacks any concern for his family and community: in the film's opening Belfast sequence he threatens the security of his family by incurring the wrath of the local IRA, and he endangers the lives of all those in the community by fomenting a riot to evade capture by British paratroopers. Forced into confinement with his father, Gerry observes the respect that Giuseppe commands among prison officials and inmates alike, and the effectiveness of his pacifist resistance that takes the form of his letter-writing campaign for their release. Gerry rejects McAndrew in the wake of his horrendous maiming of a prison warden; and his deeply ironic statement, "That was a good day's work, McAndrew," disavows this type of ineffectual, self-perpetuating violence — the product of extremism. In his last words to his fellow prisoner, Gerry stands firmly against Joe: "In all my God-forsaken life, I've never known what it was like to want to kill somebody until now. Aye, you're a brave man, Joe — brave." As Brian McIlroy states:

> Although Gerry dismisses the religious flavour of his father's spirituality, he is drawn to the basic moral goodness that it inspires. This influence allows him not only to put out the flames engulfing the English warden, but also to be confident in rejecting to his face the IRA man's ideology — an ideology, it has to be remembered, for which he is doing time [*Shooting to Kill* 60].

Gerry's compassionate assistance to the warden demonstrates his symbolic integration into a broader community, one that acknowledges the humanity of all individuals, including those who are bound to perpetuate injustice against him and his father.

Ultimately, though, the prison experience necessitates a deferral of life in the present, and thus a sort of surrender to patriarchy, for Gerry and Giuseppe. They pass their abundant idle time in their cell reflecting on the past, while often arguing over it, and it provides their one source of comfort. Prison life forces the father and son to privilege the past to survive. Giuseppe talks of continuing his old life in his mind: "They've only blocked out the light. They can't block out the light in here [points to temple]. Every night I take your mother's hand in mine, and we walk together." Finally, the ailing Giuseppe is compelled to acknowledge the disparity between life on the outside as he remembers it and his present life of deferral on the inside: "I'm gonna die. I'm scared.... I'm scared of dying in here." Throughout his fifteen-year term, Gerry copes partly through drug use, altering and denying a monotonous reality; nonetheless, he experiences bouts of extreme despair. Upon his release, his health and future seem anything but certain as, except for the triumphant final scene, the film does not move from detailing the mental and physical sacrifices he has made as a prisoner to showing his life post-exoneration.[14]

As an institution of confinement, however, the prison here also acts as a space—like the ring in *The Boxer*—within which male aggression can be mediated or perpetuated, as Gerry is forced to come to terms with his own rage. Though Giuseppe's passive resistance to their imprisonment takes years to bear fruit, and the elder Conlon never lives to attain freedom, Gerry ultimately recognizes his father's strength. As Kiberd argues, upon acknowledging an assertive father, "The child can begin the task of achieving a vision of society as a whole and the even more exhilarating challenge of framing an alternative" (391). Gerry chooses to follow Giuseppe's model, as it becomes increasingly apparent that his father's form of action, rather than violent resistance, offers the potential to accomplish "a good day's work" and enact a change in their situation.

Although Martin McLoone sees the film as lacking meaningful political commentary, I would argue that Sheridan uses *In the Name of the Father*, outwardly a mixed-genre piece (coming-of-age, prison film, family melodrama, courtroom drama), to make a statement about the process of self-discovery that leads a young, oppressed man to reject extremism in favor of a mode of masculinity that values community over militancy. In the context of the Troubles, such a statement could hardly carry more political weight. Though McLoone claims that the film's "engagement with dominant narrative forms is problematic in terms of making a film about politics" (73), several critics challenge this assertion, including Ruth Barton, Lance Pettitt and Margot Gayle Backus. The latter states, "The film's father/son dynamics shed considerable light on the very real problem of postcolonial masculine identity and self-representation, and could even be seen as offering insight into the emergence of a new political praxis" (58). One might argue, then, that its engagement with "dominant narrative forms," particularly that of the family or social melodrama, highlights the film's politics instead of obscuring them. In the context of an accessible father-son narrative, *In the Name of the Father* enacts a revaluation of the figures of the peacemaker and the extremist in Irish culture, unequivocally valorizing the former over the latter.

Hardman Versus Gunman: *The Boxer* and "Fighting Within the Rules"

In *The Boxer*, as in *In the Name of the Father*, "the family becomes metonymic for the nation" (Barton, *Jim Sheridan* ... 77). Sheridan points out that *The Boxer* begins where his previous film ends, as Danny Flynn (Daniel Day-Lewis, once again) emerges from prison in the opening title sequence.[15]

If *In the Name of the Father* concerns the successful mediation of male aggression within prison walls, *The Boxer* addresses violence on the outside in the community of Belfast, an issue that the earlier film only touches upon in its initial scenes. According to Sheridan, "[T]he film came to me after the IRA let off the bomb in [London's] Canary Wharf [in February 1996] after the Cease Fire, and I thought, 'The hell with this,' you know, [I'll] make a film about ... violence and what I think about it."

Furthermore, through the character of Maggie (Emily Watson), the film portrays the struggle for female empowerment and freedom within a community obsessed with upholding a strict moral code regarding IRA prisoners' wives. As estranged lovers Danny and Maggie attempt to navigate a cultural and physical landscape laden with booby-traps that threaten to frustrate the reestablishment of their relationship, they simultaneously seek to create, out of the ashes of the Troubles, a family unit free from the violent "circular and repetitive" history that Sheridan dramatizes so well in *The Field* (Barton 47). In *The Boxer*, Sheridan integrates a strong feminist voice, an element that is secondary at best in his previous two films, as he makes Maggie a central, rather than peripheral, figure. Her agency emerges as the controlling factor in the relationship between herself and Danny: she confronts and pursues him initially, and sets the boundaries of the relationship as it progresses. She also subverts the IRA's iron-fisted patriarchal moral code for prisoners' wives, as she says, "I'm the prisoner here." And she's given the final word of the film: "We're going home."

As in *The Field* and *In the Name of the Father*, Sheridan formulates masculinity in *The Boxer* using a triangular pattern. Danny Flynn embraces his boyhood trainer Ike (Ken Stott), while he rejects his old IRA comrade, Harry (Gerard McSorley). The latter film does not, however, dramatize the process of self-discovery that leads its young male protagonist away from violent patriarchy, but rather his subsequent struggle, having rejected regressive violence, to live within a community.[16] As *The Boxer* begins, Danny Flynn has already tried the way of the gun, seen it fail, and done time for his past association with the IRA. Danny has become alienated from his natural family during his fourteen-year imprisonment (none of his blood relatives play a part in the film), and the story ultimately propels him toward the formation of a new family based on tolerance and reconciliation. Although the film's politics have been attacked by critics such as Ruth Barton, Brian McIlroy and Martin McLoone as being "too formulaic" (McIlroy 65) and "ludicrous in terms of realism" (McLoone 78), Sheridan's political stance here can be appreciated in terms of its weary idealism. Characteristically, he channels his political statements through a family portrait:

> [T]he film ... crosses from the politics into the personal and becomes ... a family story, which is what the Greeks understood as that you could basically reduce

everything down to the family, and when you X-rayed the family, you could see what was wrong with society.

Thus, *The Boxer* deals with Danny and Maggie's loss and recovery of family.

Like Tadgh in *The Field*, Danny is initially all but silent; his voice emerges as his identity solidifies. His reunion with Ike Weir, his childhood trainer, is the catalyst that leads Danny to become a unifying emblem in his community through boxing and the space the sport affords for mediating Catholic/Protestant tensions. The force of violent dissolution maintains its power in the community in the figure of Harry, the hard-line paramilitary nationalist whose bigoted extremism prevails throughout the Cease Fire and continues to influence the younger generations of Belfast, including Maggie's son Liam (Ciaran Fitzgerald). Harry's weapons are guns and polarizing rhetoric, while Ike's only weapons are his hands and "a bit of truth," as Danny puts it.

Ike functions not only as a paternal figure but also as a dramatic soothsayer: his two drunken outbursts of cathartic truth frame the film. In the first, he lectures Danny, "You tell them Ike Weir doesn't need a gun to fight. IRA? Fuck your IRA! Put your gun down, Danny Flynn, fight me like a man." Here Ike sets up the ethical framework that Danny employs throughout the film, as he fights within the rules of the ring; and in his final bout against an equally colonized Nigerian opponent, he refuses to extend the contest to the point of brutality. In his last speech, Ike confronts Harry, Danny's one-time friend turned nemesis: "I know you, Harry. You're only interested in hurtin' people.... You killed this district, Harry. You killed the one thing you loved. Your own son. You filled his head full of shit, and you sent him out to die." Harry responds by killing Ike, but this murder is the action of a weak man, an exercise of "mere power" in the face of actual male authority.

In many ways a successor to Ford's dissolute sages, Ike, as an alcoholic, conforms to a negative characteristic shared by both the "stage Irishman" and the weak, colonized father Kiberd describes. Nevertheless, he functions as an agent of change in a community so long at the mercy of men like Harry, who are insulated from their own self-deceptions by violent, patriarchal rhetoric, the same sort of language that his enemies, the British, use to justify their continued occupation in the North.[17] Thus, Sheridan uses Ike's bouts of drunkenness as a plausible pretext for this good father to reveal the suppressed truth that Danny and Harry, as well as their community at large, will not articulate.

Through Ike, Sheridan makes the pivotal distinction between the "hardman" (Danny) and the "gunman" (Harry), between "fighting" and deliberately "hurting people." In *Formations of Violence*, anthropologist Allen Feldman includes a discussion of these different forceful masculinities, drawing on interviews with Northern Irish people.[18] Before the Troubles, "The 'hardman' was the local bare-fisted street fighter intimately associated with specific neighborhoods ... a semiprofessional trained pugilist (Belfast has a rich tradition of boxing families) or simply a street tough." Gunmen can be simply defined as "paramilitaries, irrespective of political affiliations" (46). One of Feldman's interviewees designates the essential difference between the two kinds of men: "The hardman fight was more for the excitement than the actual fight, but with paramilitaries it turned violent here and it was all for to inflict bodily harm" (48). The advent of the Troubles and the predominance of "gunmen" pushed the "hardmen" from a culturally central to a marginal position in the North: "They fought with fists on the street ... but when the guns came out the hardmen disappeared" (47). Thriving on their disregard for rules and the constant threat of fatal violence, gunmen seemed to invalidate the ethical significance of hardmen; the same source attests:

> The paramilitaries put an end to that because once somebody lifted a hand to punch you, you just stuck a .45 up their nostril and they didn't want to fight then.... There was no more of this waiting for your opponent to get up again after you had knocked him down [48].

When Ike tells Danny, "Put your gun down ... fight me like a man!" he asserts Sheridan's valuation of the hardman. In telling Harry, "You're only interested in hurtin' people — that's your only pleasure," Ike confronts the ethical void at the heart of the "gunman." Harry's manhood and political practice rely on the threat of unmitigated violence, and, characteristically, he counters Ike's ideological attack with brutal force: he kills an unarmed, drunk man with a bullet to the head. This encounter underscores the ethical as well as the physical destruction wrought by the "gunman." As another of Feldman's sources puts it:

> I see a clear distinction here. You couldn't be a hardman if you were willing to terrorize women or young people or engage in petty thieving. There is a terrible difference between that and the man who stands on two feet and says, "Okay I'll take your best man and fight him" [49].

Thus, at the cost of his life, the paternal figure Ike advocates the primacy of the hardman as a masculine model for Danny and the rest of their community.

Ike's identification as spiritual father figure becomes clear in Sheridan's extended shot of Maggie's son Liam cradling the trainer's body. Liam, the character whose masculine identity hangs in the balance throughout the film, clearly chooses his ideological alignment in this scene and subsequently accepts Danny, Ike's disciple, as a father figure. Here Sheridan reclaims and reconstructs masculinity by uniting three generations of Irish manhood in a spirit of familial peace and reconciliation in the face of patriarchal violence.

Employing the hardman/gunman distinction, Sheridan advances a masculine practice based not on pure pacifism but on the ethical circumscription of violence. As Feldman states, "The narratives that contrast the hardman to the gunman are a veiled political discourse on the ethics of violence" (46). Sheridan points to this issue as central to his own narrative:

> I think I wanted to make the film about ... growing up, and I had in the back of my mind that the boxer fought within the rules and that he wasn't a terrorist, I mean somebody who fights without rules; in other words, who dehumanizes the opposition to the point where any means necessary will work. And I thought that the boxer was somebody who didn't do that, who ... stood up for himself in a way honestly, in the ring. And that was the story I wanted to do ["Fighting for Peace..." featurette, *The Boxer* DVD].

Therefore, if we view *The Boxer* either as strictly a Troubles film or a "formula" film with a "specific message" of peace, as Ruth Barton does (121), we fail to appreciate its cultural significance, in terms of both masculinity and history:

> The hardman and gunman are elements of a folk narrative that encodes the historical transition from territorialized to deterritorializing violence. They personify the historical experience of communities that once laid claim to rule-bound performances of violence, and subsequently experienced the development of violence beyond traditional social institutions and ethics [Feldman 46].

Thus, Sheridan's examination of these two figures assumes a critical role in the cultural history of Irish masculinity. Furthermore, in addressing the marginalization of women, *The Boxer* moves far beyond the ambiguously critical celebration of Irish patriarchy and violent male rites of passage in Ford's *The Quiet Man*.

Assessing Sheridan's film also requires us to take into account another influential Hollywood forebear of *The Boxer*: Elia Kazan's *On the Waterfront* (1954). Both films center on a boxer past his prime—Danny Flynn is 32, Marlon Brando's Terry Malloy is "pushing 30"—whose career has been compromised by his personal affiliation with a violent organization (Danny with the IRA, Terry with Irish-American mobsters).[19] Kazan's film, like *The Boxer*, sets up a triangular construction of masculinity, with Father Barry (Karl Malden) as the male moral authority and Johnny Friendly (Lee J. Cobb) as the powerful masculine figure of violence. Both protagonists find redemption in loving a woman — in both cases an Irish Catholic woman — and in enduring a particularly traumatic process of disavowing violence, as Danny loses his friend/mentor and Terry loses his brother. Each of these characters ends up physically battered—Danny by Harry, Terry by Johnny Friendly—but with his integrity intact. Finally, both films seem to dramatize and vivify the maxim, spoken by Father Barry at the end of *On the Waterfront*, "You lost the battle, but you have a chance to win the war." In each case we are left with a hero staggering into the distance, defeated physically yet spiritually undaunted, embodying a principled figure of masculinity in a community beset by violence and corruption.

Crucially, though, Sheridan's work moves beyond merely reviving a traditional figure of masculinity — the hardman — for in many obvious respects the hardman not only fails to challenge but actually affirms patriarchal ideology in pugilism's insistence on the primacy of masculine bodily spectacle and aggression. With *The Boxer*, Sheridan redefines the hardman and confronts the ideological formation of masculinity in marginalized societies. Sheridan's interpretations of ideology contribute to class-consciousness by revealing the "imaginary" and deceptive operation of patriarchy. I am not suggesting that Sheridan — or Althusser, or anyone else — effectively creates critical discourse free of ideology; class-consciousness certainly constitutes an ideology and is thus potentially exploitative. Through disrupting the mechanism of a dominant ideology, however, Sheridan exposes its illusory nature, even while advancing a counter-ideology. According to Althusser:

> While admitting that [ideologies] do not correspond to reality, i.e., that they constitute an illusion, we admit that they do make allusion to reality, and that they need only be "interpreted" to discover the reality of the world behind their imaginary representation of that world (ideology = *illusion/allusion*) [87].

By confronting pervasive ideologies and redefining masculinity and femininity in the context of the Troubles and the late 1990s Peace Process, Sheridan's film enacts a profound demystification of extremist violence and patriarchal social structures.[20]

In *The Boxer*, Sheridan effectively creates a space where patriarchy can be tested and deprivileged. Danny Flynn's parents, if he has any, never appear in the film, and many young men in Belfast, including Liam, have fathers in prison. As Luce Irigaray writes, "*Father-son relationships* ... guarantee the transmission of patriarchal power and its laws, its discourse, its social structures" (574). Thus, within a community of estranged fathers and sons, patriarchy is open to destabilization.

As a masculine figure, Danny Flynn effects subversion, not only by "fighting within the rules" but by repeatedly embracing male lack rather than disavowing it. His extreme reticence after 14 years in prison represents a kind of surrender, a disavowal of phallic authority. As he explains to Maggie, "Silence becomes your best friend.... You feel as though your voice isn't welcome." Harry, the "gunman," also reminds Danny that he owes his life to keeping silent: "All you had to do was ... say hello to some of your old friends in the IRA. It's not nice snubbing people. But you didn't name names. That's why you're a healthy man, understand?" As a former IRA member, Danny realizes that if he stays in Belfast he remains under threat, both from the Catholic extremists he used to serve and the Loyalist Protestant paramilitaries who continue to associate him with their enemies. Danny cannot fully protect himself, and he chooses not to carry a gun — he has no illusions of phallic mastery. He has no place to hide, and he knows it.

Thus, Danny's masculine practice does not function through material or martial symbols that disavow his lack. By confining his aggression to the ring, a space that in a way parallels his position in the community at large, he leaves himself constantly open to the violence of his opponent. To vent aggression Danny must endure it as well. He understands this condition of vulnerability as something existential, as he tells Maggie: "For 14 years I was locked up. My feelings were locked up inside of me. And when I got in the ring again, you can't imagine the relief it was to feel the pain, to be back in the world again." Danny faces pain and lack; he does not run from them or wield guns or other phallic symbols to deny them. In the ring his only weapons are his hands, blunted by boxing gloves.

Harry's masculinity, on the other hand, functions through unmitigated violence and the weapons that threaten and perpetrate it; he denies his lack through the phallic symbols of guns and bombs. He wreaks destruction on his enemies while constantly evading their reprisals. His most profound illusion is that of control — mastery — of his weapons, both in their material and symbolic manifestations. While guns deny his male lack as long as they are directed at others, once turned against him they reinforce his vulnerability and the limits of his phallic power. At the same time, Harry's ideology bears him ceaselessly into the past: he must keep killing to avenge his son. As his murder of Ike dramatizes, to stop killing would be to acknowledge his own complicity in the boy's death. Although IRA leader Joe Hamill (Brian Cox) warns him, "Get yourself into the future!" Harry invariably reads the present through the lens of the past, clinging to an ideology that perpetuates vengeance. Harry condemns Danny, declaring:

> He's filling people's heads full of shit, Joe. "Leave the fightin' to Danny" means that all the people who are in prison, who died, who didn't surrender to the Brits — it means that all their sacrifices aren't worth a lousy fuckin' boxing match. He's spreading dissent.... A lot of the active servicemen won't accept this peace bullshit anymore. You're going soft, Joe.... You had men in prison who starved themselves to death for you, Joe — ten of them — and now you have Danny Boy Flynn making a mockery of everything you stood for, and you don't even see it.

Because he is beholden to a backward-looking ideology and is a member of a colonized, fractured society, Harry will never be at a loss for justification of his vengeance. As in *The Field* and *In the Name of the Father*, Sheridan here dramatizes the ideological force of patriarchy as propelling men into the past, and once again the threat of a stagnant future is very real: in the wake of Harry's final bombing, young Liam and his friends burn down the Holy Family gym.[21] Only as Liam comes to regret this act, showing contrition, and accepting Ike and Danny's forgiveness, does a future free of vengeance seem conceivable.

Danny poses a profound ideological threat to Harry on two fronts. First, by staging, through his bouts, a tentative version of a peaceful community, he fights to ease sectarian tensions. Second, he commits a cardinal sin against IRA doctrine and patriarchal mores by pursuing a relationship with Maggie, a prisoner's wife. Harry responds to both of these challenges with violent acts, in addition to killing Ike.[22] Even in the wake of his mentor's death, however, Danny looks to the future: "I'm gonna build a gym for the kids…"; and when Joe Hamill asks, "Are you back for revenge, Danny?" he responds, "No … I'm back for Maggie." Danny sees a future, forgoing vengeance. But Harry refuses to let go of the past, and as a threat to Maggie and Danny, as well as the authority of Joe Hamill, his IRA superior, he compels Joe to order him killed. Harry never recognizes his real condition of lack and vulnerability, and his final words to Danny, "End of story, peacemaker," precipitate his own death. He lives and dies under an illusion.

Similarly, in the final sequence of *On the Waterfront*, Terry Malloy identifies the illusory nature of Johnny Friendly's authority: "You take them heaters away from you and you're nothing! Your guts is all in your wallet and your trigger finger." Although the gunman in this case doesn't end up dead, Terry successfully demystifies the exploitative ideology at work and enables the dockworkers to confront and change their situation. Through Harry, Sheridan reveals the principles upon which violent patriarchy is founded: denial of lack and maintenance of the phallic "dominant fiction," along with deferral of life in the present. Against the gunman he pits a peaceful, confrontational figure, a man with the authority to upset this ideological mechanism and offer hope of a future.

Through Danny, Sheridan redefines the "hardman" as one who refuses to use physical prowess as a disavowal of male lack. To use Silverman's terms, Danny embodies a "deviant" masculinity, which "says 'no' to power" (2). As she puts it, "Saying 'no' to power necessarily implies achieving some kind of reconciliation with … (castration, alterity, and specularity), and hence with femininity" (3). As I will suggest, many of the men portrayed in boxing films, perhaps unsurprisingly, reinforce rather than defy phallocentrism. Boxing can obviously be a vehicle for ego aggrandizement and fuel illusions of phallic mastery, as when Danny's first opponent, Eddie Carroll, repeatedly tells him, "I'm gonna kill you." Even Danny reverts to patriarchal discourse and violence at moments in the film. When Maggie suggests that Harry will threaten their lives if they continue their relationship, Danny explodes:

> You don't understand. Half my fucking life I pissed away, and all the good things in it, because of that sickly bastard and his dirty little … world.… And now he's trying to turn us into a dirty little secret.… Let him know that I love you, Maggie.… I'll not crawl around in the fucking gutter for him. I'll kill him first! I'll rip his fucking throat out!

Danny's hubris at this moment can be understood as resistance not only to Harry's physical threat but to his manipulation of representation as well. When Harry provokes Danny to a physical confrontation near the end of the film, Danny fights, but only after Harry threatens Maggie and calls her a "whore." Although he struggles to avoid it, violence outside the ring catches up with Danny. His patriarchal community and his extremist past inevitably lead to severe tests of his peaceful ethos. Ultimately, however, Danny's project is one of reconciliation, as he vows to build another boxing gym for the young men of Belfast. He will "try and teach them something" about discipline and understanding, not rage and division.

The Boxer's progressive ethos, as well as its reconfiguration of boxing genre conventions, hinges in large part on Sheridan's ability to forcefully challenge patriarchy in his portrayal of women as well as men. In the opening sequence of the film, during a wedding reception for a prisoner's bride, young women adapt and appropriate the Rolling Stones' anthem of frustrated male desire, "(I Can't Get No) Satisfaction." Maggie, one of these singers and the main female character, occupies a central narrative position in her social roles as mother to Liam, daughter to IRA leader Joe Hamill, wife to a political prisoner (another IRA man), and estranged lover to Danny. At several key moments of the film, however, she asserts her own agency and defies patriarchal ideology.[23] As Elizabeth Butler Cullingford writes, "If incarceration suggests impotence, an unfaithful wife evokes emasculation, and an army marches on its masculinity. Republican morale had to be sustained by keeping the prisoner's sexual property safe" ("The Prisoner's Wife" 8). By pursuing Danny and refusing to maintain her loveless fidelity to Thomas, her incarcerated husband, Maggie reevaluates the position of the prisoner's wife. Early on she interprets her father's morale management of the IRA's sexual property — "You women who stood by your man will be remembered as the bravest of the district" — as the manipulative blarney it is; late in the film Maggie lets Joe know her mind: "My marriage was over before Liam was born. I'm the prisoner here. You and your politics have made sure of that." Thus, she sees through the "imaginary" spin of Joe's discourse and recognizes her own subjection.

Maggie also asserts her agency in her relationship with Danny. Separated from her during his fourteen-year term in prison, Danny makes no attempt to reconnect with Maggie. Refusing to accept his evasive manner, however, she confronts him: "When we see each other, all I get from you is the odd grunt." When Danny remains reticent, she stalks off in frustration. In their next encounter she approaches him with a warning from the IRA; Danny shrugs off her words of caution and says casually, "If you ask me to leave, I'll go." Maggie then upbraids him: "Turn around, start walking, and when you've walked for 14 years, stop and think about what you did to me." Danny responds, "I did it for you," and Maggie slaps him, apparently harder than she intended, and bloodies his nose.

Danny (Daniel Day-Lewis) and Maggie (Emily Watson) pursue their relationship despite the social and political repercussions in *The Boxer* (Universal, 1997, dir. Jim Sheridan).

This moment represents a critical gap in the ideology holding sway over this community. Maggie, speaking as subject to patriarchy (as part of the mechanism) by claiming that she was willing to put her life on hold during Danny's prison term, illuminates the deferral of life the ideology requires for the woman on the outside, as well as the man on the inside. This is a moment of recognition for them both. Throughout the course of the film Danny comes to realize the price Maggie has paid for his actions, as well as the way a prisoners' culture—like the Irish "death culture" Sheridan later addresses with *In America*—contributes to a collective privileging of the past that fuels patriarchy and violence and devalues the future. Maggie must now come to realize how her agency has been denied her ("I'm the prisoner here") and her own life deferred in the interest of politics. Thus, this ideological break provides a basis for Maggie and Danny's new vision of the future.

It is appropriate that, before we ever see Danny hit an opponent in the ring, we witness Maggie striking him. By smiling, rather than restraining her or retaliating, Danny defers to her judgment, defies patriarchy, and presents himself as a most extraordinary hardman. Later, Maggie initiates the first physical contact of their renewed union, as she commands Danny, "Give us a hug." She clearly drives their relationship in its early phases and ultimately embodies a woman with critical and symbolic agency in this highly fraught society and culture. The couple's redefinition of gender roles contributes to the film's project of depriviliging the turbulent past and imagining a future of peace and greater equality for Northern Ireland.

With its assault on patriarchal ideology, *The Boxer* occupies an unusually complex position within the genre of the boxing film. For Danny, the sport offers something other than the chance to hurt people or redeem his own wounded masculinity. In the Northern Irish context, the sport provides a space where sectarian tensions can be eased and representations challenged. Sheridan remarks on the creative genesis of the film:

> It started about 13 years ago [circa 1984] when I was in New York ... and all the news from Ireland was ... shootings and bombings and this young kid come on [television]. He was a boxer named Barry McGuigan, and he said ... "Leave the fighting to McGuigan" was his catchphrase. So I thought it was kind of innocent and ... naïve a little bit, but great. Here was a guy in a violent profession saying, "Stop fighting." That contradiction interested me ["Fighting for Peace ..." featurette, *The Boxer* DVD].

After spending several months as part of McGuigan's camp, Sheridan published his "official biography" of the boxer, entitled *Leave the Fighting to McGuigan* (1985). A Catholic who grew up just south of the Northern Irish border in Clones, McGuigan married a Protestant woman. As an amateur pugilist, he represented the national boxing teams of both Northern Ireland and the Republic. Likening the Troubles to a "plague," Sheridan recounts: "Barry had two countries; he boxed for both of them. Each country blamed the other for the plague. McGuigan blamed neither, he just fought" (123). Thus, as an icon, McGuigan had tremendous representational power in the political arena, and he exploited it to counter violent ideology. As a professional, he carried neither the Irish Tricolour nor the Union Jack into the ring; instead, the white peace flag was his banner. McGuigan's politics were simple — as he said, "I'm for peace." He fought to unite, not to divide (Sheridan 136–7).

McGuigan's story also informs *The Boxer* as the tale of a hardman's regret, though his personal demons spring from a different source than the film's protagonist. As McGuigan explains: "One traumatic time in my life, 1982. In the Grosvenor House Hotel in London, I had a tragic boxing match with a young guy called Young Ali, or Alami Mustafa was his name. And he died. And it had a ... profound effect on me." He goes on to explain how this event is manifested in Sheridan's film: "[T]he story had an effect on Jim, too. He wanted to tell that story, only he changed the outcome of the fight.... The difference is, the ending to Jim's fight is brilliant" ("Fighting for Peace ..."). In the wake of Young Ali's death,[24] McGuigan, 21 at the time, considered retiring from boxing (Sheridan 124), but he decided to continue and later dedicated his title win to the Nigerian boxer, telling the media in his post-fight comments, "I want to dedicate it to him.... I would not like it to be an ordinary fighter who beat him ... but the world champ" (Sheridan 204).

By dramatizing a revised history of McGuigan's "tragic fight," Sheridan allows Danny to embody the peaceful, unifying ethos of the "Clones Cyclone," while confronting and averting the psychic trauma that the real-life boxer experienced. In his own London fight with a Nigerian boxer, Danny gets the upper hand in the late rounds, and his opponent, reeling from two successive knockdowns, can barely stay on his feet. Far behind on points, Danny can win only by a knockout, and with the fatigued Nigerian on the ropes, the Irishman unleashes a barrage of punches that staggers the other man, rendering him defenseless. Danny is in position to win if only he obeys the referee's command to keep hitting the Nigerian until he collapses and cannot get up.[25] But Danny defies the order to continue fighting: "It's over," he says, and he walks away from degradation. He loses the fight but maintains his constructive ethos.

Though *The Boxer* has been described as an "overtly generic work" (Barton 99), it resists such narrow categorization. Manipulating the conventions of the boxing film, it deviates from the genre to reveal Sheridan's program of reconstructing affirmative masculine figures in a post-colonial setting. For Ike, Danny and Liam, boxing acts as a means to personal and community enfranchisement. By contrast, in many other boxing films the sport promotes vices like alcohol abuse, drug use, philandering, and gambling (as in *The Champ* and *Body and Soul*), as well as ethical decay: boxers often develop a taste for violence (as in *Champion* and *Raging Bull*) and "forget their roots," alienating family and friends, as in *Raging Bull*, *Body and Soul* and *The Great White Hope*. Physical decay also often overtakes boxing film heroes, as they commonly fight past their prime and in some cases die in the ring. In conventional fight films the one thing that the sport does generate is money, though money itself almost invariably leads to the corruption of the boxer, thus reinforcing the anti-capitalist critique of many movies in the genre.

In Sheridan's film, Danny never covets the money and fame that appeal to pro athletes in film and in reality. He is past his prime and only wants to get a few fights and "set the record straight." Danny never speaks of pursuing a title or public acclaim, although a common trope of boxing films includes once-great fighters making a comeback. As he says, he is "just boxing." He seeks personal redemption through a sport that has the potential to transcend religious and ideological differences in his community.

Unlike the conventional boxer hero—or, as is often the case, anti-hero—Danny doesn't win many fights. He loses his first fight, wins his second, and is disqualified from his third and presumably last fight. In this way Sheridan's film promotes ethical over material success, as we have seen in the England episode when Danny leaves the ring rather than continue a bout that he believes he has already won. When the officials fail to uphold the rules, he enforces them himself, saying, "The fight's over." He refuses to allow his sport, potentially full of generative power, to become a spectacle of brutality.

With this act Danny avoids the material exploitation dramatized in many boxing films. His English manager informs him, "You'll never fight in this country again," meaning he will probably never make money as a pro fighter, which is a great blessing judging by many other boxing films. For instance, in *Body and Soul* (Robert Rossen, 1947) the naïve young Jewish boxer Charlie Davis (John Garfield) has a friend who warns him not to become a "money machine" for managers and promoters: "It's not enough to be great, Charlie ... we're infested with rats. [You're] not just a kid who can fight, [you're] money. And people want money so bad, they make it stink. And they make you stink." Disregarding this wise counsel, Charlie soon embarks on a long career turning out money for just such "rats," before cutting ties with them in the end. Having spent his peak physical years in prison, and refusing to do the bidding of managers and promoters once he gets out, Danny avoids the capitalist morass of professional fighting.

Danny resists ideological exploitation as well as ethical and material corruption, thus embodying the central dilemma of boxing films: the question of whether or not a fighter is willing to "sell out" in his quest to achieve greatness. In a twist on this formula, though, Danny almost invariably manages to maintain his integrity. Since he has already hit rock bottom before the narrative begins, he needs no fall from grace to solidify his identity. Early on he warns Ike not to accept donations of equipment from "cops"—the Protestant Royal Ulster Constabulary (RUC)—and later, when a sneaky cameraman snaps a publicity photo of the boxer and a police captain shaking hands, Danny fumes: "I don't like being used." Accepting the police sponsorship ultimately costs Ike and Danny dearly,[26] as it gives Harry a pretext for car-bombing the police captain (as he leaves Danny's second fight) and setting off a riot that renews sectarian tensions, momentarily nullifying all the positive communal effects of the Holy Family gym. In a community where one wrong move can ignite a blaze of hatred, Danny learns to be absolutely uncompromising in his vision and representation of peace, as he finally determines to rebuild the gym. Indeed, *The Boxer* is deeply concerned with psychic, as well as physical, resilience in the face of devastation and bitterness.

A film that is illuminating in the way it both parallels and contrasts with *The Boxer* is *The Great White Hope* (Martin Ritt, 1970). Initially set in the U.S. in 1910, the narrative depicts the struggles African-American boxer Jack Jefferson (James Earl Jones), a character loosely based on Jack Johnson, the first black heavyweight champion of the world, faces in his attempt to win and defend the world heavyweight title. Jefferson steadfastly resists the corrupting and dehumanizing effects of the fight game, in spite of the additional adversity he faces in the form of racism. He explains his trademark habit of smiling during his bouts by saying, "I'm a happy sort of person ... so what I want to put a face on for? And anyway, it's a sport, right, like a game. Well,

I likes whoever I'm hitting to see I'm still his friend." He also refuses to be appropriated as part of any cause, as he flippantly tells white reporters: "I ain't fighting for no race. I ain't redeeming nobody. My mama told me Mr. Lincoln done that. Ain't that why you shot him?" After he wins the heavyweight championship, though, the white establishment determines to destroy him, and he must escape the country to evade conviction for being romantically involved with a white woman. His career ruined, Jack no longer smiles in the ring. He eventually becomes as bitter as his oppressors, drives away his lover Eleanor, and agrees to take a dive to relinquish his championship: "Champ don't mean piss-all to me, man." After Eleanor commits suicide, Jack is shocked into self-recognition: "What have I done? What have they done to us?" The power of hatred finally overcomes Jack's will, a power that Danny Flynn, in a different but parallel context, finds the strength to resist.

In stopping the London fight, Danny transcends the dehumanizing effects of the sport. Though the referee and audience demand that he "Box on!" Danny embraces his devastated opponent rather than continuing to hit him, refusing to be, as Ike puts it, "a performing monkey" in "a bloody circus." In other boxing films the dehumanization engendered by the sport becomes a central theme. Promoters and managers frequently deny boxers their humanity, as in *The Harder They Fall* (Mark Robson, 1956) when a backer states, "Fighters ain't human," and in *Body and Soul* when Charley's manager says glibly, "I like fighters better than horses." Many of these films plead for the souls of boxers, detailing the degradation to which the business end of the game subjects them. In *Requiem for a Heavyweight* (Ralph Nelson, 1956), "Mountain" McClintock's friend and trainer, Army, pleads with his manager to stop exploiting his credulously loyal fighter, whose body has been ravaged by "111 fights": "He's a decent man. He's somebody with a heart. He's somebody with flesh and blood. You can't sell this on the market by the pound." In *Raging Bull* (Martin Scorsese, 1980), Jake LaMotta is pervasively dehumanized even by his own family: "You're a killer.... You're a sick bastard.... You fuckin' wacko," says his brother; and his wife calls him a "fat pig ... bastard ... you sick animal ... you piece of shit." At the film's climax the brutal and seemingly remorseless LaMotta breaks down during a night in jail, sobbing, "They call me an animal. I'm not an animal.... I'm not that bad.... I'm not that guy."

In contrast, the only moment of *The Boxer* when Danny's humanity is questioned occurs during his bout in London against his Nigerian opponent. After a slow-motion sequence of pummeling that recalls the discomfiting ring violence of *Raging Bull*, Danny asserts his humanity by opting out of the fight. Back in Belfast, IRA men ridicule Danny — not for lack of fighting prowess or animal aggression, but for appearing too humane, as one of Harry's men jeers: "Flynn should win the Nobel Peace Prize for boxing." As opposed to the corrupted, exploited fighters portrayed in many boxing films, Danny fights on his own terms, as an ethical human being — as an aggressive yet compassionate man.

The passage into manhood — in the sense of maturing emotionally — is central to *The Boxer* in several ways. Joe Hamill implores Harry to get past bigotry and vengeance and "Grow up," while all the boxers Ike eulogizes at Danny's first fight were killed before they had the chance to reach adulthood. In Troubles-era Belfast, children are indoctrinated into violence before they understand what their actions and sacrifices mean, as Liam and his friends throw petrol bombs at the police and set fire to Ike and Danny's non-sectarian Holy Family gym. There is no space here, physical or temporal, in which to grow up, and thus men and women like Harry and his wife suffer from the same stunted development. Young people who were never children become full-grown without ever maturing. Maggie's father, Joe, a man who has long fit this mold, finally breaks out of it and commits himself to the Peace Process. Joe also allows his daughter to express her resentment about his callous exploitation of her late mother's life, which enables him to mourn for his lost wife and neglected family, and offers him some hope of salvaging his relationship with Maggie and Liam.

By the same token, when Maggie tells Danny, "We're not kids anymore," he responds, "Yes, we are." This statement is much more than idle romantic sentimentality. Danny is reclaiming their compromised, abridged youth and acknowledging that only by recapturing some of the idealism and hope of childhood can they grow to love each other as adults. In the course of the film he and Maggie reconcile youth and experience, refusing to perpetuate patriarchy and vengeance. Commenting on the film in the context of the Troubles, Sheridan says:

> I think it's kind of a tragedy that this stuff goes on in any country ... the police and army and all that bullshit having to be around. You'd think they'd just sit down and solve it and say ... "I'll swap with ya ... you be Catholic for a day and I'll be Protestant" [*The Boxer* DVD Commentary].

This sort of disarming whimsicality, though mostly absent from the depleted world Sheridan creates in *The Boxer*, shows up at particular moments in the film, such as when Joe Hamill lectures Harry: "We're going to have to live with them some time.... The Protestants — the other half of the population." These words have such pathos that one wants to believe a man like Joe would speak them, yet to the critical ear they may ring false and mark Sheridan's own political orientation as naïve. Yet these statements echo those of champion boxer Barry McGuigan from a decade earlier: "It's our country, let us all live in peace. No more of this [fucking] bigotry. Bring up your children and say, 'So you're a protestant, you're a Catholic.' Live with them, mix with them. Marry them" (Sheridan 186). McGuigan's grandfather, who was in the IRA in the 1920s, was imprisoned by the RUC for over three years without being charged; the fact that he maintains such an outlook, despite his family's past, validates hope for a peaceful future. Such is the spirit of Sheridan's final statement in the biography of the fighter: "Until there are one million Barry McGuigans Ulster will never sleep" (216).

Undoubtedly the progressive idealism clearly reflected in Sheridan's work leaves the politics of his films (or lack thereof, according to some) vulnerable to criticism by those seeking a more realistic or sympathetic portrait of Irish Republicanism. Rather than discount the filmmaker's work as inadequate for reflecting his openly acknowledged political stance, however, I would argue that Sheridan's films should be read as narrative counterarguments—cogent responses to the ideologies of extremism and patriarchy—as he invites us to do. He says of *The Boxer*, "I wanted to endorse the people who were giving up violence [in Northern Ireland]. That's what it is about. It's a propaganda film made with Hollywood money and, OK, it lost money but it did some social good, I think, I hope" (Barton 147). As imaginative works, then, Sheridan's films not only reflect the world, but at some level they produce it.

Events in Northern Ireland subsequent to *The Boxer*'s release have proven Sheridan's progressive viewpoint to be prophetic. Splinter groups of extremists do remain, and they have committed some terrible atrocities, most notably the 1998 Omagh bombing that claimed 29 lives. The mainline Catholic and Protestant paramilitary organizations, however, have consistently upheld the cease fire initiated in 1997, and, more recently, they have vowed to pursue their goals through exclusively peaceful political means: the Irish Republican Army decommissioned in 2005, and the Ulster Volunteer Force renounced violence in 2007 (*International Herald Tribune*, "IRA Is Committed"; "Ulster Volunteer Force Pledges"). Meanwhile, the government of Northern Ireland, still dominated by Protestant leaders, has been making slow but meaningful steps toward integrating the Catholic minority and sharing power.

Sheridan's Personal, Political Cinema

In all of his work Sheridan manages to portray violence as an intensely personal experience. He often places his characters in positions of isolation: Christy Brown confined in a body that allows him to move and communicate only through Herculean efforts; Tadgh as an only child in a practically silent household; Gerry in prison; Danny first in prison and then often silent and alone outside of it. In these films male rites of passage are predicated on the recognition of the consequences of violence, and only individual, constructive responses to such acts make sense. Conversely, the rhetorics of extremism and empire both employ language that does no justice to individual loss or suffering but incorporates it into a biased narrative history, as in *The Field* when Bull rants about the Great Famine and the evil Brits; in *In the Name of the Father* when Inspector Dixon ignores the evidence of the Guildford Four's innocence, claiming, "They all did it"; and in *The Boxer* when Harry invokes the Long Kesh Hunger Strikers to stigmatize the peace negotiations as a betrayal. Sheridan leads us to mistrust such statements, which trivialize individual experience in the interest of ideology. The director's progressive portrayal of maleness in the 1990s reaches its apex in *The Boxer*, as only in the latter film does a man ultimately move out of isolation and begin to live as part of a community.

Sheridan shows the tragedy of old-world patriarchy in *The Field*, as the sins of his father finally condemn Tadgh to death. Through *In the Name of the Father* and *The Boxer*, however, Sheridan constructs a viable alternative mode of masculinity in which individual experience and conscience effectively neutralize the vertiginous pull toward violence and its by-product: the dehumanization and negation of the perpetrator as well as the victims, who are cast into the narrowly proscribed, dichotomized roles of "terrorist/freedom-fighter" and "collateral damage/martyr," respectively. Sheridan dramatizes the destructive potential of regressive Irish nationalism and patriarchy, and depicts male figures endowed with constructive agency, thus completing a complex formation of affirmative masculinity. His work powerfully dramatizes the weakness of violent men and the strength of the peaceful.

CHAPTER 5

Alternative Masculinity and Irish Historical Trauma in Paul Greengrass's *Bloody Sunday* and *Omagh*[1]

> I object to violence because when it appears to do good, the good is only temporary; the evil it does is permanent.— MOHANDAS GANDHI[2]

> Since [nonviolence] is not a natural response, we need to be schooled in it. We need models, and we need to rehearse nonviolence in our daily lives if we ever hope to resort to it in crises.— WALTER WINK[3]

So far I have examined the representations of gender in the work of two Irish artists who have made highly original and provocative films that operate largely within the confines of Hollywood genres in order to appeal to the lucrative U.S. market. In this final chapter I will consider the cultural implications of two recent films that fundamentally deviate from commercially popular genre conventions. Both *Bloody Sunday* (2002) and *Omagh* (2004) use the techniques of direct-cinema documentary filmmaking to present pivotal Irish historical traumas with uncompromising immediacy and respect for victims of violence. At the same time, both works fill a crucial cinematic void as narratives focusing on male figures who engage in political conflict through exclusively peaceful means. My contention is that these works represent a type of film with the potential to positively impact sociocultural and political conceptions of gender and conflict resolution. They turn acts of violence on screen into visceral experiences of vicarious trauma for viewers, as opposed to the sort of narcotic, jingoistic high proffered by many Hollywood war, action, and western films.

Just as John Ford's work offered Jim Sheridan a set of culturally resonant narratives and archetypes to interpolate and critique, Sheridan's cinema has helped pave the way for *Bloody Sunday* and *Omagh*, both artistically and financially. Addressing politics in a remarkably nuanced way in the context of widely recognized narrative formulas and family conflicts, his films have spawned a broader interest in Irish history and culture, thereby creating an artistic space for further, more experimental cinematic explorations of Irish society and the Troubles. Furthermore, in practical terms, Sheridan's production company, Hell's Kitchen, provided backing for both of the Paul Greengrass films discussed in this chapter.

Questions of Genre and Terminology

Although *Bloody Sunday* and *Omagh* are not documentaries *per se*, in terms of substance they have as much in common with historical reenactments as with generic fiction films like political thrillers and docudramas. Stylistically, *Bloody Sunday* and *Omagh* achieve an unsettling, at times devastating intimacy with people and events through the use of handheld camerawork, quick zooms, and a complete lack of artificial lighting and non-diegetic sound.

A new and radically hybrid filmmaking practice created these two works, and therefore new critical terms are needed to describe them adequately. Brian McIlroy has devised the helpful word "Monumentary" to describe *Omagh* (and, to a lesser extent, *Bloody Sunday*), while the term I prefer is "dramatic reconstruction." Both of these generic categorizations emphasize essential aspects of these complex visual texts: "Monumentary" underscores the enduring value of these works as testaments to the suffering of victims and the actions of those who sought to prevent and/or seek justice for these atrocities; my term refers more directly to the ethically sound collaborative process that went into the making of the films. Nevertheless, I am equally concerned here with the way in which these pictures pay tribute to radically deviant, peaceful conceptions of heroism and the exemplary filmmaking practice that went into them.

Throughout the productions of both *Bloody Sunday* and *Omagh*, the filmmakers sought the input of those directly affected by these tragedies, and they made concerted efforts to portray these historical events as accurately as possible while incorporating conflicting ideological points of view. The main creative force behind both films is Paul Greengrass, the English director who honed his skills for ten years making television documentaries for the acclaimed, activist-oriented Granada Television series *World in Action* (*The Times Online*). During this time he did work on the Troubles in Northern Ireland, becoming the first filmmaker to be granted access to Long Kesh prison, where in 1979 he filmed a segment on the IRA prisoners' dirty protests (*Variety*).[4] Addressing Ireland's turbulent late-twentieth-century history,

5. Masculinity and Trauma in Greengrass's Films 141

Greengrass states, "There are two events that frame the Troubles: one was Bloody Sunday — the moment at which the progress towards conflict became unstoppable and Omagh, which marked the moment at which everyone knew the conflict had to end" (*Omagh* Press Pack 6). In recreating these events cinematically, Greengrass has said he wanted to avoid being "polemical."[5] Speaking specifically of *Bloody Sunday*, he declares:

> What I wanted to do was create a version of that day [in Derry, N.I.] so that, whether you were a British soldier, a demonstrator or you lived in Dublin, you could say, "Well, it must have been a bit like that." It wasn't a conspiracy, it was definitely a most terrible thing, but it's what happens when you get trapped in these things; you dance to the edge and then over [*Times Online*].

While Greengrass clearly evinces a progressive, pro–human rights ethos in these two works, I take him at his word that his intention was to document these traumatic moments of Irish history in a manner that is artistically interesting and intellectually rigorous, as well as factually correct. The proof is in the remarkable alignment between the historical record and the films themselves.

Although in some respects they are as much fiction films as documentaries, in terms of ethical integrity and artistic purpose, *Bloody Sunday* and *Omagh* fulfill one of the noblest and most vital functions of documentaries: investigating marginalized historical narratives and giving a voice to oppressed people. As far as the presentation of facts, of course, we should always be wary of looking at any film, documentary or otherwise, with less skepticism than politically motivated fiction films, such as docudramas or biopics. Theorist Bill Nichols argues:

> The definition of "documentary" is always relational or comparative.... Were documentary a *reproduction* of reality, these problems would be far less acute.... But documentary is not a reproduction of reality, it is a *representation* of the world we already occupy. It stands for a particular view of the world [20].

Stella Bruzzi qualifies Nichols by stating that while "[d]ocumentary is persistently treated as a representational mode of filmmaking ... at its core is the notion of film as record" (419). More definitively, Brian Winston declares, "Documentary is not fiction," and argues that, in terms of the development and purpose of the documentary form, "By 1948 ... 'sincere and justified reconstruction' was as good as 'factual shooting.'" From the earliest phases of the documentary, then, filmmakers were often compelled to make necessary adjustments, using sets and choreographed scenes and re-stagings to achieve a coherent documentary narrative. Winston determines that "the central question for documentary ethics" lies in a film's degree of "mediation," which he sees as extremely difficult to gauge (181–85).

Attempting to establish the degree to which filmmakers embellish or alter facts in the course of re-staging and/or editing footage of actual events—trying to define how much they "can be trusted" to present the truth or a version of it—may seem like a fool's errand. According to Errol Morris, however, filmmakers, as well as viewers, should not abandon the quest for truth and settle for a state of cynical relativity. Morris argues that filmmakers have a moral responsibility to strive for accuracy, especially in their use of reenactments:

> Critics argue that the use of re-enactments suggest[s] a callous disregard on the part of a filmmaker for what is true. I don't agree. Some re-enactments serve the truth, others subvert it.... The engine of uncovering truth is not some special lens or even the unadorned human *eye*; it is unadorned human *reason*.... It's not re-enactments *per se* that are wrong or inappropriate. It's the use of them. I use re-enactments to burrow underneath the surface of reality in an attempt to uncover some hidden truth ["Play It Again, Sam"].[6]

In my view, the respectful, transparent and collaborative manner in which *Bloody Sunday* and *Omagh* were made renders them "sincere and justified" reenactments; they are ethically sound "dramatic reconstructions."

Bloody Sunday: Chronicle of a Peacemaker's Courageous Failure

When a film addresses and redresses history, as *Bloody Sunday* does, questions of genre and representation become central to our understanding of its aesthetic, cultural and social value. Through its successful manipulation of disparate genre elements, and its lack of adherence to any single set of conventions, the film achieves a dynamic account of a pivotal historical trauma. It takes part in a discourse of reparation for a series of atrocities that had long been shrouded in controversy, coercion and cover-up. As scholar Margaret O'Neill writes of the massacre itself: "Bloody Sunday is not history in the sense of something that is over, but rather memory of an unhealed wound. And embedded in the trauma of that wound is the further injury inflicted by Lord Widgery's official version of events" (97). Through its technical and generic fluidity, *Bloody Sunday* the film goes beyond attempting to set the record straight about the past; it offers a fleeting vision of a revolutionary future in the person of Ivan Cooper. It is in valorizing a real, uncompromisingly peaceful masculine practice that this work transcends genre definitions and becomes a visionary work of cinematic art.

Bloody Sunday successfully employs film modes common to both the observational documentary (the entire film is shot with handheld cameras and no artificial lighting) and the docudrama (professional and amateur actors substitute for historical personages). These technical choices, though, emphasize the reconstructive aims of the filmmakers, while their employment of more conventional narrative elements, such as the love stories between Gerry (Declan Duddy) and Hester (Edel Frazer), and Ivan (James Nesbitt) and Frances (Kathy Keira Clarke), as well as Ivan's dramatic final speech, allows them simultaneously to recreate history in convincing detail and craft a compelling narrative of individual human tragedy.

Drawing on Brian Winston's terms, I classify Paul Greengrass's film as a "dramatic reconstruction" of what took place in Derry, Northern Ireland on Bloody Sunday, January 30, 1972. *Bloody Sunday*'s claim to ethical viability rests on its origins in cross-cultural creative collaboration. The film's depiction of events accords closely with the accounts of witnesses compiled by the British government in the Bloody Sunday Inquiry (www.bloody-sunday-inquiry.org/uk) and is substantially based on the book *Eyewitness Bloody Sunday* by Don Mullan (an Irishman who was present at the massacre, appears in the film as a priest, and is credited as a co-producer). Crucially, the filmmakers and actors are both English and Irish: Greengrass and producer Mark Redhead are English; while Irish director Jim Sheridan serves as an executive producer, and his company, Hell's Kitchen, helped finance the film. The actor who plays Protestant MP and civil rights leader Ivan Cooper is James Nesbitt, himself a Northern Irish Protestant, and many of those who portray the soldiers and paratroopers occupying Derry are, in fact, former British servicemen. As Don Mullan attests:

> I genuinely believe that *Bloody Sunday* is one of the most important films to be made about the "Troubles" in the last 30 years. It contextualizes the destruction of the non-violent Civil Rights Movement and the accendency of the armed struggle.... Those participating included families of the victims, the wounded, eyewitnesses to the massacre in 1972 and former British soldiers who had served in Northern Ireland. The making of the film was, in reality, a mini peace process.... Everyone on its production worked with integrity to tell the truth about the horror and consequences of that terrible day ["Bloody Sunday — the Movie"].

Indeed, the film takes great care to portray the Irish — Catholic and Protestant, working- and middle-class, official and civilian — and English, both belligerent and well-intentioned, who exacerbated the already tense situation in Derry, as well as those who attempted to defuse it. Nevertheless, as the main titles declare that the film is "written and directed by Paul Greengrass," we should be wary of treating it as entirely factual. About the incidents of the massacre, it seems overwhelmingly accurate. The director necessarily condenses and unifies his narrative, however, while privileging the stories of certain characters and leaving many of the victims' stories untold. In the final press conference scene, Greengrass also creates a more definitive conclusion to his account of the day than what actually occurred. Therefore, once again, the term "dramatic reconstruction" seems appropriate.

The central character of the film, Ivan Cooper, is trapped in his contradictory roles, which allow him to navigate a treacherous landscape and mediate between conflicting groups, but constrain his personal life to the extent that he is an outsider in almost every situation. He is a Protestant leading a group of mostly Catholic civil rights protestors, including Frances, his girlfriend. Early in the film she is angry with him for neglecting her, and he tries to placate her by explaining his difficult position:

> My father was in the UVF [Ulster Volunteer Force], for Christ's sake. You know that.... Your brother was shot by the RUC.... So I don't take you out; we don't go to the pictures. I go to the meetings, I go to the marches, and all the time I'm thinking, "If I can just sort this ... one day, maybe soon, we can be normal, and we won't have to worry."

His motives, therefore, are as much personal as political. As a Member of Parliament, he is opposing his own government's colonial policies, and every time he encounters resistance from British paratroopers he repeats almost mechanically, "My name is Ivan Cooper, I'm a Member of Parliament." He also strictly adheres to peaceful methods of political resistance in a context where violent uprising has been valorized for centuries. He is alone in his world, but his isolated vantage point grants him a kind of ideological distance that is a precious commodity in any highly fraught political context.

Cooper is constantly moving, navigating, defusing situations. In his first moments on screen he says, "Can I get through here?" as he weaves through a crowd of supporters on his way to a press conference. He makes it clear that the march on January 30, 1972, is to protest "mass internment without trial," a special power that the British had claimed in Northern Ireland as of August 9, 1971: to incarcerate Irish people indefinitely without due process of the law.[7] In Northern Ireland the policy of internment was broadened and extended by the subsequent "Prevention of Terrorism Act of 1974" (*Cain Web Service*). To counter Cooper and other civil rights protestors, the British government also outlawed marches in Ulster prior to the demonstration on Bloody Sunday, giving Cooper and his fellow protestors no recourse but to march amidst barricades and occupying troops. Thus, Cooper is forced to run an ideological and physical gauntlet through the course of the film.

The physical limitations the occupied city space places on Cooper reinforce his limited power as a civil rights leader. Early in the film, on his way to the march, he walks on the street, passing out ads for the march, among civilians, police, soldiers and snipers. Cooper continually repeats, "It's a peaceful march we're having." Intercut with his actions are scenes of the paras going over their game plan of "maximum aggression." Directly following the last of these para sequences and images of prospective rioters at a military barricade, one brilliantly compressed shot epitomizes Cooper's position in the city. First we see a wall with "IRA" and "PROVO RULE" emblazoned in graffiti. As a tank rolls by this wall, Cooper appears in the left of the frame, and as the tank recedes off camera, Cooper walks past the paramilitary slogans into the open — with a residential district and half the horizon visible in the distance — to see his fellow organizer, Kevin McCorry, giving directions to their march stewards. Juxtaposing this striking image of physical and ideological confinement with one of the most expansive spaces portrayed in the film creates a sense of pervasive claustrophobia throughout the entire city space.

Even within his protest movement, Cooper faces an intense struggle to maintain unity of purpose. Those marching with Cooper are working-class and middle-class, male and female, Catholic and Protestant (mostly Catholic), young and old. Though they emulate American civil rights protestors led by Martin Luther King, Jr. in singing "We Shall Overcome," their group struggles to maintain the kind of unified vision that King and his supporters evinced. As the confrontation begins between Irish rioters and British soldiers on Bloody Sunday, Cooper speaks to the greater part of the crowd, the peaceful protestors, amid the noise of rioting and the echoes of rubber bullets; he valorizes their struggle and tacitly condemns the hooligan element:

> It's been a difficult day, but a glorious day here together.... Civil rights isn't a soft option. Not when the bricks fly and the police and the army ... charge down. It's not easy keeping to the non-violent road when other people say, "This isn't working. Let's get the guns out and take revenge." But if you believe in the civil rights movement with all your heart and your soul, as I do; if you believe in what Gandhi and Martin Luther King believed in with a passion, as I do; then in the end, with one single united march, we shall overcome.

The ironic disconnect between his words and the events of the day is all too apparent, as the confrontation continues to escalate, leading to rash and vengeful decisions by the British military that ultimately take the lives of fourteen people. Cooper's non-violent rhetoric has been confined to a space among soldiers, bombs, hooligans and barricades, where it becomes increasingly ineffectual.

The reasons Cooper struggles for solidarity among protestors are extraordinarily complex. Cooper himself follows in the footsteps of other prominent Protestant leaders who have advocated for the liberty of Irish Catholics: Wolfe Tone and Henry Joy McCracken died in the 1798 Rising; Isaac Butt founded the Home Rule League; and Charles Stewart Parnell was the man who came nearest to making Home Rule a reality before his life and political career were ruined by scandal. Tone, McCracken and Parnell all ended their lives as great martyrs of the Irish Nationalist cause, and the valorized figure of the martyr in Irish history has everything to do with the intellectual and physical obstacles that Ivan Cooper encounters in *Bloody Sunday*. Ultimately conceding that the fourteen victims of English oppression are likely to be viewed as martyrs,

As he leads a march for Irish Catholic civil rights, Ivan Cooper (James Nesbitt) must contend with threats of Irish paramilitary violence and aggression from British colonizers in *Bloody Sunday* (Paramount, 2002, dir. Paul Greengrass).

Cooper bitterly denounces the English for making his peaceful march into a bloodbath that energizes the IRA and its tactics: "And I just want to say this to the British government: You know what you've just done, don't you? You've destroyed the civil rights movement, and you've given the IRA the biggest victory it will ever have." Such killings serve only to destroy everything that Cooper and his movement represents.

In contemporary Irish culture many artists and intellectuals are actively engaged in the demystification of martyrdom and rebel violence. Roddy Doyle's 1999 novel *A Star Called Henry*, for example, deconstructs the legends surrounding the Easter Rising of 1916 and the subsequent Irish Revolution. The protagonist, orphan Henry Smart, is loyal to James Connolly and the working-class Citizens' Army, and detests Padraig Pearse and the Irish Volunteers. He wants to fight a class war, not struggle against English oppression. When the rag-tag band of freedom fighters—Henry is "one of the few real soldiers there"—finally engages the British Army, Henry aims not for the attacking force, but for the institutions and business establishments of greater Dublin: "I shot and killed all that I had been denied ... all the injustice, unfairness" (119). Henry despises all the institutions that have driven apart and destroyed his family, and he fights only because he has nothing to lose and considers the rebellion as good a way as any to die. He is a far cry from the sanctified, glorified figures of the Rising, immortalized in verse and song.

Henry even sneers at Michael Collins when he first sees him, sizing up his "well-fed puss" and wondering, "When was the last time Collins had been hungry?" (117).

Henry later becomes an assassin for Collins and the IRA, killing more men than he can count. As he matures—at the end of the book he's still only 20—he realizes that he has been used as a pawn in a game that really never concerned a poor "trouble-maker" like him: "I was a slave, the greatest fuckin' eejit ever born.... The dead men weren't coming back. But I'd kill no more" (355). Henry doesn't mourn the death of his friend Michael Collins, and he ultimately has no interest in the continued struggle for a unified Ireland. As he says, "Fuck Ulster" (368). Finally, he feels that the revolution has been a movement to benefit high- and middlebrow types like de Valera and his cronies, and he sees no change on the horizon for working-class people like himself. The novel also suggests that the IRA provoked and benefited from English atrocities against civilians; as Henry declares, "They [the English colonial forces] were our greatest ally." Doyle's work, along with Sebastian Barry's novel *The Whereabouts of Eneas McNulty* (1998), which chronicles the post–Irish Independence exile of a Sligo-born member of the Royal Irish Constabulary, represents a welcome antidote to Neil Jordan's beautiful but simplistic and jingoistic biopic *Michael Collins* (1996), a film that keeps alive the tradition of mythic Irish martyrdom.

In the same vein as Jordan's film, several of the urban Northern Irish murals collected in Bill Rolston's book *Drawing Support* (1992) connect twentieth-century Irish rebel martyrs to the legend of Cuchulain. Cuchulain is mythologized as a kind of Irish Achilles, the "Hound of Ulster" who lives a brief but glorious life and dies defending his country; he is less known for having unwittingly killed his only son, Connla, an act of filicide that marks him as a hero whose commitment to violence destroys the future. One mural from 1984 Belfast depicts "mythological hero Cuchulain dying upright with shield and sword"; and next to it is a plaque with the names of IRA dead from the community (39). Like Cuchulain, many of these men have killed (and been killed by) their own—their countrymen—and thus their martyrdom is often a peculiarly self-immolating one.[8] Bobby Sands and the Long Kesh Hunger Strikers of 1981, referenced in Sheridan's *The Boxer*, are a perfect case in point: they are martyrs who killed themselves. Their leader, Bobby Sands, refused to end his strike, even after he was elected to Parliament; his eventual death by peaceful protest sparked riots and murders, resulting in the deaths of many civilian men, women and children. In a sense, then, *Bloody Sunday* both reflects and further anticipates this cycle of martyrdom and violence.

Colonial oppression frequently gives rise to an overprivileging of martyrdom. People feeling trapped and powerless have little to lose but their lives, which some give freely. The Cameroonian scholar Achille Mbembe describes this colonial situation as one wherein "resistance and self-destruction are synonymous" (36). If one people deprives another of land, wealth and opportunities, they engender a culture of hatred and desperation; and, as Ivan Cooper puts it at the end of *Bloody Sunday*, "They ... reap a whirlwind."

Greengrass's film takes pains to depict the callous indifference of the British high military command, as well as the genuine concern and subsequent remorse of others. Tim Pigott-Smith's gung-ho Major General Ford ultimately declares, "I've seen nothing today that reflects in any way with discredit on our forces, who have behaved, as ever, with restraint, and I believe, with great professionalism."[9] Brigadier MacLellan, however, the general ostensibly in command of the Derry forces, is portrayed by Nicholas Farrell as a man forced to follow orders against his own conscience and better judgment. He repeatedly mediates his orders to the paratroopers by telling them to act "with discretion" in subduing the crowd. Chief Superintendent Lagan (Gerard McSorley), the police (RUC) chief who tries all day to avert the conflict by advising both Ivan Cooper and the British high command, finally upbraids MacLellan, noting the tragic disparity between the general's benign intentions and his utter failure to put them into action: "You call that minimum force?"

Among British soldiers at the locus of the massacre, Private Lomas (Mike Edwards), the 1 Para radio operator, is the embodiment of remorse for the day's events. Greengrass portrays Lomas as a decent man who is part of a violent mechanism designed to escalate conflict. He first appears onscreen entering Derry in a troop transport. Using a partially occluded point of view shot, Greengrass conveys the discomfiting nature of the soldier's duty, as Lomas looks outside the truck and views the graffiti message "BRITS OUT" writ large on a building. Edwards' almost child-like face and demeanor emphasize Lomas' role as a figure of conscience within an apparatus of brutality, and his constant expression is one of abiding anxiety — in sharp contrast to the confident postures and declarations of his fellow paras: "Let's teach them a fucking lesson. Let's do the business.... I want to show the brigade what One Para are made of." Later, once the paras open fire and the atrocities begin, Lomas objects to the killing, yelling, "There's nothing there.... There's no targets!" When he finally receives the "Cease Fire" order over the radio, he strives desperately to restrain the other paras, but they continue their slaughter of fleeing civilians. After the massacre is over, Lomas confronts his comrades as they rationalize their actions: "What the fuck did you do? I saw it. I saw you shoot civvies."

Lomas's lone voice of conscientious dissent, however, is lost amid the institutional push to justify the indiscriminate killings, and he last appears in the film reluctantly concocting a phony account of the paras' actions for superior officers in a debriefing. Lomas is essentially a dramatization of "Soldier 027," as he is referred to in *The Bloody Sunday Inquiry*.[10] In his testimony

5. Masculinity and Trauma in Greengrass's Films

In *Bloody Sunday* (Paramount, 2002, dir. Paul Greengrass), Private Lomas (Mike Edwards, right) doubts his mission and regrets the killing of civilians, but as a British paratrooper his moral agency is severely circumscribed.

thirty years after Bloody Sunday, this soldier of the 1 Para unit expresses regret for the atrocities:

> [D]uring that period of gunfire ... a number of fairly unfortunate, to say the least, decisions were made by individuals on the ground which led to some shameful and disgraceful acts being perpetrated.... I think that an acknowledgment [of] what happened ... is ... long overdue.... I think the shootings which I witnessed were unjustified [*Bloody Sunday Inquiry*, 027–97].

The tenor of his comments expresses his ambivalence as a loyal soldier who knows he was involved in horrendous and unconscionable actions. As represented by Lomas, he is yet another man caught amidst a perilous landscape where rash actions, misdirected vengeance and insidious deceptions rule the day.

The film also details the impulsive resentment of a contingent of young men among the protestors— the "hooligan element." They are part of a larger group of marchers that takes a wrong turn after the route is changed to avoid the military barricade erected to block access to the Guildhall, the seat of power in Derry. Greengrass puts a human face on the hooligans by investing a considerable amount of his narrative in the story of Gerry Donaghy, a conflicted young man with a Protestant girlfriend who associates with friends prone to rioting.[11]

Though they never meet in the film, Gerry seems to represent the type of youth that Ivan Cooper is trying to reach: one whose future hangs in the balance between aimless rebellion and concerted resistance. Despite Cooper's diligent effort to ensure that everyone involved follows the right path, many protestors, including Gerry and many other hooligans, join the march late and abide by the initial plan to proceed to the Guildhall. Thus, when the latecomers go astray, they run up against a barricade manned by British paratroopers. This group of protestors is penned in by those behind them, and the close confrontation with the soldiers, exacerbated by the young men's stone-throwing, soon escalates into lethal violence. Though Cooper rushes to the front of the breakaway group and exhorts them to turn back, all the pent up tension between occupier and oppressed comes to a head in this compressed space, as the young men bombard the soldiers with rocks until, upon the pretext of having seen a gun among the crowd, the paratroopers open fire, gunning down Gerry and thirteen others. Thus, *Bloody Sunday* represents many points of view on the day's events, depicting very different men — Cooper, MacLellan, Lagan, Lomas, Gerry — as well-intentioned people constrained by ideology and association to the point of direct or indirect complicity in the massacre.

Cooper's attempts to keep the peace ultimately have little effect, yet the heroic idealism he represents ratchets up an emotional and moral tension that would otherwise be absent in a film where the outcome is never in doubt. In addition to rerouting the march away from the Guildhall to avoid a confrontation, earlier in the day Cooper approaches, one after the other, British soldiers at an army barricade, young men primed for a riot, and provisional IRA men, exhorting them all to minimize conflict, declaring, "This is our day." The local provo leader dismisses Cooper's efforts: "It's all very well for you, Ivan. You're sitting pretty with your wee Westminster paycheck. Marching's not going to solve this." Yet Cooper responds with determination: "Watch us." The film gives an accurate and compelling portrayal of Cooper in this regard. According to his own testimony in the *Bloody Sunday Inquiry*, leading up to that fateful day, Cooper had sought and received assurances from the local IRA that they would not interfere with the march (KC 12–13).[12] The extent to which they kept their promise to Cooper, however, has been a subject of intense controversy.

In *Bloody Sunday*, Greengrass portrays the IRA as agitators attempting to exploit the confrontation with the British in Derry and escalate the violence. They pose a threat to Cooper and his fellow protestors as well as to the British. In two instances, IRA men appear with guns and turn them toward the paratroopers, but both times civilians collectively restrain them. Therefore, though they simultaneously loom as a threat to Cooper's movement and serve as a justification for British intervention (the military brass wants to make a few token arrests of suspected militant leaders), the IRA in Derry remain marginal figures in the massacre. As Greengrass emphasizes, however, by the end of the day's events the Republican extremists stand to benefit most from the atrocities, as the penultimate scene of the film shows a group of young men, including a friend of Gerry's, lining up in a dark hallway to join the IRA.

Thus, Ivan Cooper fights a losing battle, not only as a politician but as a pacifist attempting to advance alternative models of conflict resolution and manhood. Once the shooting begins, Cooper struggles among the crowd to reach the locus of conflict, and by the time he does the fourteen victims of Bloody Sunday are already dead or dying. Two middle-aged men and seven teenagers are among the dead, while two women are among the wounded. In its depiction of the military brass, the film suggests that the British high command, specifically Major General Ford, intended to send a grisly message; from the perspective of the paratroopers actually doing the shooting, it seems they wished to take satisfaction on a people they had feared and resented in a place where they themselves were feared and hated. Early in the film one embittered soldier equates all protestors with hostile rioters: "I'm sick of being shot at, spat on, all the other shit that goes with this place. It's about time we go out there and show these fuckers." Ultimately, too many physical and ideological forces align themselves against Cooper and the civil rights marchers in Derry. His failure to navigate this volatile terrain is starkly symbolized by the indelible image of his group's banner, emblazoned with "Derry Civil Rights Association," placed over the bloody head and body of one of the massacre's victims, Bernard McGuigan.

On its release, *Bloody Sunday* was analogized to *The Battle of Algiers* (Gillo Pontecorvo, 1966) for its similar use of documentary realism to portray resistance against colonial oppression. The two films are technically and thematically alike. Both have casts that include many non-actors, and both meticulously recreate historical events using a neo-realist style (one of the most memorable scenes in *The Battle of Algiers* is the staged but stunningly realistic dramatization of the Algerians' final and successful uprising against French authority in 1961). Both films depict soldiers and military operations on one side, and the activities of a resistance movement on the other, demonstrating that a colonial administration, even the most efficient and ruthless, cannot prevail over people who are systematically dehumanized to the point of desperation.

During a press conference scene in *The Battle of Algiers* the French military commander, Colonel Mathieu (Jean Martin), succinctly sums up the problem of colonial occupation: "[They want] to throw us out of Algeria, and we want to stay." Like the British, the French colonizers maintained a willful ignorance of their inability to win "the hearts and minds of the people" by depriving them of land and rights. Pontecorvo's film emphasizes the consequences of colonial occupation by cutting directly from Mathieu's speech to a harrowing sequence of the French military torturing suspected Algerian insurgents.[13] Yet Greengrass's film ultimately valorizes Ivan Cooper's non-violent form of political action, while Pontecorvo's work persuades viewers to side with the colonized in a conflict in which both sides deliberately go beyond military/guerrilla conflict to commit atrocities against civilian populations. Greengrass's achievement is harder and greater: he sets his hero's pro-human rights ethos above any political loyalty.

Bloody Sunday concludes with Cooper's largely condensed and fictionalized speech that serves as a lucid assessment of the day in cross-cultural colonial terms; this is certainly a "sincere and justified" departure from the factual record, especially considering Cooper's actual subsequent comments regarding Bloody Sunday's inspiration of increased IRA membership and activity.[14] At a press conference a few hours after the massacre, the film's Cooper makes the following statement:

> They were innocent. We were there. This is our Sharpeville; this is our Amritsar massacre. A moment of truth, and a moment of shame. And I just want to say this to the British government: you know what you've just done, don't you? You've destroyed the civil rights movement, and you've given the IRA the biggest victory it will ever have. All over this city tonight, young men, boys, will be joining the IRA. And you will reap a whirlwind.

These words would prove only too prophetic.[15] Both the Sharpeville (March 21, 1960) and Amritsar (April 13, 1919) massacres were crucial turning points in the respective struggles of South African blacks and Indian natives against colonial oppression. For Ivan Cooper, this parallelism is not only an attempt to make sense of trauma and locate it historically, it is a profound admission of the failure of his peaceful movement in the face of violent oppression. He can read the writing on the wall, and when a reporter asks him what he would say to young men thinking of signing on with the IRA, he replies, "I feel very ill-equipped to do any preaching to them after today." He is deeply saddened as well as outraged, knowing that this day will only perpetuate and increase violence and political and sectarian divisions, exactly what he sought to avoid. At the same time, Cooper's fictionalized speech in the film, punctuated by Bernadette Devlin's vow, "We will not rest until justice is done," lends the film a sense of emotional and narrative finality. In this instance, as writer and director, Paul Greengrass intrudes on the factual record in order to make sense of the day's tragedy and atrocity in a way that a conventional documentary on the subject could not. This scene also completes Cooper's tragic character arc as a visionary man who strives and fails to put his pacifist ideas into practice.

Another important cinematic precedent for *Bloody Sunday* is John Sayles's *Matewan* (1987), which also addresses traumatic historical events from the point of view of a visionary pacifist. This historical drama substantially follows the events leading up to the Matewan massacre, which occurred on May 19, 1920, in the eponymous West Virginia town. Like Ivan Cooper, Sayles' protagonist, Joe Kenehan (Chris Cooper), acts as a strong, peaceful figure struggling to create solidarity and solidify a non-violent front of resistance among a diverse group of oppressed miners. Kenehan is a union organizer who tries to unite assimilated ethnic Americans,[16] African Americans and Italian immigrants into "one big union" (the slogan of the International Workers of the World). Like *Bloody Sunday*, *Matewan* privileges cross-cultural constructions of masculinity and resistance. Ivan Cooper's pacifist role models are Gandhi and Martin Luther King; Joe Kenehan, as an imprisoned conscientious objector during World War I, had learned from a group of Menonites the meaning of uncompromising pacifism. During a pivotal scene Kenehan recounts to one of the embattled miners, "Few Clothes" Johnson (James Earl Jones), how these devout men, fellow inmates in the Leavenworth Federal Prison, went on strike after the prison guards violated their religious principles:

> So they refused to work. And they went on a strike right there in Hell's half-acre. They was hand-cuffed to the bars of a cell house eight hours a day for two full weeks.... Eight hours a day, day after day. But still they wouldn't work. Still they tore the buttons off their uniforms every time they were sewed back on. They tore 'em with their teeth because their hands wouldn't close no more. So, now, I don't claim a thing for myself. But them fellas, they never lifted a gun in their lives, and you couldn't find any braver in my book.

Much like Cooper in *Bloody Sunday*, however, Kenehan provides a model of resistance that ultimately becomes impracticable when a longstanding conflict (workers against corporations) once again erupts into violence. In Sayles' film, Kenehan himself becomes an innocent victim caught in the crossfire, and his spiritual son, Danny (Will Oldham), is left to carry on his work.[17] Yet *Matewan*, like *Bloody Sunday*, depicts the power of a peaceful man inspired by examples of masculine pacifism across religious and cultural boundaries, and exhibiting compelling courage in the face of violent dissolution.

Ultimately, both *Bloody Sunday* and *Matewan*, while allowing viewers to experience historical trauma, also engage in the process of demystification and healing. Cooper does not condone the methods of the IRA at the film's close, just as violence serves only to exacerbate the problems of the West Virginia miners. In Greengrass's film, Cooper is finally forced to concede out of sorrow and frustration that, considering what has just happened, his non-violent form of resistance has lost all credibility, and violence now seems like the only practical means of fighting oppression. As Cooper attests in a 2002 interview with *BBC News*:

> It's difficult for people [today] to appreciate the ethos of the non-violence movement at the time.... Before Bloody Sunday, I believe there were no more than 30

to 40 IRA volunteers in Derry.... The support was with John Hume and Ivan Cooper.... The IRA's campaign of violence that followed in the wake of Bloody Sunday ... changed all that.

Despite the subsequent ideological shift toward violent resistance in Irish Republican politics and the breakdown of Cooper's movement, the film successfully preserves the revolutionary possibility that he embodies as a leader and as a man.

Greengrass underscores his film's agenda by playing U2's "Sunday Bloody Sunday" over the closing credits. Singer and lyricist Bono has often introduced this searing meditation on the Troubles with the words, "This is not a rebel song." While remembering the massacre, the song challenges its audience to break the cycle of violence in Northern Ireland and recognize the urgent need for reconciliation.

Likewise, the film recalls trauma in order to move beyond it, and in focusing on the story of Ivan Cooper in the midst of the massacre, rather than on each of the individual victims, the film portrays the tragedy of a man valiantly moving through volatile terrain, charting a path toward peace that he never attains. Such an intimate focus and characterization would be difficult to achieve in the context of a conventional documentary reconstruction. Ivan Cooper himself speaks of the film's dual artistic role:

> I've seen the film six times now.... And my first thoughts were that it was an emotional experience. I'm able to say with confidence that it was made with great integrity.... But I also think that the film has been very helpful — it's going to help make it possible to put Bloody Sunday behind us much faster than otherwise [*BBC News*].

Thus, the film's blurring of genre distinctions enables it to construct a harrowing re-enactment of the day's events as an important and suppressed chapter in Irish history, while also offering a compelling character study of a man struggling to make a powerful peaceful statement in a community beset by violence and division. As Greengrass attests:

> The reason why I made *Bloody Sunday* in the way that I did is because guys like Ivan Cooper had seen the truth that it's taken the rest another 20 or 30 years to understand.... If you're going to resolve conflicts, you cannot resolve them on the basis of conflicting nationalisms, you can only resolve them on the basis of developing shared rights [*Variety*].

In *Bloody Sunday*, the movement of the protagonist in physical space constitutes a form of resistance. As Michel de Certeau writes, "Walking affirms, suspects, tries out, transgresses, respects, etc., the trajectories it 'speaks'" (99).[18] Ivan Cooper believes that a peaceful demonstration delivers a stronger message than riots and reprisals, and his actions as an organizer promote an ethos that extends outside the seat of government to his embattled community and nation. In an urban landscape that challenges his non-violent masculinity at every turn, his success is constantly limited, yet his resolve remains unbending. Thus, the film is a testament not only to great atrocity but to great heroism as well. As a brave leader striving for unity amidst fear, hatred and violence, Ivan Cooper is an extraordinarily subversive and revolutionary peacemaker.

Facing Atrocity and Its Victims: *Omagh*'s Demystification of Political Violence

In essential respects *Omagh* serves as a "bookend" to *Bloody Sunday* (Greengrass, *Omagh* Press Pack 6). It does so in terms of plotting the trajectory of the Troubles from 1972 to 1998 and beyond, but also in dramatizing one family's emotional devastation in the aftermath of atrocity. Whereas *Bloody Sunday* is principally concerned with the actions that precipitated the massacre of January 30, 1972,[19] *Omagh* begins by dramatizing the horrific events of August 15, 1998, in the town of Omagh, County Tyrone, Northern Ireland, before turning its attention to the family members of the victims. The film's particular focus is on the Gallagher family, and the bulk of its narrative portrays their mourning process and quest for justice. At minute 17 (of its 99-minute running time) the film depicts the single most deadly act of the Troubles: the explosion of the Real IRA car bomb in Omagh that killed 29 people, all civilians, twelve of them eighteen years of age or younger (*CAIN Web Service*, "The Omagh Bomb—List of Those Killed").[20] The remaining 80-plus minutes of the film show the aftermath of this devastation, depicting how the people of Omagh have dealt with the loss of loved ones.

Speaking of the film as representing a new kind of genre, that of the "Monumentary," Brian McIlroy explains:

> If we accept that genre films pose specific common questions in society, and hence their reproducability, then what kind of question does the Monumentary ask? Whereas the Western asks how is it lawful to kill a man, and whereas the Musical asks how is it possible for individual artists to work together as an ensemble, the Monumentary asks how do the suddenly bereaved grieve and move on from that grief? ["Memory Work..." 266].

This is a vitally important question that cinema can pose powerfully but rarely does, as Hollywood genre films and their foreign imitators normally function to suppress such concerns in favor of focusing on the actions and, to a lesser extent, the motivations of violent men. In order to assuage social anxieties, movies tend to encourage audience identification with the enactors of violence, as opposed to those affected by it.[21] As a dramatic reconstruction of a horrendously traumatic event, *Omagh* fundamentally breaks with this pattern.

The film begins by intercutting scenes of the Real IRA bombers' clandestine activities with images of the Gallagher family and other citizens of Omagh, including shop workers and tourists, going about their Saturday business. In a film that tends to maintain a striking intimacy with whatever characters are onscreen at any given moment (through the routine use of extreme close-ups), the figures that remain most remote from viewers are the bombers. As they concoct their fertilizer-based weapon, the camera peers in at them from behind various screens and obstacles, thus creating an occluded view of the extremists. When their faces are shown, they're in profile, shadowed, or at a distance; no traditional close-ups are used in portraying the bombers. These men have no conversation beyond talking about their violent endeavor. These stylistic choices undoubtedly reflect a desire on the part of the filmmakers to prevent viewer investment in the people responsible for the deaths at Omagh, as well as the reality that the true identities of the bombers are still not known, and no one has yet been brought to justice in a criminal court for the atrocity itself.[22]

The scenes leading up to the bombing build tension by alternately showing the RIRA men moving closer to their destination (shots of road signs—"Omagh 5"—indicate their progress) and providing expository images of those who will become their victims: Aiden Gallagher goes into town to buy some jeans; Anne McCombe opens up her boutique; tourists arrive on a charter bus. In this way the film elicits horror of the violence that is to come. Just as the 74 minutes leading up to the massacre in *Bloody Sunday* have the potential effect of moving viewers to dread the inevitable bloodshed, the first 17 minutes of *Omagh* seem agonizingly interminable. Once the bombers enter the town, park the red car carrying their deadly payload, and leave the area, there is a series of shots of people unwittingly milling about the bomb. This dramatic irony engenders a sense of despondency and powerlessness. As viewers, we are closely observing people who are about to be suddenly, brutally killed. Again, this move to encourage viewer identification with victims is in stark contrast to the formulaic violence of most Hollywood genre pictures, in which collateral damage—when any is shown—is persistently marginalized onscreen.

Crucially, when the atrocity finally occurs, the film is unrelenting in portraying the experience of the victims. The moment before Omagh is torn apart, 21-year-old Aiden Gallagher (Paul Kelly) stands with a friend chatting and laughing only a few yards away from the red car. When the bomb explodes, the film's vantage point remains on the street, right in the middle of the blast. Debris comes flying at the camera, and then a cloud of gray dust pervades the entire frame. For a few seconds an eerie silence descends, but when the smoke and haze clears, chaos ensues: a barrage of images shows the wounded, maimed, and dying; blood, gore and trauma are everywhere. There are screams of pain, sirens wailing, and cries for help. These sounds and images contribute to a profound demystification of political violence and establish the tone of the remainder of the film as a somber search for answers rather than a quest for vengeance. Indeed, the film seems to ask, what revenge could possibly be commensurate with such carnage and suffering?

From this point the narrative quickly shifts from functioning as a large-scale drama with multiple plot threads to recounting the story of one man, Michael Gallagher (Gerard McSorley), who, along with his wife and two daughters, must completely reconfigure his life and family as a result of the atrocity. Having lost his son Aiden in the bombing, Michael gradually emerges from isolation and takes on the role of spokesman for the Omagh Support and Self-Help Group. This leadership role is thrust upon him when, during their first meeting, Michael proves capable of mediating the tensions between the ideologically diverse group members. When the meeting escalates into a series of acrimonious accusations and allegations regarding which nation or political entity is most to blame for the bombing, Michael steps forward to calm everyone down. Having become the center of attention, Michael hesitates, telling his friend Stanley McCombe (Ian McElhinney), "I'm not very good at public speaking." After Stanley encourages him to continue, Michael explains the need for cooperation among the group:

> There's Catholics in this room, and Protestants, and Presbyterians, and Mormons.... And ... some of us believe in God, and now maybe some of us have no God. But I can tell you this: we're not going to get anywhere unless we do it together, that's the truth of the matter.

Although Michael is himself a Catholic (apparently non-practicing), his best friend among the group members is Stanley, a Protestant. The two other group members featured most prominently in the film are Laurence Rush (Alan Devlin), an Irish Catholic whose confrontational nature is a stark contrast to Michael's placid demeanor, and Victor Barker (Stuart Graham), an English transplant who is most likely a Protestant. Following his brief, unifying speech, Michael is elected chairman of the group. Thus, his ability to achieve consensus— the antithesis of an alpha-male style of leadership — along with his soft-spoken, respectful manner, makes him the ideal person to head up the families' campaign for justice. Additionally, as is the case with Ivan Cooper in *Bloody Sunday* and Danny Flynn in *The Boxer*, Michael's nonsectarianism is vital to his success as a leader and indicative of a radically progressive political and masculine practice.

Reflecting this spirit of cooperation, the film itself was made in consultation with the actual Omagh Support and Self-Help Group. The Anglo-Irish team of Paul Greengrass and Don Mullan (co-producer of *Bloody Sunday* and author of the book *Eyewitness Bloody Sunday*) began by contacting the group to request their permission and support for a film on the bombing and its aftermath. As the project developed, the filmmakers sought the input of the victims' family members on the script and received their approval before shooting began. Once filming wrapped, the families were the first to see the finished product at a screening (*Omagh* Press Pack 6–8). According to the filmmakers, "Without the consent of the Support Group and the individual families depicted in this film, this project could never have been made" (Press Pack 6). Additionally, the real Michael Gallagher advised Gerard McSorley, the actor portraying him in the film. McSorley, himself an Omagh native, has proved amazingly versatile in his many roles in Troubles films, which range from sinister (in *In the Name of the Father* and *The Boxer*) to sympathetic (in *Some Mother's Son* and *Bloody Sunday*, as well as *Omagh*). As Gallagher, McSorley invests his character's every action and expression with quiet sorrow, moving between determination, frustration, and resignation.

As a bereaved parent, activist, husband and father to his daughters, Michael faces four distinct challenges over the course of the film:

1. He seeks justice for his son and the other victims.
2. He holds together the Support Group as best he can by smoothing over personal and ideological conflicts, especially those flaps caused by the contentious Laurence Rush.
3. He tries to provide emotional support to his wife and daughters in the wake of tragedy.
4. He goes through his own process of mourning.

None of these challenges can be met effectively with macho posturing or coercion; patience, persistence and sensitivity are Michael's best assets. Frequently, however, his work toward the first two goals detracts from his ability to care for his family, particularly after his wife, Patsy (Michèle Forbes), leaves the Support Group, citing her need to mourn out of the public eye.

As Michael is consumed with phone calls and interviews for newspapers and television, Patsy's frustration at their lack of privacy grows, and she finally tells Michael, "I can't do this anymore." When he replies, "But we have to know what happened," she declares, "I know what happened.... Someone killed Aiden, that's what happened. And I don't care about why, or what or how—any of it. All I want to know is that he's at peace. That's it, that's all." Although Michael voices his intention to continue the campaign, the film gives weight to Patsy's divergent way of grieving; as Michael leaves the room to take another phone call, the narrative stays with Patsy standing still, staring out the window, starkly lit against a bright white curtain. While this statement represents her progression through an important stage of mourning, indicating her acceptance of their loss, it also serves to drive a wedge between Patsy and Michael.

Furthermore, as the group's campaign for justice intensifies and Michael is less and less emotionally and physically present at home, his daughter, Cathy (Fiona Glascott), begins to question his priorities. Having been away at college, Cathy returns home during a break to find her mother in a depressive state, and she upbraids her father for his negligence. Michael tries to placate her, stating, "Look, we're doing OK. Your mommy likes to be on her own, doesn't she?" Cathy rejects this assessment, countering: "It's not true! She's too sad to get up." Throughout this scene there are cuts to Patsy's reactions as she listens from the stairs above the kitchen. In her anger, Cathy proceeds to belittle Michael's campaign:

> You're always at a meeting. Every time I've rung you're at a meeting, or on *TV*.... What's the use of all this running around? I mean, do you really think they care about what you're doing? Do you think they're going to stop the shooting and the bombing just because you gave an interview to the *Belfast Telegraph* or the BBC?

Cathy finally starts crying as she tells her father, "Aiden's dead! ... You should be here, Daddy, looking after us!" At this point Michael appears somber and chastened; he makes no response to his daughter's charge. Such clashing of domestic and public roles and priorities has been a common theme of films with female protagonists, but it is rare to see it treated in such depth with a male figure at the center of the narrative. These moments of family conflict seem strikingly true-to-life: they are not well-defined communicative breakthroughs yielding epiphanies or catharsis, but everyday flare-ups in which feelings are expressed but little resolution is achieved.

Michael seems to internalize the very doubts about his progress that Cathy expresses so forcefully. Later, following a particularly fruitless and divisive encounter of the Support Group with an RUC official, he offers his own brutal assessment of their endeavors, telling Stanley and Victor Barker:

> It's not working, is it — none of it.... I mean, the whole campaign. What have we achieved? ... What have we actually achieved? ... They're still shooting and bombing. They're still walking around the place, drinking in bars, having a good life, laughing at us. I mean, there've been over 2000 unsolved murders since the beginning of the Troubles. Why should we be any different?

Following this statement of resignation, Michael temporarily abandons his work on behalf of the Support Group. During this period he is finally able to focus on his own stunted progress through the stages of mourning. Crucially, he expresses his grief to Patsy for the first time, explaining the jealousy, resentment and guilt that exacerbate his sense of loss: "Inside, I feel he meant more to me, and I know that's awful—to feel like that. Because I know how much you loved him. But I can't feel the way you feel, only the way I feel." Patsy remains silent as he speaks these words; she listens, looking deeply relieved, and seems to accept what Michael says without judgment. This scene represents only a small, though meaningful, step on the family's long and tortuous path to healing.

As in its portrayal of the bombing and the Omagh community's grief, the film is extraordinarily accurate and sophisticated in terms of depicting politics. In particular, it reveals two fundamental aspects of the Northern Irish situation, both of which are significant in terms of gender and genre. First, it takes account of many of the sects, factions, and breakaway organizations involved in the Troubles that have contributed to the immensely complex, gradually shifting stalemate of the Peace Process. As reflected in *Omagh*, each of these distinct groups compromises and shares information with great reluctance, when they do so at all.

Michael's meeting with the president of the Sinn Fein Party, Gerry Adams, provides the best illustration of this point. To the film's credit, Adams is portrayed not as a menacing villain, but as no better and no worse than a normal politician who is limited to fulfilling the demands of his constituency. When Michael refuses to shake Adams' extended hand,[23] the former IRA leader takes this gesture of disrespect in stride. Adams proceeds to express his sympathies, while explaining to Michael why Sinn Fein and the Provisional IRA refuse to participate in the official investigation of the Omagh bombing: "[A]ssisting the RUC is only going to alienate hard-liners in our community, the very people we have got to keep on board if we're to keep this thing moving forward. This is the reality we face. We cannot jeopardize the Peace Process."

Stylistically, the scene has the feel of a western showdown, as it employs tight close-ups on the eyes of Michael and Adams, thus ratcheting up the tension. Although some confrontation or mini-climax seems imminent, nothing of the sort ensues. The scene ends abruptly without any sense of what consequences will follow this meeting. In fact, the status quo will be maintained: Sinn Fein and the Provisional IRA will continue to be uncooperative in the official Omagh investigation, and there is little Michael can do about it. He can no more bend Gerry Adams to his will than he can push the police force to do their job and find the killers.

The second aspect of this political situation that *Omagh* captures, and the most important one in terms of the film's avowed aims, is the human cost of political negotiations and compromise — specifically, that of the Northern Irish Peace Process. This kind of commentary is an important extension of the discourse begun in earlier Troubles films like Sheridan's *In the Name of the Father* and *The Boxer*. As Michael tells a TV reporter during a protest, "Everybody wants us to walk away ... go quietly, so that they can get on with their Peace Process." The families of those killed in the Omagh bombing have their grief compounded by indignity, as their desire for justice is repeatedly met with bureaucratic indifference, despite the British government's pledge, in the words of Tony Blair, to "do everything in our power ... to hunt down those responsible for this outrage."

Almost every law enforcement and government official Michael and his fellow campaigners encounter gives them the same scripted condolences and condescension. The most egregious example is Chief Constable Ronnie Flanagan of the RUC, who tells them, "I understand the frustration that you all feel — that we all feel," before placating them with the emptiest of assurances: "You have to trust us. Otherwise, what else is there?" In this way the film actually justifies Gerry Adams and Sinn Fein's enduring mistrust of the RUC, even as it portrays the former as no more helpful, though somewhat more sympathetic and courteous, than the latter. Overall, the film seems to lend credence to the suspicion shared by many commentators and critics— Brian McIlroy among them — that the UK authorities "made a deal" with the Real IRA, secretly promising that none of their members would be prosecuted in exchange for the outlying paramilitary group's commitment to the Peace Process ("Memory Work..." 265).

Thus, any progress that Michael and his group make is always partial and incomplete; their successes are more than mitigated by their failures. In this way the film subverts the generic pattern of "rites of order," in which a macho social savior employs further violence to quell violent threats to a community (Schatz 34). *Omagh* is really about the way a community *re*orders itself in the wake of trauma through affirmative, nonviolent means, even as their prospect of achieving success through their campaign remains unlikely. As the films closes, there is no sense that regular people can "take on city hall" and win, as no definitive end to this quest for justice is on the horizon. By the same token, the Omagh families' grieving will not cease. The narrative pays tribute to their losses and their constructive response to trauma by focusing on the struggle of one man, Michael, who summons the courage to seek healing, as well as justice and peace, while resisting the allure of bitterness and vengeance. Together with his group members, he manages to use the tragedy of the bombing as an occasion to broaden and deepen the bonds of community, endowing them with the collective strength and resources to take action in lieu of their ineffective government and police. The group finally remains determined to pursue a civil case against the bombers, which in reality they would win — in a "landmark multi-million pound" decision — in June 2009, five years after the release of the film in Ireland and the UK (*Belfast Telegraph*, "Omagh Bomb Families Win...").

Omagh ends by looking beyond the Northern Irish context, accurately representing the Omagh Support and Self-Help Group as an organization that maintains visionary goals of justice, peace and human rights for all those affected by atrocity, regardless of nationality or religion. After hearing RUC ombudsman Nuala O'Loan (Brenda Fricker) issue a revelatory report

In *Omagh* (RTÉ [Raidió Teilifís Éireann]/Sundance, 2004, dir. Pete Travis, co-written and produced by Paul Greengrass), following the ombudsman's damning report, Michael Gallagher (Gerard McSorley, center) gives his statement to the press, as his daughters (Pauline Hutton and Fiona Glascott, back left), wife (Michèle Forbes, center) and friend Stanley (Ian McElhinney, back right) look on.

acknowledging the egregious failures and oversights in the official investigation of the bombing, Michael walks outside with Patsy, their daughters, and other members of the Support Group, who urge him to issue a statement to the assembled press on behalf of the Omagh families. In a finale that is a subdued echo of Gerry Conlon's vow to pursue justice at the end of *In the Name of the Father*, Michael declares that the ombudsman's report, "however distressing, however shocking," will allow them to "move forward." He announces their intention to pursue a civil action against the Real IRA and to "call into account the security forces and the police and the politicians in London, Belfast and Dublin who have promised us so much but have so far singularly failed to deliver." In closing, Michael expresses solidarity with all those victimized and traumatized by political violence, irrespective of ideology: "We speak not just for ourselves; we speak for the victims of the Troubles of whatever tradition, and all those victims of terror wherever it happens. We will not go away. We will not be quiet. We will not be forgotten."

Like Ivan Cooper in *Bloody Sunday*, Michael evinces a progressive masculine ethos based in collaboration, reconciliation, and a determination to achieve peace and justice. Modeled after real men, these two figures are the political consciences of Paul Greengrass's dramatic reconstructions of Irish historical trauma. Rather than compelling us to pick sides in past and present ideological battles, these films move us to think about history and political struggle in new and empowering ways, offering us a vision of a more peaceful, egalitarian future. As Greengrass puts it:

> I always felt that Northern Ireland, far from being this defigured, violent abscess on the body politic, was in fact the most interesting dynamic melting pot in which much of today's, indeed tomorrow's politics, first took shape. The solutions to the problems in Northern Ireland have given inspiration to solving conflicts in many parts of the world because they mirror most modern conflicts: namely two tribes, two traditions, two nationalisms wanting to occupy the same piece of land [*Variety*].

Thus, while his films depict terrible atrocities and their devastating consequences, Greengrass is equally concerned with showing the hopeful possibilities that can emerge from these traumas. His work helps establish new models of male leadership and conflict resolution in Irish cinema and culture.

Conclusion[1]

In closing, I would like to consider two key questions about the future of Irish cinema and take note of two emerging *auteurs* of Irish-themed films. I will also say some final words about John Wayne and consider the implications of an Irish rock singer's peacemaker ethos. In the process, I will underscore affirmative conjunctions of gender, art, and politics.

My first question is this: with their representations of alternative gender identities, how much of an impact can experimental, niche market films like *Bloody Sunday* and *Omagh* make on mainstream culture? I am not so naïve as to think such works will ever achieve blockbuster status. One can hope, though, that the critical and (modest) financial success of these two releases can help create momentum for a steady stream of films using alternative narrative structures and stylistic techniques in the service of portraying progressive heroes and heroines. The visual poetics of the dramatic reconstruction could be used effectively to represent all kinds of marginalized historical events and perspectives. Furthermore, this filmmaking practice carries the distinct advantage of being relatively cheap to employ; *Bloody Sunday* was made for only $4.3 million (£3 million) (Mullan, "Bloody Sunday — the Movie").

A consistent output of dramatic reconstructions could constitute a dynamic sociopolitical counternarrative standing in opposition to hegemonic, imperialist historical accounts, as well as those of violent extremist movements. Judging from Greengrass's work, if there is one guiding ethical and aesthetic imperative of this new genre, it is a determination to resist pat moral judgments and to humanize individuals regardless of their ideological orientations, while casting suspicion on colonial, military, legal, and other bureaucratic systems that grind human lives beneath their wheels as they function to preserve the status quo. Expressing outrage at injustice is something that cinema does exceptionally well — perhaps more effectively than any other medium — yet doing so on film without resorting to villainization and dehumanization is a rare feat. Greengrass has managed to achieve just such a level of nuance in both his Irish films, as Jim Sheridan has done in *The Boxer*.

Second, what reasons do we have for cautious optimism about genre filmmaking in Europe and the U.S.? In the case of Irish cinema, both Jim Sheridan and Paul Greengrass have demonstrated that genre-driven narratives can be exciting, politically engaged works of art. Sheridan's Irish films are brilliant in their manipulation of genre, whereas Greengrass has gone from making experimental works concerning Irish culture and history to crafting exceptionally challenging and commercially successful political thrillers (with *The Bourne Supremacy* and *The Bourne Ultimatum*), thereby becoming "Hollywood's favourite Brit" (*Guardian*). Both Sheridan and Greengrass now appear committed to working within the Hollywood system, with all its attendant perks and constraints, for the near future.

Sheridan's first Hollywood film, *Get Rich or Die Tryin'* (2005), a biopic about (and starring) rap star 50 Cent, flopped critically while only breaking even at the box office. Sheridan fared much better, however, on his next film, *Brothers* (2009), which achieved modest critical and financial success and delivered yet another of his poignant, nuanced portraits of family life rocked by violence and its aftermath. A remake of a renowned film by Danish director Susanne Bier (2004), *Brothers* concerns a contemporary American family in the midst of crisis: the narrative centers on Sam (Tobey Maguire), a Marine officer gone missing in Afghanistan, and his wife (Natalie Portman), two young daughters and brother (Jake Gyllenhaal) at home coping with his apparent death. When Sam returns, he struggles to come to grips with his traumatic war experiences, alienation from his wife and children, and jealousy stemming from his brother's newly close connection to his family. As a document of war, Sheridan's film succeeds where many Hollywood combat movies fail: it effectively dramatizes the emotional toll paid by military families at home, as well as the long-term psychological consequences for the soldiers serving in U.S. wars of occupation.

As for Greengrass, his latest film deals directly with the early stages of the war in Iraq.[2] *Green Zone* (2010) portrays a U.S. Army officer, Roy Miller (Matt Damon), attempting to unearth evidence of Saddam Hussein's alleged Weapons of Mass Destruction in the Baghdad area amidst the chaos unleashed by the American invasion. Examining the Bush Administration's now notoriously flimsy rationale for preemptive war affords Greengrass ample opportunity to further dramatize the human consequences of colonial aggression and bureaucratic indifference.

As a political thriller with the Iraq War as its setting, the film enacts catharsis through the revelation of truth, not via a military victory. Ultimately, Miller confronts a duplicitous Department of Defense official and tells him,

"The reasons we go to war always matter — it's all that fucking matters," before asking a fundamental question about the future of American foreign policy: "What's going to happen the next time we need people to trust us?" Furthermore, through film technique and narrative structure, *Green Zone* encourages viewer identification with two fully developed Iraqi characters — "Freddy," a civilian turned informant (Khalid Abdalla), and a Ba'athist ex-general (Igal Naor) with vital intelligence regarding Weapons of Mass Destruction, who at the film's climax is on the run from an American Special Forces unit. Late in the movie Freddy articulates the film's anti-colonial message to Miller: "It is not for you to decide what happens here." While engaging controversial subject matter, both Sheridan and Greengrass's most recent works play to their strengths in terms of genre: Sheridan stays within the friendly confines of the family melodrama, and Greengrass does the same with another political thriller.

That these new works by Sheridan and Greengrass are two of the latest in a fairly long line of Hollywood films critically addressing recent U.S. wars represents another reason to feel somewhat sanguine about the state of mainstream genre filmmaking. Despite the commercial failure of recent well-reviewed pictures such as *In the Valley of Elah* (Paul Haggis, 2007) and *Stop-Loss* (Kimberly Peirce, 2008), and the slim box office returns of numerous acclaimed documentaries on U.S. foreign policy in the Middle East, including the masterful and damning exposé *Taxi to the Dark Side* (Alex Gibney, 2007) and the sobering year-in-the-life combat unit narrative *Restrepo* (Sebastian Junger and Tim Hetherington, 2010), studios have continued to put up money for films addressing a subject that seems to inspire more disaffection than interest in the American public. The summer of 2008 saw the premiere of HBO's acclaimed 7-part series *Generation Kill*, which offers an unvarnished depiction of one Marine battalion's march of destruction into Baghdad. In late 2009 came the release of *The Messenger* (Dir. Oren Moverman), a gritty film about the aftermath of war concerning two Army men charged with delivering death notices to bereaved family members of soldiers killed in action. Though it benefited from numerous rave reviews and two Oscar nominations, *The Messenger*, following the pattern of its Hollywood predecessors, fared poorly at the box office, taking in only $1.1 million compared to its $6.5 million budget (*Box Office Mojo*). The most successful war-themed American film of 2009 was *The Hurt Locker* (Dir. Kathryn Bigelow), a critical darling and the year's big Oscar winner.[3] Unfortunately, this movie reverts to clichéd war genre formula by using action and thriller elements to reduce the meaning of the Iraq War to one man's quest for self-determination and vindication, focusing on a bomb removal expert who dispenses macho bromides like "If I'm gonna die, I'm gonna die comfortable."

Though the case of *The Hurt Locker* makes me doubt that we are witnessing a total paradigm shift in the way Hollywood and other national cinemas make war films, I do see a number of positive recent developments in that genre. For example, two of the most recent high-profile American World War II films, Clint Eastwood's diptych of *Flags of Our Fathers* (2006) and *Letters from Iwo Jima* (2006), address the U.S.'s most unambiguously celebrated war in a somber, revisionist tone, focusing on the human costs of war to the virtual exclusion of glorified acts of combat heroism.[4] Additionally, some recent German films revisiting World War II, particularly *Downfall* (2004), *Napola* (2004), and *Sophie Scholl — the Final Days* (2005), act as powerful affirmations of humanity in the face of fascist oppression. If mainstream cinema functioned more consistently as a vehicle for demystifying violence, it could productively impact public consciousness, feeding a critical mass of opposition that might help prevent future imperialist wars of aggression.

Furthermore, with *The Wind That Shakes the Barley* (2006), Irish cinema has taken a great leap forward in critically treating its War of Independence and subsequent Civil War. Although Ken Loach's anti-colonial, pro-socialist sympathies are front and center throughout the film, his sobering depiction of Republican guerrilla warfare and internecine conflict results in a work that effectively expresses ambivalence over revolutionary violence, even as it valorizes revolutionary leftist principles. *Wind* relegates Neil Jordan's simplistic *Michael Collins* (1995) to second-tier status as an Irish war film.

Clearly the cultural shifts of the past two decades have manifested themselves in the form and content of Irish film and other media, as well as the backgrounds of the artists themselves. In addition to Paul Greengrass and Ken Loach, both English filmmakers who openly question the morality and practicality of British imperialism, the meteoric rise of Martin McDonagh offers an illustrative case in point. The London-bred progeny of working-class Irish expatriates, McDonagh, already an accomplished playwright and filmmaker at the age of 43, renders rural Ireland, the setting for five of his seven plays and one of his two films to date, as a hyper-real land of repressed passions, brutal humor, and atrocious outbursts of gory violence. Yet his characters remain identifiably human and somehow sympathetic, even as they ruthlessly torment their victims — most frequently their own family members.

Irish purists can attack McDonagh, and not without reason, for his glib representations of politically charged events and figures that still touch deep emotions and provoke intense controversy. One of his most successful plays, *The Lieutenant of Inishmore* (2001), which is set in 1993, features a paramilitary psychopath — a man so violent he was denied membership in the IRA — terrorizing his native island to avenge the death of his beloved cat. Nevertheless, McDonagh's artistic concerns are deeply serious, and by constantly focusing on internal Irish conflicts on an absurdly small scale, his plays, which the critic Fintan O'Toole aptly describes as "merciless rebukes to literary sentimentality," represent Irish drama at its most daring and uninhibited ("A Mind in Connemara").

In addition, McDonagh has now made two provocative, award-winning films—a short, *Six Shooter* (2004), and the feature *In Bruges* (2008)—that function brilliantly both as darkly comic crime films and as searing commentaries on contemporary Western masculinity. The main characters of both films seem to suffer from a sort of postcolonial traumatic stress disorder, rendering them at once callously indifferent to the suffering of others and grotesquely sentimental and self-absorbed. McDonagh's work points to a promising future for Irish artists on the global stage and a seamless fusion of creative media.

Productively complicating this artistic landscape further is another phenomenal Irish film from 2008, *Hunger*. This is the work of Steve McQueen (b. 1969), also a Londoner, who is the son of West Indian immigrants. A renowned photographer and fine artist, McQueen transitioned to cinema to craft his visceral interpretation of the IRA hunger strikes at the Maze Prison in 1981. An astounding, revelatory debut, *Hunger* is by equal turns horrifying and breathtakingly beautiful, as well as restrained and careful in its attention to the humanity of pro–British guards and IRA prisoners alike.

McQueen followed up *Hunger* with a second collaboration with the versatile and enigmatic Michael Fassbender, the Irish-German actor who portrayed hunger striker Bobby Sands with harrowing depth and conviction. Their 2011 film *Shame* is another meditation on human degradation—one that reveals, through its portrait of sex addiction, the angst and excesses of modern Western masculinity with unflinching, clinical precision and insight. Fassbender's Irish-American protagonist, Brandon, spends much of the film plundering New York City for increasingly lurid erotic stimulation, leading him to the brink of psychological breakdown and alienating him from his only close human connection, his fragile sister, whom Brandon abandons in her time of direst need. McQueen's film leaves viewers in a Beckettian state of penultimacy, wondering if someone as damaged and self-destructive as Brandon, so far gone down the road of addiction, can ever lead a remotely normal, healthy life again. The movie is a devastating critique of the half-truths, self-deceptions and outright lies upon which patriarchal masculinity relies to maintain its ascendancy.

Nevertheless, we can be assured that most mainstream films will continue to trade in destructive sociohistorical myths and distortions that privilege dominant, regressive modes of masculinity. As critics, our skepticism should be unrelenting. Kurt Vonnegut offers an example of a model iconoclast in the autobiographical opening of *Slaughterhouse-Five* (1969): that of Mary O'Hare, the wife of a friend and fellow veteran. Vonnegut relates O'Hare's defiant reaction when she hears of his intention to write a book about his experience in World War II:

> You were just babies in the war.... But you're not going to write it that way.... You'll pretend you were men instead of babies, and you'll be played in the movies by Frank Sinatra and John Wayne or some of those other glamorous, war-loving, dirty old men. And war will look just wonderful, so we'll have a lot more of them. And they'll be fought by babies like the babies upstairs [14].

Vonnegut dedicates his book to Mary O'Hare, whose eloquent indictment of Hollywood's collusion with American militarism stands as the most cogent statement of outrage against war in the text and a stirring incitement to vigilance.

As the many 2007 centennial celebrations of his birth attested, the spirit of John Wayne remains alive and well, validating O'Hare's concerns. Millions of fans continue to view the Duke as the epitome of American masculinity — the quintessential figure of a time "when men were men" (Wills 14). That Wayne was the sheep in wolf's clothing hardly dents his admirers' esteem; perusing forums and blogs that address his evasion of military service, one finds ardent followers citing a litany of their hero's excuses, which, as Garry Wills says so well, all boil down to "the dog ate his homework" (109). It is thus tempting to trace the evolution of the Bush administration's "chickenhawk" U.S. leaders, including Bush and Dick Cheney, straight back to Wayne, as liberal columnist Glenn Greenwald does in his book *Great American Hypocrites: Toppling the Big Myths of Republican Politics* (2008). Yet U.S. imperialist wars in Korea and Vietnam were engineered and executed by Democratic presidents, who were no more averse to worshipping at the altar of the military-industrial complex than their Republican counterparts have been in recent years.

As consumers and critics of cinema and culture, it is essential that we understand John Wayne: his appeal, what he represents, what he conceals, and what he tells us about ourselves, whether we like it or not. As Garry Wills states, "The less we advert to what he did to us, the less we can cope with it" (27). For Americans and those who admire our country, the Duke gracefully reconciles our democratic values with our frequently opportunistic, morally careless actions. Shortly after Wayne died, the U.S. government commemorated his passing by issuing a special coin; it featured the star in his 1950s heyday sporting a bandana, and it bore the deceptively simple inscription "John Wayne — American." My grandfather gave me one of these golden medallions when I was a preschooler, and for years it was one of my most prized possessions. Although I now staunchly oppose most of what he stood for — blind patriotism, dogged anti-intellectualism, misogyny with a thin veneer of chivalry — I cannot deny that he once mesmerized me.

It is not enough to indignantly reject Wayne and gleefully retreat to our progressive enclaves. We need to interrogate our own values and find ways to reclaim the moral, as well as the political, high ground. We need to point to models of male and female leadership as empowering alternatives. In the process, we should make moral judgments without resorting to dehumanizing those we oppose. The great irreconcilable moral contradiction of militarism is that it requires us to posit ourselves as more worthy of life and safety than those our forces blast and bomb in the name of "liberty." Near the end of his life, Paul Tibbets, the pilot of the plane that decimated Hiroshima, told Studs Terkel that his use of the atomic bomb had helped create "a free world." When Terkel proceeded to ask if he would support using nuclear weapons against foreign enemies today, Tibbets made the following reply:

> Oh, I wouldn't hesitate if I had the choice. I'd wipe 'em out. You're gonna kill innocent people at the same time, but we've never fought a damn war anywhere in the world where they didn't kill innocent people. If the newspapers would just cut out the shit: "You've killed so many civilians." That's their tough luck for being there [54].

So much for a free world! Nevertheless, while this man might seem grotesquely callous, his statement is merely a frank assessment of the message behind the action he carried out, part of a consistent pattern in American foreign policy over the past seventy years.

Paul Tibbets was only in reality the logical extension of what John Wayne represents on the screen — the John Wayne who in *The Comancheros* (Michael Curtiz, 1961) allays an inexperienced Indian fighter's anxiety about being able to tell "a Comanche from a tame Indian" by drawing a comparison to snakes: "Just like your first rattler. One look and you'll know." In those few words Wayne expresses the essence of American Exceptionalism, the myth that moral superiority results from superior strength. The allure of John Wayne — his easy confidence and seemingly pre-ordained dominance over all he surveys— needs to be contested, and it needs to be countered with images and examples of moral, humane, attractive masculine identities. In short, we need stars and popular narratives that make peacemaking look cool and sexy.

Irish cinema and popular culture have given the world a number of such extraordinary figures in recent years. In addition to compelling characters in the films of Sheridan and Greengrass, Irish musicians such as Sinead O'Connor, the Cranberries, and, in particular, U2 have achieved worldwide popularity while espousing progressive principles in their work. Although he freely admits to having a "messianic complex," U2's Bono has become one of the most effective peace activists in the world today. He is a rock star who has successfully lobbied the U.S. government for increased aid to Africa and been nominated for a Nobel Peace Prize, as well as named one of *Time* magazine's 2005 "Persons of the Year" in recognition of his work fighting AIDS and poverty on that continent. He describes this activism for "justice" as driven by "a belief that where you live should no longer determine whether you live" ("Bono remarks..."). On stage as well, Bono and U2 use their performances to promote tolerance and human rights. During shows of their 2005-06 Vertigo tour, they prominently displayed a banner integrating the Muslim crescent, the Jewish star, and the Christian cross into the word "Coexist," which was projected during the song "Love and Peace or Else," a performance featured in the groundbreaking concert film *U2 3D* (2007).

As I mention briefly in Chapter 5, Bono has also long been an outspoken advocate for peace in Ireland. Having grown up in Dublin with a Catholic mother and a Protestant father, he has repeatedly used his songs to call for an end to sectarian divisions and the violence of the Troubles. In addition to 1983's "Sunday Bloody Sunday," U2's "Please," released in 1997 in the midst of the Peace Process in Northern Ireland implores Irish leaders to help bring about a definitive end to the Troubles. The cover art for the "Please" single dispels any doubts about whom Bono is addressing in the song: it features pastel-colored photographs of rival Northern Irish politicians Gerry Adams, David Trimble, John Hume, and Ian Paisley. Later, in "Peace on Earth" (2000), Bono expresses frustration at the lack of resolution to the conflict in Northern Ireland and laments the lives taken in the Omagh bombing. Bono emphasizes the indiscriminate cruelty of the attack by underscoring four of the youngest victims: Sean McLaughlin, 12; Julia Hughes, 21; Gareth Conway, 18; and Breda Devine, 20 months (*CAIN*, "The Omagh Bomb...").

During U2's performance of "Sunday Bloody Sunday" at Slane Castle near Dublin on September 1, 2001, Bono referenced Omagh once again as part of a stunningly cathartic artistic response to the Troubles.[5] In front of 80,000 countrymen and women, he sings the refrain "How long, how long must we sing this song?" before departing from the original lyrics and screaming, "We're not going back there!" He then leads the crowd in chants of "No more!" and calls out a series of terms seared into the Irish collective memory: "No paratroop! No petrol bombs! No Saracens! No UDA! No IRA!" Expressing disgust with colonial as well as sectarian purveyors of violence, Bono wails, "I'm so sick of this! We've had enough." Finally, he connects the atrocities of January 30, 1972, and August 15, 1998 — "Three years after Omagh we turn this song into a prayer" — and ends by naming each victim of the bombing and declaring, "29 people too many."

Such theatrics might seem like idealistic blarney, and in one sense they are exactly that. At the same time, though, the singer's progressive ethos, like his band's global success, reflects the reality of an increasingly interconnected, interdependent world. Thus, there's a very pragmatic aspect to Bono's peacemaking. As he points out in a 2007 interview, "The greatest army cannot protect you from hatred that gets busy and organized and has enough of an audience to protect it.... [W]e have now entered a phase where being powerful and having the biggest nuclear arsenal leaves you completely defenseless." Therefore, he predicts:

> In the near future, distance will no longer decide who your neighbor is.... In the not-too-distant future, the rich world will invest in the education of the poor world, because it is our best protection against young minds being twisted by extremist ideologies—or growing up without any ideology at all, which could be worse. Nature abhors a vacuum; terrorism loves one [*Rolling Stone*].

As he indicates, military strength and market-driven self-interest cannot keep the U.S., Europe, and their allies fat and happy at the expense of less developed nations for very much longer. This way of life is not sustainable. Denying our vulnerability, isolating enemies, and using old imperialist ways of thinking will not bring us long-term security.[6] We need new voices and styles of leadership that express strength through words and actions that are as empathetic and forward-thinking as they are strategically sound.

As a postcolonial nation and diasporic culture, Ireland has provided the world with an exemplary success story. The Irish have endured a painful process of soul-searching as an oppressed and divided people, one reflected in their extraordinary artistic output of film, theater, literature, and music. Like many exploited countries, Ireland has witnessed revenge and martyrdom—cycles of victimization, reprisal, and self-destruction. Yet through my study of Irish films and filmmakers from the past 75 years, what I now recognize as the most constant theme of this national cinema is not outrage or despair at injustice and inequality, but an abiding faith in humanity in the face of trauma, the belief that every life has value and every death is a profound loss. Thus, Irish cinema provides the basis for a radically alternative conception of family life, politics, and manhood.

Chapter Notes

Preface

1. Alfred W. McCoy's "The Myth of the Ticking Time Bomb" offers a succinct, forceful refutation of popular misconceptions about the efficacy of torture in yielding reliable intelligence.

2. Ford directed his first film in 1917, but I focus almost exclusively on his work from 1939 onward, since many critics agree that his best and most characteristic works began appearing in that year.

3. Welles was referring to the heroine of Ford's notoriously melodramatic and maudlin 1928 silent film, *Mother Machree*, which portrays the trials and travails of an archetypal long-suffering Irish emigrant mother.

4. Describing the family melodrama genre, Thomas Schatz writes:

> Ideally, the family represents a "natural" as well as a social collective, a self-contained society in and of itself. But in the melodrama this ideal is undercut by the family's status within a highly structured socioeconomic milieu, and therefore, its identity as an autonomous human community is denied — the family roles are determined by the larger social community [227].

Ford's films constantly depict a tension between the primacy of the family and social demands and constraints, often in the form of military duty, as in *Fort Apache*. Instead of focusing on small-town, middle-class families like prototypical family melodramas, however, Ford's films tend to focus on working class or military families in frontier or other marginal communities.

5. Ford's tendency to dwell on the sentimental certainly rivaled that of Frank Capra, whose films were often derided by critics as "Capracorn" due to the perceived naïveté of the director's narratives and their insistent foregrounding of the struggles and triumphs of social underdogs. Capra's most well known films, including *Mr. Deeds Goes to Town* (1936), *You Can't Take It with You* (1938), *Mr. Smith Goes to Washington* (1939), and *It's a Wonderful Life* (1946), were ostensibly romantic dramedies that focused on social and family problems. Since Capra didn't make westerns like Ford, perhaps his corniness was more open to criticism. Yet Ford's emotional investment in favoring "the little guy" is equally apparent in his films.

6. Ann Cvetkovich's study of Victorian sensational novels, *Mixed Feelings*, establishes that since the mid–nineteenth century melodrama has been widely viewed as a feminine genre: "[T]he association of femininity with affect has led to the simultaneous devalorization of both" (1).

7. Ford directed 59 fiction features in the sound era, and 113 features total, not including the many combat documentaries he made as an officer in the U.S. Navy's Field Photo unit (McBride 9–10; 797–803).

8. I feel compelled to offer my rationale for excluding Neil Jordan from this study. First, although his films are deeply concerned with complex male identities, including queer masculinities, Jordan has rarely portrayed women with much sympathy or complexity. While this project looks primarily at representations of alternative masculinity, I am equally interested in deviant heterosocial relationships enacted on film (which Jordan seldom explores very compellingly, in my opinion) and complex homosocial relationships (which Jordan dramatizes extraordinarily well). Second, with the notable exception of the fractured family at the center of *The Butcher Boy* (1997), Jordan has little narrative investment in the functioning of the Irish family. Finally, his engagement with Irish history has at times bordered on the jingoistic and simplistic, as it does in the wildly uneven *Michael Collins*. For all these reasons I feel that Jordan does not fit well in a study that includes Ford, Sheridan, and Greengrass and is principally concerned with gender and politics.

9. No doubt *Valley* was made more palatable to audiences and censors by virtue of its foreign setting. Nevertheless, had it been released during the Hollywood Blacklist era (1947–60), it would almost certainly have created a storm of controversy due to its sympathetic portrayal of labor unions and critical treatment of organized religion.

10. In a telling sign of the times, Oscar Wilde's 1895 public humiliation and incarceration was precipitated by his dispute with John Sholto Douglass, the 9th Marquess of Queensberry, the man who leant his family name to the now standard set of boxing ring regulations, the Queensberry Rules.

11. Dempsey was born William Harrison Dempsey but took the name Jack as an homage to another great boxer with Irish roots, "Nonpareil" Jack Dempsey (1862–1895), the world middleweight bare-knuckle boxing champion born in County Kildare.

12. See Gail Bederman's great study, *Manliness and Civilization: A Cultural History of Gender and Race in the United States, 1880–1917*, for an account of boxing's central significance to Western ideas of gender.

13. For a helpful chart that demystifies boxing weight divisions see http://www.boxrec.com/media/index.php/Weight_divisions

14. Joseph R. Svinth, editor of the *Journal of Combative Sport*, has documented 1355 boxing deaths since 1890, 923 of which were professional fighters. According to Svinth, over half of these fatalities occurred in the U.S. and U.K.

15. Like any mass medium, Hollywood cinema has molded and responded to public taste in an ever-changing, reciprocal relationship. In some respects, mainstream films reflect a degree of social progress over the past 100 years—perhaps most notably in terms of racial representations. With regard to gender (and probably social class as well), however, mainstream cinema has seemed to run in cycles, with high incidences of complex representations of femininity and masculinity coming in the 1930s (especially in screwball romantic comedies and Jean Renoir's work during this time) and then again in the 1960s and '70s (arguably, the greatest artistic period for the Italian, French, English, and American cinemas). Perhaps with the rise of independent cinema, the exponential growth of small film festivals, and the emergence of relatively inexpensive digital technologies, we are on the verge of another peak time for depictions of gender on screen.

16. *Gandhi* earned over $52 million at the U.S. box office. The twelfth-highest-grossing film in the U.S. that year, it amazingly outperformed the original Rambo film, *First Blood* ($47 million) domestically. *The Passion of the Christ* earned over $370 million domestically (and $611 million globally), becoming the highest-grossing R-rated film of all time (*Box Office Mojo*).

17. Sadly, only in the wake of her husband's assassination did Ms. King assume a position of leadership worthy of her talents—as founder and chair of the King Center in Atlanta.

Chapter 1

1. Quoted in her 2004 memoir *'Tis Herself* by O'Hara and John Nicoletti (160–61).

2. *The Rising of the Moon* is a series of three cinematic vignettes, the last of which is an expanded version of Lady Gregory's one-act play that gives the film its title.

3. Due to health problems, Ford had to relinquish the shooting of the film to Jack Cardiff, who finished it and received full directing credit.

4. One exceptional Ford film in this regard is *The Quiet Man*, which portrays a pastoral Irish community virtually untainted by class conflict.

5. Ford's Hemingway-lite safari adventure *Mogambo* (1953) also features dozens of singing African villagers who are little more than an element of the scenery.

6. Although *Drums* certainly has some western elements, I see it as more akin to early American frontier adventure tales (and films) like *The Last of the Mohicans*. The setting is upstate New York in 1776, and thus in many respects *Drums* is more of a war film than a western.

7. Ford's only subsequent film was a documentary about a U.S. Marine general, *Chesty: A Tribute to a Legend*, which was released in 1976, three years after his death.

8. Frank S. Nugent, one of Ford's most frequent collaborators, wrote the screenplays for both *The Quiet Man* and *Fort Apache*.

9. Ford's other 1941 release was *Tobacco Road*, also an adaptation of a successful novel about struggling working-class people. This broad comedy, while certainly showcasing Ford's sympathy for the downtrodden at a few key moments, exuberantly trades on stereotypes of poor Southerners, particularly in the figure of the lazy, bumbling patriarch Jeeter Lester (Charley Grapewin), whom Ford characterizes as a slightly more good-hearted dissolute father than those found in Sean O'Casey's drama. The most mature and least pathetic member of the Lester clan by far is Jeeter's wife Ada (Elizabeth Patterson), who is wise to all his schemes and evasions, marking her as another strong and fairly nuanced Fordian mother figure from this period. Very much in contrast to *How Green Was My Valley* and *The Grapes of Wrath*, however, the ending of *Tobacco Road* features two beneficent upper-middle-class men miraculously bailing out the struggling Lester family, thus blunting any critical edge the film has in terms of social or political commentary.

10. In the most famous passage of John 8, prior to blessing and forgiving the adulterous woman himself, Jesus tells her accusers, "He that is without sin among you, let him first cast a stone at her" (8:7).

11. Earlier, Parry fumes at one of the Morgan brothers, "Unions are the work of the devil!"

12. Befitting one of the most popular and successful actors of the 1930s and '40s, Colbert is the top-billed star of the film, and thus the script and Ford's direction may have been tailored to give her performance at least as much prominence as Fonda's.

13. Ford relentlessly stereotypes Native Americans throughout *Drums Along the Mohawk*. They speak child-like English, run by bounding and leaping like deer, and in one scene two "Indians" enter a white settler's home and set fire to it while one of them holds a whisky jug in the midst of their arson. All the Native Americans in the film except Blue Black side with the British baddies, represented principally by Caldwell (John Carradine), who wears a black eye patch to make his dastardly intentions completely unambiguous. To be fair, Caldwell is almost as much of a stereotype as the Native Americans in the film. He's perfectly articulate, but although he leads the British and Indian forces, he's portrayed as just as much, if not more, of a bigot as the American settlers who oppose them. At one point in the heat of battle he orders his underling officers, "Call the filthy [Indian] beggars back!"

14. As I will discuss in Chapter 2, the final thirty minutes of *The Quiet Man* contain some very similar stick-wielding business involving the central married couple of that film, and its placement so late in the latter movie is just one contributing element to the much more troubling depiction of spousal abuse in *The Quiet Man*.

15. Many war movies and westerns employ revenge plots. Star vehicles for Clint Eastwood (circa 1970s) and Mel Gibson often fit this mold: for example, *High Plains Drifter* (Clint Eastwood, 1973), *The Outlaw Josey Wales* (Clint Eastwood, 1976), *Braveheart* (Mel Gibson, 1995), and *The Patriot* (Roland Emmerich, 2000). The latter three films strip away any ambiguity about their protagonists' motives for going to war by endowing them with deeply personal reasons for enacting revenge on their enemies in combat: in each case, the murders of

multiple family members provide the motivation. Thus, the hero's killings of people who side with the bad guys are justified as he pursues his revenge against the principal villain.

16. Again, *Valley* is set in Wales, but many of the characters seem Irish, and many of the film's actors (Maureen O'Hara, Sara Allgood, Arthur Shields, Barry Fitzgerald) *are* of Irish descent.

17. Abigail Clay in *Young Mr. Lincoln* is another idealized mother figure from Ford's work of this period. Near the end of the film, in one of his courtroom speeches, Abe declares, "I've seen Abigail Clay precisely three times in my life. And yet I know all there is to know about her." He goes on to say of her and other mothers like her: "They ask for nothing, and give everything."

18. Ma is the only character to use this childish nickname to address Tom.

19. Although he acknowledges Ma's familial authority near the end of the novel (423), Pa Joad remains an active figure in the family throughout Steinbeck's book and doesn't suffer the same degree of emasculation that he does in Ford's film.

20. This dialogue *is* derived from Steinbeck's novel. It's a close approximation of Ma's dialogue from page 423.

21. Perhaps the only parallel in his work is Mrs. McKlennar's declaration of autonomous widowhood in *Drums Along the Mohawk*.

22. Many folk and country artists, including Arlo Guthrie and Marty Robbins, render the last line of the chorus as "And the cowboy who has loved you so true," which seems to be the standard version of the song.

23. By contrast, the novel features only a handshake farewell for Ma and Tom (420).

24. Much credit for the lighting artistry in *The Grapes of Wrath* is due its cinematographer, the great Gregg Toland.

25. In the case of *Fort Apache*, Fonda portrayed an unconventional villain: Thursday, a man on the side of the "good guys" who is really the most evil person in the story.

26. In a 1975 BBC television interview included on the *Young Mr. Lincoln* Criterion DVD, Fonda reflects on this scene and his personal connection to it. He explains how, when he was a twelve-year-old growing up in Omaha, Nebraska, his father took him to witness the formation of an actual lynch mob, which ultimately murdered a young African American man.

27. This speech is strikingly similar to one Fonda would make in a later masterpiece dealing with the issues of lynching and mob injustice: William Wellman's *The Ox-Bow Incident* (1943). In the film's penultimate scene, Fonda reads a letter — aloud to a barroom full of men — from one of the three victims of a lynching he failed to prevent; he says, in part: "A man just naturally can't take the law into his own hands and hang people without hurting everybody in the world, 'cause then he's just not breaking one law but all laws."

28. While interviewing the aging Ford, Peter Bogdanovich raised this point — "By the end of the picture, though, it seemed that Vera Miles was still in love with Wayne" — and Ford responded, "Well, we meant it that way" (qtd. in Schatz 63).

29. I am not including the Fonda showcase *Mister Roberts*, a film in which Ford is credited as director but one he did not finish. He was replaced midway through the shoot by Mervyn LeRoy.

30. Late in his life Fonda offered an incredibly candid (and sad) description of his demeanor on screen: "[I]f there is something in the eyes, a kind of honesty in the face, then I guess you could say that's the man I'd like to be, the man I want to be" (*Time*, "The Permanent Star").

31. When Wyatt Earp catches Chihuahua tipping off other poker players against him, he threatens to send her back "to the Apache reservation, where you belong."

32. Once again the double-edged nature of Ford's cultural representations comes into play. As Ramírez Berg argues, *My Darling Clementine* can be categorized as one of the director's "Conversion-to-the-Margin" plots. Although Clementine is converted to the marginal community in the end, there is no place here for women like Chihuahua, or for other Latinos, except perhaps for the ones we see in the singer/prostitute's backing mariachi band. Likewise,

no black people or Native Americans are present in this community, except for the one "drunken Indian" whom Wyatt Earp throws out of town for shooting up a saloon in the film's opening reel.

33. The women in *Clementine* are a few shades less complex than Donna Reed's Sandy Davys in Ford's 1945 war movie *They Were Expendable*, in which she starts out as a tough nurse who confronts John Wayne's Rusty Ryan and criticizes him for his recklessness. After Sandy falls in love with Ryan, however, she quickly morphs into a submissive nonentity, following the pattern of so many Ford women.

Chapter 2

1. Wills, *John Wayne's America: The Politics of Celebrity* (75).
2. Quoted in McBride, *Searching for John Ford* (641).
3. *Fort Apache* (1948) had Fonda, as the second-billed star, playing the villain. John Wayne was first-billed and played the film's protagonist.
4. I would argue that Fonda's apparent asexuality in these films is more a reflection of the roles he played. Except for Gil Martin in *Drums Along the Mohawk*, in which Fonda exhibits a remarkable amount of romantic passion for Claudette Colbert's Lana, all of his characters in Ford films are essentially loners.
5. According to Joseph McBride, General Douglas MacArthur, who advocated spreading the Korean War into Chinese territory, loved *She Wore a Yellow Ribbon* and used to view it "once a month." Ford was a big MacArthur booster, and he sided with the general and turned against Truman when the president fired MacArthur in 1951, reflecting Ford's shift from Democrat to Republican during this time (McBride 504).
6. Other members of the CFA included Katharine Hepburn and Spencer Tracy.
7. According to Joseph McBride, "When Bond invited Ford to a party honoring Joseph McCarthy, Ford reacted with unequivocal disgust: 'You can take your party and shove it. I wouldn't meet that guy in a whorehouse. He's a disgrace and a danger to our country'" (476). Furthermore, Ford would temporarily revert to being a Democrat in 1960 when he became a strong supporter of his fellow Irish-American and New Englander John F. Kennedy (Eyman 483).
8. In case clarification is needed: I would have no problem whatsoever with John Wayne's lack of military service if not for his blatant and well-documented hypocrisy on the subject, as well as his deeply destructive acts of "patriotic" overcompensation. The pernicious influence he wielded during the Hollywood blacklist years (more on this below) helped destroy many of his peers' professional lives. By the same token, his open contempt for others who would avoid military service during subsequent wars contributed to the social stigma against an already marginalized group of men — a group to which he, in fact, very much belonged. "This is a man who called on other generations to sacrifice their lives, and called them 'soft' if they refused" (Wills 110). In short, people like Wayne who live in glass houses should not throw stones.
9. According to McBride, "In a letter to [his wife] Mary that March [1942], Ford made an acerbic comment about.... Wayne sitting on a California mountaintop listening for a possible Japanese attack: 'Ah well — such heroism shall not go unrewarded — it will live in the annals of time'" (343).
10. Although the tempestuous romance at the heart of the narrative has strong parallels with the tragic love story of Christy and Pegeen in *The Playboy of the Western World* (1907), Ford's characteristic emphasis on community togetherness as an extension of ethnic identity stands as a stark contrast to the ideological orientation of Synge's plays, which frequently depict the suffocating and dehumanizing aspects of life in rural Irish communities. As opposed to Sean Thornton, Synge's Christy Mahon finally and permanently leaves the village where he had briefly found a home.
11. Both Gibbons and Ford biographer Joseph McBride marshal Brandon French's overly optimistic take on the film's final moments to lend credence to their readings of the

film. French apparently originated the argument that the throwing away of the stick represents Mary Kate's "break with tradition" (qtd. in McBride 516).

12. Compared to members of other marginal groups, Asian characters tend to fare much less well in Ford films, particularly in *Donovan's Reef* and *7 Women*.

13. According to Maureen O'Hara's memoir, Ford described himself precisely thus when the two first met in the early 1940s (60).

14. The most recent boxing film mini-renaissance includes American movies like *Girlfight* (Karyn Kusama, 2000), *Million Dollar Baby* (Clint Eastwood, 2004), *Cinderella Man* (Ron Howard, 2005), and *The Fighter* (David O. Russell, 2010), as well as the Irish film *The Boxer* (Jim Sheridan, 1997), *Beutiful Bockser* (Ekachai Uekrongtham, 2004) from Thailand, and *Napola* (Dennis Gansel, 2004) from Germany.

15. Additionally, some exceptional westerns of this period deal effectively with issues surrounding patriarchy and assimilation, particularly George Stevens' *Shane* (1953) and William Wyler's *The Big Country* (1958). These films center on men who, though adept at using violence, express moral aversion to force. In contrast to Sean Thornton, both of these protagonists defy a community's expectations and fight exclusively on their own terms. Furthermore, as opposed to *The Quiet Man*, these films feature mature female characters invested with significant agency: Marian Starrett (Jean Arthur) in *Shane* and Julie Maragon (Jean Simmons) in *The Big Country*.

16. Lana Martin's materialism, a vestige of her urban, WASP upbringing, is exposed as a flaw in her character—one that she corrects in the course of *Drums Along the Mohawk* as she adapts to frontier life and thus "converts to the margin."

17. Additionally, though some may cite Eloise Kelly (Ava Gardner) in *Mogambo* (1953) as a progressive figure of femininity, I would counter that Ford systematically humiliates this initially strong-willed character in a manner similar to his treatment of Mary Kate: by making her repeatedly "fall down on her derrière" and ultimately requiring her to humble herself before a dominant macho figure—in this case, the roving-eyed hunter Victor Marswell (Clark Gable).

18. At the same time, though, she is initially too embarrassed to acknowledge the fact that she is keeping Sean out of their bed. When Will's agents and Michaeleen arrive the morning after the wedding to deliver her furniture, she urges Sean to put away his sleeping bag, pleading, "Don't be shaming me, please, in front of your friends."

19. In her commentary on the 2002 Artisan DVD edition of *The Quiet Man*, O'Hara explains that she initially refused to use the line that Ford himself suggested. Only when the director promised to keep it a secret from the rest of the world did she finally consent to say the words in Wayne's ear.

20. Richard Llewellyn, who wrote the novel *How Green Was My Valley*, wrote the first draft of the script for *The Quiet Man*, but he received no credit in the film itself.

21. According to Eyman, "When [first assistant director Andrew] McLaglen asked Ford if he should clean the sheep dung from the meadow grass, Ford thought about it for a bit, then snapped, 'Leave it there.' 'Ford really dragged Maureen through a lot of it,' chortled McLaglen" (406).

22. In her 2002 DVD commentary O'Hara contradicts this account. According to her, she and Wayne only did this scene (in which they kiss in a graveyard in the rain) just once.

23. Slip case description of *The Quiet Man* DVD (Artisan, 2002).

24. Accompanying the first full scene, an expository voiceover proclaims: "This is the hearing room of the House of Representatives Committee on Un-American Activities. We, the citizens of the United States of America, owe these, our elected representatives, a great debt. Undaunted by the vicious campaign of slander launched against them as a whole and as individuals, they have staunchly continued their investigation, pursuing their stated beliefs: that anyone who continued to be a communist after 1945 is guilty of high treason."

25. Nevertheless, some Hollywood westerns of the 1950s did go to great lengths to portray American Indians as dignified, complex human beings. Delmer Daves' poignant, though heavy-handed *Broken Arrow* (1950), which, like Ford's *Fort Apache*, features the Apache leader Cochise as a central and sympathetic character, stands as one notable example.

26. In the liner notes to his earlier album *The Ghost of Tom Joad* (1995), Springsteen proclaims his admiration for Ford and cites his film of *The Grapes of Wrath* as a major inspiration for the record.

27. In *The Last Hurrah*, Ford focuses on the exclusively male social network of a long-serving mayor and his political cronies.

28. This argument is the one that Luke Gibbons attempts to refute in the introduction to his book on *The Quiet Man*.

29. James Edward Grant co-scripted both *Donovan's Reef* and *Big Jim McLain*, in addition to many other Wayne pictures.

Chapter 3

1. Director's Commentary, *In America* DVD.

2. Orson Welles uses this phrase in his narration for Bogdanovich's *Directed by John Ford*. Welles gushes on about Ford's *oeuvre*: "His hero has most often been a man alone, silhouetted against the moving background of history, whether played by Henry Fonda or Jimmy Stewart or Spencer Tracy. From Harry Carey to John Wayne — the same." I would beg to differ with that last statement.

3. Even more unfortunate than Ford's underdevelopment of these characters is the fact that he largely wasted the efforts of great actresses in these roles. Maureen O'Hara (who played Kathleen Yorke and Mary Kate Danaher), Vera Miles (Laurie Jorgensen), Shirley Jones (Marty Purcell) and Anne Bancroft (Dr. Cartwright) were all dynamic actresses capable of complex performances. O'Hara (as Angharad Morgan) and Miles (as Hallie Stoddard) both did give excellent performances in other Ford films.

4. One could argue, though, that Gareth Peirce (Emma Thompson), Gerry Conlon's lawyer in the film, acts as a surrogate mother for the protagonist. Peirce persuades him to emerge from his apathetic lethargy concerning his imprisonment, and she boldly takes on the old boys' network of the British legal establishment.

5. Three of Sheridan's Irish-themed films were commercially successful in relatively limited theatrical release. According to *Box Office Mojo*, *My Left Foot* took in $14,743,391 at the American box office, with its widest release being only 510 theaters; *In the Name of the Father* had a box office take of $65,796,862 worldwide ($25,096,862 in 688 U.S. theaters); and *In America* had a worldwide haul of $25,382,911 (with American receipts of $15,539,656 in just 403 theaters). These three films also received many critical accolades, including a total of 14 Academy Award nominations among them, with *My Left Foot* winning Oscars for Best Actor (Daniel Day-Lewis) and Best Supporting Actress (Brenda Fricker). *The Field* and *The Boxer*, on the other hand, were commercial flops, particularly at the American box office: *The Field* took in only $1,494,399 (40 theaters) in the U.S., while Sheridan's $40 million *The Boxer*, by far his biggest budget Irish picture to date (Barton 99), grossed just $5,980,578 domestically (523 theaters) and a total of $16,534,578 worldwide (*Box Office Mojo*). *The Field* did, however, garner a Best Actor Oscar nomination for Richard Harris's performance.

6. Much like the father in *My Left Foot*, Mr. Morgan goes to the pub as a form of therapy, though he is never brutal with his family.

7. Lord Castlewelland (Cyril Cusack) makes light of this fact, as he reads from Christy's book during the benefit near the end of the film. Again, though, the deaths of the Brown children are never dramatized in the movie.

8. The patriarchal Catholic Church is likewise a subject of pronounced ambivalence for Sheridan's hero. When a priest lectures pre-pubescent Christy (played by Hugh O'Connor) about purgatory and hell, he is horrified and shrinks from the clergyman's touch; on the other hand, when his mother takes him to mass shortly thereafter, he is much more placid, telling her to light an additional candle for some poor soul in purgatory.

9. Throughout his work, Sheridan displays an occasional command of black humor — obviously, a very Irish trope — that Ford could rarely get a handle on, as the Irish-American

filmmaker's attempts at humor usually veered toward the maudlin, especially when executed by John Wayne.

10. Earlier, when introducing Christy to the audience at the cerebral palsy foundation benefit, Castlewelland calls Christy "quite the bravest chap I've ever come across."

11. Sheridan himself was a playwright, stage actor and director in Dublin before he moved to the U.S. and pursued a career in theater (and later film) in New York City. Among his projects in the late '70s, he adapted Christy Brown's novel *Down All the Days* for the Irish stage (Barton 150).

12. At the close of the film a title states, "Dedicated to the memory of my brother / Frankie Sheridan."

13. The Sullivans are also analogous to E.T.: they are "illegal aliens," people living in the U.S. without documentation.

14. The heads of the Joad family never call each other anything but "Ma" and "Pa" throughout the film, an indicator of the desexualized nature of their relationship.

15. Sheridan's older two daughters, Naomi and Kirsten, co-wrote the screenplay for *In America* with their father.

16. Similarly, at the close of Ford's *Fort Apache* a child is born who is named after several of the main characters—but in this case, Michael Thursday York O'Rourke bears the appellations only of militarist patriarchs: his father and late grandfather, both named Michael O'Rourke; the awful Lieutenant Colonel Thursday, his other deceased grandfather; and John Wayne's York.

Chapter 4

1. An earlier, shorter version of this chapter was published as "Fighting Within the Rules: Masculinity in the Films of Jim Sheridan" in *National Cinema and Beyond* (Dublin: Four Courts Press, 2004).

2. *The Irish Times*, "Pray for the Dead...."

3. Kiberd is similarly quoted in Barton 55–56.

4. During this period Sheridan also wrote the screenplay for *Into the West* (1992), and co-wrote and co-produced *Some Mother's Son* (1996).

5. All these narrative structures are variations on genres that enact "rites of integration," as Thomas Schatz calls them.

6. Like colonialism and capitalism, patriarchy is no doubt both an ISA, as well as an RSA (Repressive State Apparatus), since for Althusser, "every State Apparatus, whether Repressive or Ideological, 'functions' both by violence and by ideology..." ("Ideology and Ideological State Apparatuses" 74).

7. The following is a compendium of the Oedipus complex: son desires mother, father sexually possesses mother and prohibits the son's desire, thus psychically castrating him; son accepts the prohibition/castration and surrenders or represses his initial desire, ultimately aligning himself with his father and repeating the cycle with his own son. As Althusser would say, this is "the reproduction of the means of production" (62) for patriarchy, and, by extension, for capitalism and colonialism.

8. Sheridan notes this connection in an interview with Ruth Barton (Barton 153).

9. In this way, "habitus" functions much like an Althusserian Ideological Apparatus.

10. For a fuller discussion of this point, see Elizabeth Butler Cullingford, *Ireland's Others: Gender and Ethnicity in Irish Popular Culture* 181–82, 231.

11. *In the Name of the Father* was co-written by Sheridan and Terry George.

12. Kiberd's use of "authority" is akin to Foucault's sense of "power": "[W]hat defines a relationship of power is that it is a mode of action which does not act directly and immediately on others. Instead it acts upon their actions" (Foucault 220).

13. For one such example, see Richard Grenier's essay "In the Name of the IRA." The title accurately summarizes his patently negative, unnuanced view of the film.

14. During his time in prison, the real Gerry Conlon spent, by his own account, over

three years in solitary confinement (Conlon 141–2) — something not dramatized in Sheridan's film. It is hard to fathom the traumatic effects such prolonged isolation would have on an individual's life.

15. Director's Commentary for *The Boxer* Collector's Edition. Unless otherwise noted, all subsequent Sheridan quotations in this chapter come from the same source.

16. Secondarily, however, the film does employ a conventional *Bildungsroman* sub-plot through the character of Liam, an issue I address below.

17. I am referring to the traditional colonial rhetoric casting the colonizer as a benevolent father protecting an unruly child unable to care for himself. The inverse is that of the hard-line Republican, which simply casts the colonizer as an insensible brute that can only be persuaded by violent resistance.

18. Ruth Barton draws on Feldman's work and the hardman/gunman distinction in her discussion of *The Boxer* (112).

19. For more on the cultural and political context of *On the Waterfront*, which was inspired by actual events and the real figure of an Irish-American priest who fought for social justice, see James T. Fisher's penetrating study *On the Irish Waterfront*.

20. I would argue that violence (at least the political kind) and patriarchy cannot function independently of one another, like Althusser's ISA and RSA (repressive state apparatus). Violence is a disavowal of male lack (even if the agent is a woman, as Silverman indicates), and patriarchy constantly relies on the threat of violence: e.g., "Wait until your father gets home!"

21. Such a stagnant future comes to fruition in *The Field* after Tadgh is destroyed, and Gerry's future is threatened by his initial rejection of his father and acceptance of Joe McAndrew in *In the Name of the Father*.

22. Harry counters Danny's peaceful statements with his own violent ones: by blowing up an RUC (police) captain in his car following Danny's victory over Eddie Carroll; by killing Ike after Danny pulls out of his fight in London against a battered Nigerian opponent; and by attacking Danny and Maggie as they drive home together after Ike's funeral.

23. Harry's wife Patsy is also an extremely influential, though sinister, female figure. Patsy plays a Lady Macbeth–like role, exhorting Harry to reject Joe Hamill's negotiations for peace, as she looks at their dead son's picture and whispers audibly, "Did you die just so Joe Hamill could sell us out?" Patsy actively drives Harry toward destruction.

24. Young Ali, whose wife was pregnant at the time, remained in a coma for six months following the fight, and died on Sandra and Barry McGuigan's first wedding anniversary, just a few days after Sandra learned that she, too, was pregnant (Sheridan 121–2). This series of events occupies a substantial part of Sheridan's biography.

25. If the referee had been properly enforcing Marquess of Queensberry rules, he would have stopped the fight — declaring a technical knockout — once a boxer was obviously hurt or no longer able to defend himself, regardless of whether or not he was still on his feet.

26. This is a move that symbolically privileges the Loyalist cause over the Republican — exactly the kind of polarizing political stance that Danny seeks to avoid. Similarly, Danny's involvement with the Republican cause in his youth had alienated those on the other side of the sectarian divide; as Ike explains, "After you were arrested, the Protestant boys didn't show up [to the gym]. They took it hard."

Chapter 5

1. An earlier, shorter version of this chapter appears under the title "Genre Politics: *Bloody Sunday* as Documentary and Discourse" in the book *Genre and Cinema: Ireland and Transnationalism*, edited by Brian McIlroy (London and New York: Routledge, 2007).

2. Gandhi, *The Essential Gandhi* (175).

3. Wink, "Christian Nonviolence."

4. Outside of Ireland and the UK, Greengrass is best known for his work on Hollywood-produced films. He is the writer and director of the Oscar-nominated *United 93* (2006),

and the director of the blockbuster political action thrillers *The Bourne Supremacy* (2004) and *The Bourne Ultimatum* (2007). The first of these has many of the same reconstructive aims as his films on Northern Ireland: *United 93* attempts to recreate the events of September 11, 2001, from the vantage point of those involved in and affected by the titular hijacked flight, which crashed in rural Pennsylvania, killing everyone aboard. While Greengrass' two Bourne films are genre pieces intended for mass consumption, they feature his signature handheld camera techniques, creating a discomfiting edge to violent scenes, and they go to some lengths to portray the eponymous CIA assassin's dehumanization, as well as his remorse for the murders he has committed. Tellingly, the main villains in these films are CIA bureaucrats who demonstrate no more concern for their agents' lives than they do for their human targets. According to Greengrass, Jason Bourne (played by Matt Damon) is James Bond's polar opposite:

> Bond is an insider, he loves being a secret agent, he worships at the altar of technology, he's a cruel character who kills without regret and remorse, he's a misogynist, he's an imperialist, all the values I wouldn't accept, even if they make for great entertainment.... Bourne is the reverse of all that. He's an outsider, mistrusts authority, he's not misogynistic, and he's filled with doubt and anxiety [*The Times Online*].

5. Greengrass is the writer and director of *Bloody Sunday*, and the co-writer and producer of *Omagh*, which was directed by Pete Travis. Since Greengrass developed the *Omagh* project, and the latter film seems to appropriate many of the techniques and elements of *Bloody Sunday*, I speak of it as a Greengrass film.

6. There is perhaps no more powerful example of a film uncovering the truth than Morris' own *The Thin Blue Line* (1988), which helped free an unjustly imprisoned man who had been erroneously convicted of murder. Morris says of the film: "It wasn't a cinéma vérité documentary that got Randall Dale Adams out of prison. It was a film that re-enacted important details of the crime. It was an investigation—part of which was done with a camera" ("Play It Again, Sam").

7. This government-sanctioned violation of human rights is similar to the power invoked more recently by the Los Angeles Police department with the "Street Terrorism Enforcement and Prevention Act of 1988 (STEP)" (Davis 282) and by the U.S. government with Section 412 of the Patriot Act. The latter statute amends immigration law by giving the Attorney General the power to incarcerate suspected "Terrorist Aliens" (or non-resident aliens) indefinitely, severely limiting internees' rights to due process (EPIC).

8. Many IRA members, as well as Irish Protestant paramilitaries, have been killed by their own bombs rather than colonial agents. The IRA has also inflicted huge casualties on civilian populations, both Catholic and Protestant. According to a *BBC News* report, from 1969 to 1999 the number of Catholic and Protestant civilians killed as a result of the Troubles (1931 non-militants) was considerably greater than the numbers of Republican, Loyalist, RUC and British army combatants combined (1404) ("Provisional IRA: War, Ceasefire, Endgame?").

9. Ford's remarks here bear a chilling resemblance to a statement of the U.S. secretary of war in 1901. Speaking of the U.S. colonial occupation of a Pacific island nation and the accompanying massacre of tens of thousands of its residents he said, "The war in the Philippines has been conducted by the American army with scrupulous regard for the rules of civilized warfare ... with self-restraint and humanity never surpassed" (Zinn 316).

10. Edwards' character is also listed in the end credits of *Bloody Sunday* as "Soldier 027."

11. According to Malcolm Sutton's *"Bear in Mind These Dead..." An Index of Deaths from the Conflict in Ireland, 1969–1993*, Gerry Donaghy was, or had been, a member of the Irish Republican Army Youth Section (IRAF). By Sutton's account, Donaghy was the only one of the fourteen victims of Bloody Sunday who had any affiliation with paramilitary groups.

12. In his testimony, Cooper states the following:

> I was concerned that the IRA would view the march by the dynamic and powerful civil rights movement as an opportunity to create a confrontation with the military and the security forces. Therefore, a few days prior to the march I approached an intermediary and asked him to make arrangements, on my behalf, for me to meet a representative of the IRA. I met four members of the IRA, three of whom I already knew. I made it absolutely clear that the march would have to be a non-violent march with no involvement by the IRA, failing which I would use my influence to seek to have the march cancelled. I sought an assurance to this effect.... I received confirmation 48 hours after my meeting with the IRA that the IRA would ... confine itself to the Creggan Estate whilst the march proceeded. I was, therefore, fairly satisfied that there was a realistic chance that the march could take place without the threat of serious violence [*Bloody Sunday Inquiry*, KC 12–13].

13. The goal of "winning the hearts and minds of the people" was emphasized time and again by U.S. President Bush in his remarks on the War in Iraq, his own colonial enterprise.

14. Both in the *BBC News* article quoted below (225–6) and in his testimony to the *Bloody Sunday Inquiry* (specifically, in KC 12–1, page 16 of his testimony) Cooper maintains that the IRA benefited from Bloody Sunday.

15. According to Cooper, while the *Irish Independent* attributed the Sharpeville comparison to him, Cooper himself doubts that he spoke to reporters after the massacre: "I spent a lot of time at the hospital, probably hours. I would not have thought that I would have given interviews at the hospital — but I could be wrong. I just cannot see where I would have spoken to reporters for all these newspapers." But he certainly concurs that Bloody Sunday and Sharpeville are comparable events: "The article in the *Irish Independent* ... refers to 'another Sharpville' [sic]. I am absolutely certain that the army opened fire first. There were no nail bombs or petrol bombs, and if there was firing from the Provisionals or some other group it came about 10 minutes after the army opened fire" (*Bloody Sunday Inquiry*, KC 12–29).

16. Based on their names, Joe Kenehan is most likely an Irish-American character, and his surrogate son, Danny Radnor, probably has Welsh heritage.

17. In his final voiceover, Danny, narrating as an elderly man in the present, explains the aftermath of the Matewan massacre and Kenehan's death: "That were the start of the Great Coal Field War, and us miners took the worst of it, like Joe said we would. 'It's just one big union, the whole world over,' Joe Kenehan used to say. And from the day of the Matewan massacre that's what I preached. That was my religion."

18. In her article "Memory and Mapping in *Bloody Sunday*," Margaret O'Neill also connects de Certeau's ideas to the characters and physical space portrayed in *Bloody Sunday*.

19. The first 74 minutes of *Bloody Sunday* portray the events leading up to and including the massacre; the final thirty minutes depict the remaining hours of 30 January, 1972, in Derry.

20. Additionally, 220 people were injured by the bomb (*Guardian*). One of the victims, Avril Monaghan, was seven months pregnant with twins when she was killed. Therefore, some listings put the Omagh death toll at 31. Ms. Monaghan was killed along with her mother, Mary Grimes, 65, and her daughter, Maura, eighteen months (*BBC News*, "Hundreds Gather for Omagh victims' funeral").

21. The attitude such narratives often serve to promote is summed up nicely by a line presidential candidate John McCain used in a campaign speech in early 2008: "We are the makers of history, not its victims." This is his view of Americans, but it certainly reflects the brazen confidence common among the self-reliant white male heterosexual *übermenschen* that are the protagonists of so many American movies.

22. One man, Colm Murphy, was convicted of "conspiracy to cause the Omagh bombing" in January 2002 (*Guardian*, "Timeline..."), but after serving three years in prison his conviction was "quashed" (*Belfast Telegraph*, "Murphy to Launch..."). Later, Murphy was

"found to be responsible for the terrorist attack" in the landmark civil action brought by the families of the Omagh Support and Self-Help Group (*Belfast Telegraph*, "Omagh Bomb Families Win...").

23. Michael has a very legitimate reason for slighting Adams; as he tells the Sinn Fein leader during this scene:

> Mr. Adams, my brother was murdered by an IRA gunman in 1984. No witnesses came forward for that, either. So they got away. So I agree with you: let's put the past behind us. That was my brother then, but this is my son now. The war is supposed to be over. You say you want to build a new Northern Ireland, a peaceful Northern Ireland, but how can we build a peaceful Northern Ireland unless you help us to bring his killers to justice?

Conclusion

1. Substantial portions of pages 245–6, which address the work of Martin McDonagh and Steve McQueen, have been adapted from my introduction to the *FSC Review* issue on Irish culture, which was published in 2010.

2. Despite a wide release and a big advertising budget, *Green Zone*, like most Hollywood movies dealing with recent U.S. actions in the Middle East, received a lukewarm reception from American audiences. Though budgeted at $100 million, the film earned only $35 million domestically, while taking in far more at foreign cinemas—$59.7 million—enabling it to nearly break even in its theatrical run (*Box Office Mojo*).

3. Even *The Hurt Locker*, despite its exceptional critical success, barely turned a profit in American theaters: it grossed $16.4 million (compared to a $15 million budget). Like *Green Zone*, it fared far better overseas, taking in $32 million at foreign theaters (*Box Office Mojo*).

4. Countering the humane intelligence of those two films is Quentin Tarantino's crude and juvenile historical revenge fantasy, *Inglourious Basterds* (2009), which grossed over $120 million domestically and $320 million worldwide.

5. This performance is captured on the concert video *U2 Go Home: Live from Slane Castle* (2003).

6. The recognition that violence and militarism create more problems than they solve has been made by leaders from the revolutionary Gandhi to the conservative Dwight Eisenhower. The latter put it plainly in 1953:

> Every gun that is made, every warship launched, every rocket fired, signifies, in a final sense, a theft from those who hunger and are not fed, those who are cold and are not clothed. This world in arms is not spending money alone. It is spending the sweat of its laborers, the genius of its scientists, the hopes of its children.... This is not a way of life at all, in any true sense. Under the cloud of threatening war, it is humanity hanging from a cross of iron ["The Chance for Peace"].

Bibliography and Filmography

Althusser, Louis. "Ideology and Ideological State Apparatuses." *Lenin and Philosophy and Other Essays*. Trans. Ben Brewster. London: New Left Books, 1971. Print.
The Associated Press. "Experts say IRA committed to peace, has shut down units for bomb-making, arms smuggling." 4 October 2006. *LexisNexis Academic*. Web. 27 August 2012.
_____. "Ulster Volunteer Force pledges to renounce violence." 3 May 2007. *The International Herald Tribune: The Global Edition of the New York Times*. Web. 27 August 2012.
Backus, Margot Gayle. "Revising Resistance: *In the Name of the Father* as Postcolonial Paternal Melodrama." *Contemporary Irish Cinema: from* The Quiet Man *to* Dancing at Lughnasa. Ed. James MacKillop. Syracuse: Syracuse University Press, 1999. 54–70. Print.
Barry, Sebastian. *The Whereabouts of Eneas McNulty*. New York: Penguin, 1998. Print.
Barton, Ruth. *Irish National Cinema*. London and New York: Routledge, 2004. Print.
_____. *Jim Sheridan: Framing the Nation*. Dublin: Liffey Press, 2002. Print.
The Battle of Algiers. Dir. Gillo Pontecorvo. Criterion, 1966. DVD.
The Battle of Midway. Dir. John Ford. U.S. Navy, 1942. DVD. *Becoming John Ford*. 20th Century–Fox, 2007.
Beautiful Boxer. Dir. Ekachai Uekrongtham. TLA Releasing, 2004. DVD.
Beckett, Samuel. *Worstward Ho*. New York: Grove Press, 1983. Print.
Bederman, Gail. *Manliness and Civilization: A Cultural History of Gender and Race in the United States, 1880–1917*. Chicago: University of Chicago Press, 1996. Print.
The Best Years of Our Lives. Dir. William Wyler. MGM, 1946. DVD.
The Big Country. Dir. William Wyler. Perf. Gregory Peck and Jean Simmons. MGM, 1958. DVD.
Big Jim McLain. Dir. Edward Ludwig. Perf. John Wayne, Nancy Olson and Dan Liu. Warner Bros., 1952.
Bloody Sunday. Dir. Paul Greengrass. Perf. James Nesbitt, Declan Duddy, Kathy Keira Clarke, Nicholas Farrell, Gerard McSorley, Mike Edwards and Tim Piggott-Smith. Paramount, 2002. DVD.
The Bloody Sunday Inquiry. "KC12-1— Statement of Ivan Cooper (1 of 2)" [no longer accessible online]. 1998–2005. Web. 31 May 2008. <http://www.bloody-sunday-inquiry.org/index2.asp?p=6>.

The Bloody Sunday Inquiry. "KC12-2 — Statement of Ivan Cooper (2 of 2)" [no longer accessible online]. 1998–2005. Web. 31 May 2008. <http://www.bloody-sunday-inquiry.org/index2.asp?p=6>.

"Bloody Sunday leader finds faith in film." *BBC News.* 30 January 2002. British Broadcasting Company. Web. 27 August 2012.

Body and Soul. Dir. Robert Rossen. Perf. John Garfield. Artisan/Republic Pictures, 1947. DVD.

Brothers (Brodre). Dir. Susanne Bier. Universal, 2004. DVD.

Bogle, Donald. *Toms, Coons, Mulattoes, Mammies, and Bucks,* 4th ed. London: Continuum International, 2001. Print.

Bono. "Transcript: Bono remarks at the National Prayer Breakfast." *USA Today.* 2 February 2006. Web. 27 August 2012.

"Bono." Interviewed by Anthony DeCurtis. *Rolling Stone.* 15 November 2007. Print.

Bordwell, David. "The Classical Hollywood Style, 1917–60." *The Classical Hollywood Cinema: Film Style and Mode of Production to 1960.* New York: Columbia University Press, 1985. Print.

The Bourne Supremacy. Dir. Paul Greengrass. Perf. Matt Damon. Universal, 2004. DVD.

"Bourne to win: Paul Greengrass." *The Times* (London). 12 August 2004. *The Times Online.* Web. 27 August 2012.

The Bourne Ultimatum. Dir. Paul Greengrass. Perf. Matt Damon. Universal, 2007. DVD.

Box Office Mojo. "Jim Sheridan." *BoxOfficeMojo.com.* Web. 27 August 2012.

_____. "Search Site." *BoxOfficeMojo.com.* Web. 27 August 2012.

The Boxer. Dir. Jim Sheridan. Perf. Daniel Day-Lewis, Emily Watson, Ken Stott, Brian Cox, Gerard McSorley and Ciaran Fitzgerald. Universal, 1997. DVD.

BoxRec.com. "Boxing Record Search." Web. 27 August 2012.

_____. "Weight Divisions — BoxRec Boxing Encyclopedia." Web. 27 August 2012.

Broken Arrow. Dir. Delmer Daves. 20th Century–Fox, 1950. DVD.

Brothers. Dir. Jim Sheridan. Perf. Tobey Maguire, Natalie Portman and Jake Gyllenhaal. Lionsgate, 2009. DVD.

Bruzzi, Stella. "The Event: Archive and Imagination." *New Challenges for Documentary,* 2d ed. Ed. Alan Rosenthal and John Corner. Manchester: Manchester University Press, 2005. 419–431. Print.

Bryant, Wayne M. *Bisexual Characters in Film.* London and New York: Routledge, 1997. Print.

The Butcher Boy. Dir. Neil Jordan. Warner Bros., 1997. DVD.

Cahiers du Cinéma Editors. "John Ford's *Young Mr. Lincoln.*" *Movies and Methods: An Anthology.* Ed. Bill Nichols. Berkeley: University of California Press, 1976. Print.

de Certeau, Michel. "Walking in the City." *The Practice of Everyday Life.* Berkeley: University of California Press, 1988. 91–110. Print.

The Champ. Dir. King Vidor. Warner Bros., 1931. DVD.

Champion. Dir. Mark Robson. Perf. Kirk Douglas. Artisan/Republic Pictures, 1949. DVD.

Cheyenne Autumn. Dir. John Ford. Perf. Dolores Del Rio, Gilbert Roland, Richard Widmark and Ricardo Montalban. Warner Bros., 1964. DVD.

Cinderella Man. Dir. Ron Howard. Universal, 2005. DVD.

The Comancheros. Dir. Michael Curtiz. Perf. John Wayne. 20th Century–Fox, 1961. DVD.
Conlon, Gerry. *Proved Innocent: The Story of Gerry Conlon of the Guildford Four*. London: Hamish Hamilton, 1990. Print.
Cortright, David. *Gandhi and Beyond: Nonviolence for an Age of Terrorism*. Boulder: Paradigm, 2006.
Cowie, Peter. *John Ford and the American West*. New York: Harry N. Abrams, 2004. Print.
Crowdus, Gary, and O'Mare Leary. "Getting Past the Violence: an Interview with Jim Sheridan." *Cineaste* (Summer 1998). Print.
Cullingford, Elizabeth Butler. *Ireland's Others: Gender and Ethnicity in Irish Literature and Popular Culture*. Cork, Ireland: Cork University Press, 2001. Print.
_____. "'John Wayne Fan or *Dances with Wolves* Revisionist?' Analogy and Ambiguity in the Irish Western." *Ireland's Others: Gender and Ethnicity in Irish Literature and Popular Culture*. Notre Dame: University of Notre Dame Press, 2001. 161–92. Print.
_____. "The Prisoner's Wife and the Soldier's Whore: Female Punishment in Irish History and Culture." *Keeping It Real: Irish Film and Television*. Ed. Ruth Barton and Harvey O'Brien. London and New York: Wallflower Press, 2004. 8–24. Print.
Cvetkovich, Ann. *Mixed Feelings*. Piscataway, NJ: Rutgers University Press, 1992.
Darby, William. *John Ford's Westerns: A Thematic Analysis, with a Filmography*. Jefferson, NC: McFarland, 1996. Print.
Davis, Mike. *City of Quartz*. New York: Random House, 1992. Print.
December 7. Dir. John Ford. U.S. Navy, 1943. DVD. *Becoming John Ford*. 20th Century–Fox, 2007.
The Departed. Dir. Martin Scorsese. Warner Bros., 2006. DVD.
Directed by John Ford. Dir. Peter Bogdanovich. Turner Classic Movies, 2006.
Donnelly, Cathleen. "Christy Brown." *British Novelists Since 1960*. Ed. Jay L. Halio. Detroit: Gale Research, 1983. *Dictionary of Literary Biography*, vol. 14. *Literature Resource Center*. Web. 27 August 2012.
Donovan's Reef. Dir. John Ford. Perf. John Wayne, Elizabeth Allen, Lee Marvin, Jack Warden and Cesar Romero. Paramount, 1963. DVD.
Downfall. Dir. Oliver Hirschbiegel. Columbia Tristar, 2004. DVD.
Doyle, Roddy. *A Star Called Henry*. New York: Penguin, 1999. Print.
Drums Along the Mohawk. Dir. John Ford. Perf. Claudette Colbert, Henry Fonda, Edna May Oliver, Arthur Shields and Ward Bond. 20th Century–Fox, 1939. DVD.
Dyer, Richard. *Stars*. London: British Film Institute, 1979. Print.
Ebert, Roger. "Great Movies—*The Grapes of Wrath* (1940)." 31 March 2002. *RogerEbert.com*. Web. 27 August 2012.
Eisenhower, Dwight. "The Chance for Peace." 16 April 1953. *Information Clearing House*. Web. 27 August 2012.
Erickson, Glenn. "DVD Savant Review: *How Green Was My Valley*." 9 January 2003. *DVD Savant*. Web. 27 August 2012.
Eyman, Scott. *Print the Legend: The Life and Times of John Ford*. New York: Simon & Schuster, 1999. Print.
Feldman, Allen. *Formations of Violence: The Narrative of the Body and Political Terror in Northern Ireland*. Chicago: University of Chicago Press, 1991. Print.
Felski, Rita. "Feminism, Postmodernism, and the Critique of Modernity." *Cultural Critique* (Fall 1989): 33–56. Print.

The Field. Dir. Jim Sheridan. Perf. Richard Harris, Sean Bean, Brenda Fricker, John Hurt and Tom Berenger. Live/Artisan, 1990. DVD.
The Fighter. Dir. David O. Russell. Paramount, 2010. DVD.
Fisher, James T. *On the Irish Waterfront: The Crusader, the Movie, and the Soul of the Port of New York*. Ithaca: Cornell University Press, 2010. Print.
Flags of Our Fathers. Dir. Clint Eastwood. Warner Bros., 2006. DVD.
Ford, John. "John Wayne — My Pal." *John Ford Made Westerns: Filming the Legend in the Sound Era*. Ed. Gaylyn Studlar and Matthew Bernstein. Bloomington: Indiana University Press, 2001. 272–76. Print.
Fort Apache. Dir. John Ford. Perf. John Wayne, Henry Fonda, Pedro Amendáriz, Shirley Temple, Ward Bond and Victor McLaglen. Warner Bros., 1948. DVD.
Foucault, Michel. "The Subject and Power." Trans. Leslie Sawyer. *Michel Foucault: Beyond Structuralism and Hermeneutics*. Ed. Hubert L. Dreyfus and Paul Rabinow. Chicago: University of Chicago Press, 1983. Print.
French, Brandon. *On the Verge of Revolt*. New York: Frederick Ungar, 1978. Print.
The Fugitive. Dir. John Ford. Perf. Henry Fonda, Dolores Del Rio, Pedro Amendáriz and Ward Bond. Warner Bros., 1947. DVD.
Gandhi. Dir. Richard Attenborough. Perf. Ben Kingsley. Sony Pictures, 1982. DVD.
Gandhi, Mahatma. *The Essential Gandhi: An Anthology of His Writings on His Life, Work, and Ideas*. Ed. Louis Fisher. 1962. New York: Vintage, 2002. Print.
Generation Kill. Prod. David Simon. HBO, 2008.
Get Rich or Die Tryin'. Dir. Jim Sheridan. Perf. Curtis "50 Cent" Jackson. Paramount, 2005. DVD.
Gibbons, Luke. *The Quiet Man*. Cork, Ireland: Cork University Press, 2002. Print.
Girlfight. Dir. Karyn Kusama. Columbia Tristar, 2000. DVD.
Goodfellas. Dir. Martin Scorsese. Warner Bros., 1990. DVD.
The Grapes of Wrath. Dir. John Ford. Perf. Henry Fonda, Jane Darwell, John Carradine and John Qualen. 20th Century–Fox, 1940. DVD.
The Great White Hope. Dir. Martin Ritt. 20th Century–Fox, 1970. DVD.
Green Zone. Dir. Paul Greengrass. Perf. Matt Damon, Khalid Abdalla and Igal Naor. Universal, 2010. DVD.
"Greengrass' film roots in Northern Ireland." *Variety*. Grey, Tobias. 10 October 2007. *Variety.com*. Web. 27 August 2012.
Greenwald, Glenn. *Great American Hypocrites: Toppling the Big Myths of Republican Politics*. New York: Crown, 2008. Print.
Grenier, Richard. "In the Name of the IRA." *Why Docudrama? Fact-Fiction on Film and TV*. Ed. Alan Rosenthal. Carbondale: Southern Illinois University Press, 1999. Print.
The Harder They Fall. Dir. Mark Robson. Perf. Humphrey Bogart. Columbia Pictures, 1956. DVD.
The Harris Poll. "For the Second Year, Johnny Depp is America's Favorite Actor." 19 January 2012. *Harris Interactive: Vault*. Web. 27 August 2012.
Hellman, Lillian. *Scoundrel Time*. 1976. New York: Bantam, 1977.
Herbert, Bob. "Madness and Shame." *New York Times*. 22 July 2008. *New York Times Opinion*. Web. 27 August 2012.
Herr, Cheryl Temple. *The Field*. Cork, Ireland: Cork University Press, 2002. Print.
The Holy Bible. King James Version. Iowa Falls: World, 1989. Print.
hooks, bell. "Eating the Other: Desire and Resistance." *Media and Cultural Studies:*

Key Works. Ed. Meenakshi Gigi Durham and Douglas M. Kellner. Malden, MA: Blackwell, 2001. 424–438. Print.
_____. *Feminism Is for Everybody: Passionate Politics*. Cambridge, MA: South End Press, 2000. Print.
How Green Was My Valley. Dir. John Ford. Perf. Maureen O'Hara, Walter Pidgeon, Sara Allgood, Arthur Shields, Barry Fitzgerald and Roddy McDowall. 20th Century–Fox, 1941. DVD.
"Hundreds gather for Omagh victims' funeral." *BBC News*. 18 August 1998. British Broadcasting Company. Web. 27 August 2012.
Hunger. Dir. Steve McQueen. Perf. Michael Fassbender, Stuart Graham and Liam Cunningham. Criterion, 2008. DVD.
The Hurricane. Dir. John Ford. Perf. Jon Hall, Thomas Mitchell, Dorothy Lamour, Mary Astor, C. Aubrey Smith and Raymond Massey. Samuel Goldwyn/United Artists, 1937.
The Hurt Locker. Dir. Kathryn Bigelow. Perf. Jeremy Renner. Summit Entertainment, 2008. DVD.
In America. Dir. Jim Sheridan. Perf. Paddy Considine, Samantha Morton, Sarah Bolger, Emma Bolger and Djimon Hounsou. 20th Century–Fox, 2002. DVD.
In the Name of the Father. Dir. Jim Sheridan. Perf. Daniel Day-Lewis, Pete Postlethwaite, Emma Thompson and Don Baker. Universal, 1993. DVD.
In the Valley of Elah. Dir. Paul Haggis. Warner Bros., 2007. DVD.
The Informer. Dir. John Ford. Perf. Victor McLaglen. Warner Bros., 1935. DVD.
Inglourious Basterds. Dir. Quentin Tarantino. Universal, 2009. DVD.
"Interview with Stephen Rea." Conducted by Ted Sheehy. *Keeping It Real: Irish Film and Television*. Ed. Ruth Barton and Harvey O'Brien. London and New York: Wallflower Press, 2004. 198–201. Print.
Irigaray, Luce. "Commodities amongst Themselves." *Literary Theory: An Anthology*. Ed. Julie Rivkin and Michael Ryan. Oxford: Blackwell, 1998.
It's a Wonderful Life. Dir. Frank Capra. Columbia Pictures, 1946. DVD.
Keane, John B. *The Field*, from *The Field and Other Irish Plays*. Niwot, CO: Roberts Rineheart, 1994. Print.
Ketteman, Kerstin. "Cinematic Images of Irish Male Brutality and the Semiotics of Landscape in *The Field* and *Hear My Song*." *Contemporary Irish Cinema: from* The Quiet Man *to* Dancing at Lughnasa. Ed. James MacKillop. Syracuse: Syracuse University Press, 1999. 54–70. Print.
Kiberd, Declan. *Inventing Ireland*. Cambridge: Harvard University Press, 1995. Print.
Lakoff, George. *Don't Think of an Elephant! Know Your Values and Frame the Debate*. White River Junction, VT: Chelsea Green, 2004. Print.
The Last Hurrah. Dir. John Ford. Perf. Spencer Tracy, Jeffrey Hunter, Pat O'Brien and John Carradine. Columbia Tristar, 1958. DVD.
Leighninger, Robert D., Jr. "The Western as Male Soap Opera: John Ford's *Rio Grande*." *The Journal of Men's Studies* 6.2 (1998): 135–148. *ProQuest*. Web. 27 August 2012.
Letters from Iwo Jima. Dir. Clint Eastwood. Warner Bros., 2006. DVD.
Levy, Emanuel. *John Wayne: Prophet of the American Way of Life*. Metuchen, N.J.: Scarecrow Press, 1988. Print.
The Long Gray Line. Dir. John Ford. Perf. Tyrone Power and Maureen O'Hara. Columbia Tristar, 1955. DVD.

The Long Voyage Home. Dir. John Ford. Perf. Thomas Mitchell, John Wayne and Ian Hunter. Warner Bros., 1940. DVD.

The Magdalene Sisters. Dir. Peter Mullan. Miramax, 2002. DVD.

Maltby, Richard. "A Better Sense of History: John Ford and the Indians." *The Book of Westerns*. Ed. Ian Cameron and Douglas Pye. London and New York: Continuum, 1996. 34–49. Print.

The Man Who Shot Liberty Valance. Dir. John Ford. Perf. John Wayne, James Stewart, Vera Miles, Edmund O'Brien, Lee Marvin, Woody Strode and John Carradine. Paramount, 1962. DVD.

"Massacre of Amritsar." *Encyclopædia Britannica*. 2005. *Britannica Online Encyclopædia*. Web. 27 August 2012.

Matewan. Dir. John Sayles. Perf. Chris Cooper, Will Oldham and James Earl Jones. Seville, 1987. DVD.

Mbembe, Achille. "Necropolitics." Translated by Libby Meintjes. *Public Culture* 15(1): 11–40. Print.

McBride, Joseph. *Searching for John Ford*. New York: St. Martin's Press, 2001. Print.

McCain, John. "Remarks by John McCain to Potomac Primary Victory Party." 13 February 2008. *ProCon.org*. "Candidate Speeches—2008 Election." Web. 27 August 2012.

McCoy, Alfred W. "The Myth of the Ticking Time Bomb." *The Progressive*. October 2006. *The Progressive Magazine*. Web. 27 August 2012.

McDonagh, Martin. *The Beauty Queen of Leenane and Other Plays*. New York: Vintage, 1998. Print.

_____. *The Lieutenant of Inishmore*. New York: Dramatists Play Service, 2001. Print.

McDonagh, Martin, dir. *In Bruges*. Perf. Colin Farrell, Brendan Gleeson and Ralph Fiennes. Universal, 2008. DVD.

_____. *Six Shooter*. Perf. Brendan Gleeson, Rúaidhrí Conroy and David Wilmot. *A Collection of 2005 Academy Award–Nominated Short Films*. Magnolia, 2004. DVD.

McIlroy, Brian. "Memory Work: *Omagh* and the Northern Irish Monumentary." *Genre and Cinema: Ireland and Transnationalism*. Ed. Brian McIlroy. New York and London: Routledge, 2007. 261–72. Print.

_____. *Shooting to Kill: Filmmaking and the "Troubles" in Northern Ireland*. Wiltshire, England: Flicks Books, 1998. Print.

McLoone, Martin. *Irish Film: the Emergence of a Contemporary Cinema*. London: British Film Institute, 2000. Print.

The Messenger. Dir. Oren Moverman. Oscilloscope Pictures, 2009. DVD.

Michael Collins. Dir. Neil Jordan. Warner Bros., 1996. DVD.

Mies, Maria. *Patriarchy and Accumulation on a World Scale*. London and New York: Zed Books, 1998. Print.

Million Dollar Baby. Dir. Clint Eastwood. Warner Bros., 2004. DVD.

Mr. Deeds Goes to Town. Dir. Frank Capra. Columbia Pictures, 1936. DVD.

Mister Roberts. Dir. John Ford and Mervyn LeRoy. Perf. Henry Fonda. Warner Bros., 1955. DVD.

Mr. Smith Goes to Washington. Dir. Frank Capra. Columbia Pictures, 1939. DVD.

Mogambo. Dir. John Ford. Perf. Clark Gable, Ava Gardner and Grace Kelly. Warner Bros., 1953. DVD.

Morris, Errol. "Play It Again, Sam (Re-enactments, Part One)." *The New York Times*. 3 April 2008. *NYTimes.com*. Web. 27 August 2012.

Moser, Joseph. "Fighting Within the Rules: Masculinity in the Films of Jim Sheridan." *National Cinema and Beyond*. Ed. Kevin Rockett and John Hill. Dublin: Four Courts Press, 2004. 89–96. Print.
_____. "Genre Politics: *Bloody Sunday* as Documentary and Discourse." *Genre and Cinema: Ireland and Transnationalism*. Ed. Brian McIlroy. New York and London: Routledge, 2007. 245–59. Print.
_____. "Introduction." *Irish Culture* issue. *FSC Review: A Literary Magazine of the English Graduate Program*, Vol. XII (Fall 2009): I–II. Fitchburg State University, 2010. Print.
Mother Machree. Dir. John Ford. 20th Century–Fox, 1928.
Mullan, Don. "Bloody Sunday — the movie." *Newsmedianews*. 2002. Web. 27 August 2012.
_____. *Eyewitness Bloody Sunday: The Truth*. 1997. Dublin: Merlin, 2002. Print.
Mulvey, Laura. "Visual Pleasure and Narrative Cinema." *Media and Cultural Studies: Key Works*. Ed. Meenakshi Gigi Durham and Douglas M. Kellner. Malden, MA: Blackwell, 2001. 393–404. Print.
"Murphy to launch new challenge to Omagh trial." *The Belfast Telegraph*. 6 November 2007. Belfasttelegraph.co.uk. Web. 27 August 2012.
My Darling Clementine. Dir. John Ford. Perf. Henry Fonda, Linda Darnell, Victor Mature, Cathy Downs, Walter Brennan and Ward Bond. 20th Century–Fox, 1946. DVD.
My Left Foot. Dir. Jim Sheridan. Perf. Daniel Day-Lewis, Brenda Fricker, Ray McAnally, Ruth McCabe, Hugh O'Connor and Fiona Shaw. Miramax Pictures, 1989. DVD.
Mystic River. Dir. Clint Eastwood. Warner Bros., 2003. DVD.
Napola. Dir. Dennis Gansel. Picture This, 2004. DVD.
Nichols, Bill. *Introduction to Documentary*. Bloomington: Indiana University Press, 2001. Print.
Oates, Joyce Carol. "Mike Tyson: Blood, Neon and Failure in the Desert." 7 March 1987. *The Celestial Timepiece: the Joyce Carol Oates Home Page*. Web. 27 August 2012.
O'Casey, Sean. *Three Dublin Plays: The Shadow of a Gunman, Juno and the Paycock, The Plough and the Stars*. London: Faber and Faber, 2000.
O'Hara, Maureen, and John Nicoletti. *'Tis Herself: An Autobiography*. New York: Simon & Schuster, 2004. Print.
Omagh. Co-writer and prod. Paul Greengrass. Dir. Pete Travis. Perf. Gerard McSorley, Michèle Forbes, Fiona Glascott, Pauline Hutton, Ian McElhinney, Stuart Graham and Brenda Fricker. Sundance, 2004. DVD.
"Omagh bomb families win multi-million pound legal case." *The Belfast Telegraph*. 8 June 2009. Belfasttelegraph.co.uk. Web. 27 August 2012.
"The Omagh Bomb — List of Those Killed." *Cain Web Service*. 1996–2012. Web. 27 August 2012.
"*Omagh* Press Pack." *Omagh* DVD. Sundance, 2005.
On the Waterfront. Dir. Elia Kazan. Perf. Marlon Brando, Eva Marie Saint, Karl Malden, Rod Steiger and Lee J. Cobb. Columbia Tristar, 1954. DVD.
O'Neill, Margaret. "Memory and Mapping in *Bloody Sunday*." *National Cinema and Beyond*. Ed. Kevin Rockett and John Hill. Dublin: Four Courts Press, 2004. 97–104. Print.
O'Toole, Fintan. "A Mind in Connemara." *The New Yorker*. 6 March 2006. Web. 27 August 2012.

The Ox-Bow Incident. Dir. William A. Wellman. Perf. Henry Fonda, Harry Morgan, Anthony Quinn and Dana Andrews. 20th Century–Fox, 1943. DVD.

Oxford English Dictionary. "patriarchy, *n.*" June 2012. *The Oxford English Dictionary online.* Web. 27 August 2012.

Pettitt, Lance. *Screening Ireland: Film and Television Representation.* Manchester: Manchester University Press, 2000. Print.

The Plough and the Stars. Dir. John Ford. Perf. Barbara Stanwyck. RKO, 1936.

"Prevention of Terrorism (Temporary Provisions) Act 1974." *Cain Web Service.* 1996–2012. Web. 27 August 2012.

"Provisional IRA: War, Ceasefire, Endgame?" *BBC News.* 2005. British Broadcasting Company. Web. 27 August 2012.

Pye, Douglas. "Double Vision: Miscegenation and Point of View in *The Searchers*." *The Book of Westerns.* Ed. Ian Cameron and Douglas Pye. London and New York: Continuum, 1996. 229–35. Print.

The Quiet Man. Dir. John Ford. Perf. John Wayne, Maureen O'Hara, Barry Fitzgerald, Victor McLaglen, Arthur Shields and Ward Bond. Artisan/Republic Pictures, 1952. DVD.

Raging Bull. Dir. Martin Scorsese. MGM, 1980. DVD.

Ramírez Berg, Charles. "Gendered Actions, Gendered Stories." Unpublished excerpt from draft of forthcoming textbook, *A New History of the Movies.* 2005.

_____. *Latino Images in Film.* Austin: University of Texas Press, 2002. Print.

_____. "The Margin As Center: The Multicultural Dynamics of John Ford's Westerns." *Latino Images in Film.* Austin, Texas: University of Texas Press, 2002. 128–52. Print.

Reds. Dir. Warren Beatty. Perf. Warren Beatty and Diane Keaton. Paramount, 1981. DVD.

Requiem for a Heavyweight (TV production). Dir. Ralph Nelson. MGM/United Artists, 1956. VHS.

Requiem for a Heavyweight. Dir. Ralph Nelson. Columbia Pictures, 1962.

Restrepo. Dir. Sebastian Junger and Tim Hetherington. Virgil Films, 2010. DVD.

The Ring. Dir. Kurt Neumann. Alpha Video, 1952. DVD.

Rio Grande. Dir. John Ford. Perf. John Wayne, Maureen O'Hara, Victor McLaglen, Claude Jarman, Jr. and Ben Johnson. Artisan/Republic Pictures, 1950. DVD.

The Rising of the Moon. Dir. John Ford. Four Provinces/Warner Bros., 1957.

Roche, Barry. "Pray for the dead and fight like hell for the living." *The Irish Times.* 27 July 2012. *IrishTimes.com.* Web. 27 August 2012.

Rolston, Bill. *Drawing Support: Murals in the North of Ireland.* Belfast: Beyond the Pale Publications, 1992. Print.

Sands of Iwo Jima. Dir. Alan Dwan. Perf. John Wayne. Artisan/Republic Pictures, 1949. DVD.

Schatz, Thomas. *Hollywood Genres: Formulas, Filmmaking, and the Studio System.* New York: Random House, 1981. Print.

Schickel, Richard. "The Man Who Shot the West." *New York Times Book Review* 149.51262 (9 January 2000): 9. Web. 27 August 2012.

The Searchers. Dir. John Ford. Perf. John Wayne, Natalie Wood, Jeffrey Hunter, Ward Bond and Henry Brandon. Warner Bros., 1956. DVD.

Sergeant Rutledge. Dir. John Ford. Perf. Woody Strode, Jeffrey Hunter and Constance Towers. Warner Bros., 1960. DVD.

7 Women. Dir. John Ford. Perf. Anne Bancroft, Sue Lyon, Margaret Leighton and Flora Robson. MGM, 1966.

Shaheen, Jack G. *Reel Bad Arabs: How Hollywood Vilifies a People*. Northampton, MA: Interlink, 2001. Print.

Shame. Dir. Steve McQueen. Perf. Michael Fassbender and Carey Mulligan. Film 4/UK Film Council/Fox Searchlight, 2011.

Shane. Dir. George Stevens. Perf. Alan Ladd and Jean Arthur. Paramount, 1953. DVD.

She Wore a Yellow Ribbon. Dir. John Ford. Perf. John Wayne, Victor McLaglen, Ben Johnson, Joanne Dru and John Agar. Warner Bros., 1949. DVD.

Sheridan, Jim. *Leave the Fighting to McGuigan: The Official Biography of Barry McGuigan*. Middlesex, England: Viking/Penguin Books, 1985. Print.

"Show Business: The Permanent Star." *Time*. 9 October 1978. *Time.com*. Web. 27 August 2012.

Silverman, Kaja. *Male Subjectivity at the Margins*. New York and London: Routledge, 1992. Print.

Sophie Scholl: The Final Days. Dir. Marc Rothemund. Zeitgeist Films, 2005. DVD.

Stagecoach. Dir. John Ford. Perf. John Wayne, Claire Trevor and Thomas Mitchell. Criterion, 1939. DVD.

Steinbeck, John. *The Grapes of Wrath*. 1939. New York: Penguin, 2006. Print.

Stop-Loss. Dir. Kimberly Peirce. Paramount, 2008. DVD.

Studlar, Gaylyn. "'Be a Proud, Glorified Dreg': Class, Gender, and Frontier Democracy in *Stagecoach*." *John Ford's* Stagecoach. Ed. Barry Keith Grant. Cambridge, UK: Cambridge University Press, 2003. Print.

_____. "Sacred Duties, Poetic Passions: John Ford and the Issue of Femininity in the Western." *John Ford Made Westerns: Filming the Legend in the Sound Era*. Ed. Gaylyn Studlar and Matthew Bernstein. Bloomington: Indiana University Press, 2001. Print.

Studlar, Gaylyn, and Matthew Bernstein. *John Ford Made Westerns: Filming the Legend in the Sound Era*. Bloomington: Indiana University Press, 2001. Print.

The Sun Shines Bright. Dir. John Ford. Perf. Charles Winninger, John Russell, Arleen Whelan and Stepin Fetchit. Republic Pictures, 1953.

Sutton, Malcom. *Bear in Mind These Dead ... An Index of Deaths from the Conflict in Ireland 1969–2001*. Cain Web Service. 1996–2012. Web. 27 August 2012.

Svinth, Joseph R. "Death under the Spotlight: The Manuel Velazquez Boxing Fatality Collection." *Journal of Combative Sport* (November 2007). Web. 27 August 2012.

Synge, John Millington. *The Playboy of the Western World*. 1907. *The Complete Plays of J.M. Synge*. New York: Vintage, 1960. Print.

_____. "The Vagrants of Wicklow." 1901. *The Aran Islands and Other Writings*. Ed. Robert Tracy. New York: Vintage, 1962. Print.

Taxi Driver. Dir. Martin Scorsese. Sony Pictures, 1976. DVD.

Taxi to the Dark Side. Dir. Alex Gibney. Image Entertainment, 2007. DVD.

Terkel, Studs. "Brigadier General Paul Tibbets." *Hope Dies Last: Keeping the Faith in Difficult Times*. New York and London: The New Press, 2003. Print.

The Thin Blue Line. Dir. Errol Morris. MGM, 1988. DVD.

They Were Expendable. Dir. John Ford. Perf. John Wayne, Robert Montgomery, Ward Bond and Donna Reed. MGM, 1945. DVD.

This Is Korea! Dir. John Ford. Republic, 1951.

Thorpe, Vanessa. "Hollywood's favourite Brit." *Guardian Unlimited*. 5 August 2007. *The Observer*. Web. 27 August 2012.

"*Time* Names Bono, Bill and Melinda Gates Persons of the Year." *CNN.* 19 December 2005. *CNN.com.* 27 August 2012.
"Timeline: the Omagh Bombing." *Guardian Unlimited.* 8 June 2009. Web. 27 August 2012.
Tobacco Road. Dir. John Ford. Perf. Charley Grapewin and Elizabeth Patterson. 20th Century–Fox, 1941. DVD.
Two Rode Together. Dir. John Ford. Perf. James Stewart, Richard Widmark, Linda Cristal, Shirley Jones, Henry Brandon and Woody Strode. Columbia Pictures, 1961.
United 93. Dir. Paul Greengrass. Universal, 2006. DVD.
"USA Patriot Act (H.R. 3162)." *EPIC.* 2005. *Electronic Privacy Information Center.* Web. 27 August 2012.
U2 Go Home: Live from Slane Castle. Dir. Enda Hughes and Hamish Hamilton. Perf. U2. Interscope Records, 2003. DVD.
U2 3D. Dir. Catherine Owens and Mark Pellington. Perf. U2. 3ality/National Geographic, 2007.
Vietnam! Vietnam! Exec. prod. John Ford. Dir. Sherman Beck. 1971.
Vonnegut, Kurt. *Slaughterhouse-Five.* 1969. New York: Dell, 1991. Print.
Wagon Master. Dir. John Ford. Perf. Ben Johnson, Joanne Dru, Ward Bond and Alan Mowbray. Warner Bros., 1950. DVD.
Walker, Rebecca. "Putting Down the Gun." *What Makes a Man: 22 Writers Imagine the future.* Ed. Rebecca Walker. New York: Riverhead Books, 2004. 1–7. Print.
Walsh, Maurice. "The Quiet Man." 1933. *The Quiet Man and Other Stories.* Belfast: Appletree Press, 2002. Print.
Wilde, Oscar. "The Ballad of Reading Gaol." 1898. *Oscar Wilde — the Major Works.* Oxford: Oxford University Press, 2000. Print.
Wills, Garry. *John Wayne's America: The Politics of Celebrity.* New York: Simon & Schuster, 1997. Print.
The Wind That Shakes the Barley. Dir. Ken Loach. IFC, 2006. DVD.
The Wings of Eagles. Dir. John Ford. Perf. John Wayne, Dan Dailey and Maureen O'Hara. Warner Bros., 1957. DVD.
Wink, Walter. "Christian Nonviolence." *ZNet.* 17 December 2004. *ZNet Articles.* Web. 27 August 2012.
_____. *Jesus and Nonviolence: A Third Way.* Minneapolis: Fortress Press, 2003. Print.
Winston, Brian. "Ethics." *New Challenges for Documentary*, 2d ed. Ed. Alan Rosenthal and John Corner. Manchester: Manchester University Press, 2005. 181–193. Print.
You Can't Take It with You. Dir. Frank Capra. Columbia Pictures, 1938. DVD.
Young Cassidy. Dir. Jack Cardiff. Metro-Goldwyn-Mayer, 1965.
Young Mr. Lincoln. Dir. John Ford. Perf. Henry Fonda. Criterion, 1939. DVD.
"027_09 — Statement of Soldier 027 (Part 9 of 11)" [no longer accessible online]. *The Bloody Sunday Inquiry.* 1998–2005. Web. 31 May 2008. *Breakingnews.ie.* "Bloody Sunday paratrooper says shootings unjustified." Web. 27 August 2012. <http://www.breakingnews.ie/ireland/bloody-sunday-paratrooper-says-shootings-unjustified-72711.html>.
Zinn, Howard. *A People's History of the United States.* New York: HarperCollins, 2003. Print.

Index

Numbers in ***bold italics*** indicate pages with photographs

Abbey Theatre 29, 101
Abdalla, Khalid 167
Adams, Gerry 161
Agar, John 25, ***26***
Allen, Elizabeth 24, 82, 91
Allgood, Sara 28–9, 35, 36, 90, 94, 111, 178*n*16
Althusser, Louis 114, 127, 182*n*6, 182*n*7, 182*n*9, 183*n*20
Amritsar massacre 152
Arthur, Jean 180*n*15
Attenborough, Richard 13

Baker, Don 118, 119, ***120***, 121
Bancroft, Anne 81, 91, 181*n*3
Barry, Sebastian 147
Barton, Ruth 7–8, 9, 16, 84, 92, 95, 100, 103, 104, 110, 113, 116, 122, 123, 126, 137, 181*n*5, 182*ch*3*n*11, 182*ch*4*n*3, 183*n*18
The Battle of Algiers 151–2
The Battle of Midway 47–8
Bean, Sean 116–8
Beatty, Warren 17
Beckett, Samuel 14, 169
Bederman, Gail 176*n*12
Berenger, Tom 117, 118
Beutiful Bockser (*Beautiful Boxer*) 180*n*14
Bier, Susanne 166
The Big Country 180*n*15
Big Jim McLain 68, ***69***, 70, 180*n*24
Bigelow, Kathryn 167
Blair, Tony 161
Bloody Sunday (1972) 10, 141
Bloody Sunday (film) 8, 10, 13, 19, 139, 140, 141, 142–5, ***146***, 148, ***149***, 150–2, 153, 154–5, 162, 165, 184*n*9, 184*n*10, 184*n*11, 185*n*12, 185*n*14, 185*n*15, 185*n*18, 185*n*19
The Bloody Sunday Inquiry 143, 148–9, 150
Body and Soul 12, 57, 133, 134, 135
Bogdanovich, Peter 27, 34, 63, 64, 83, 178*n*28, 181*n*2
Bolger, Emma 103, 105, 108–9
Bolger, Sarah 103, 104, 108–9
Bond, Ward 33, 51, 54, 71, 75, 84–5, 179*n*7
Bono 154, 171–3, 186*n*5
Bordwell, David 23–4
The Bourne Supremacy 17, 166, 183–4*n*4
The Bourne Ultimatum 17, 166, 183–4*n*4
The Boxer 8, 10, 11, 12, 13, 19, 84, 92, 94, 102, 113, 114, 115, 118, 122–30, ***131***, 132–4, 135–37, 181*n*5, 183*n*16, 183*n*22, 183*n*23, 183*n*25, 183*n*26
boxing fatalities 11–2, 176*n*14
boxing films 12–3, 15, 57–8, 93, 129–30, 132–6, 180*n*14
Braddock, James J. 11
Brady, Alice 90
Brando, Marlon 12, 126, 129
Brennan, Walter 86
Brothers (2009) 166
Brown, Christy 100, 102, 182*ch*3*n*11
Bruzzi, Stella 141
Bush, George W. 166, 170, 185*n*13
The Butcher Boy 176*n*8

Caldwell, John 11
Capra, Frank 48, 175*n*5
Cardiff, Jack 177*n*3
Carey, Harry 181*n*2
Carey, Olive 74, 90

197

Carradine, John 13, 35, 39, 41–2, 44, 87, 88, 89, 93, 106, 177n13
The Champ 133
Champion 133
Cheney, Dick 170
Chesty: A Tribute to a Legend 177n7
Cheyenne Autumn 24, 79
Cinderella Man 180n14
Clarke, Kathy Keira 143–4
Cobb, Lee J. 126, 129
Colbert, Claudette 31–2, **33**, 34, 177n12, 179n4, 180n16
Cold War 18, 25, 42, 48, 50–1, 52, 53, 68–70, 79–80
colonialism 12, 13, 18, 19, 102, 113–14, 118, 120, 140–1, 142, 144–52, 168, 182n6, 182n7, 183n17
The Comancheros 171
Communist Blacklist (in Hollywood) 49, 50–2, 68–71, 80, 176n9, 179n8, 180n24
Conlon, Gerry 119, 182–3ch4n14
Considine, Paddy 103, 104–5, 106, 107–8, **109**, 110
Cooper, Chris 153
Cooper, Ivan 150, 153–4, 185n12, 185n14, 185n15
Corbett, James J. "Gentleman Jim" 11
Cortright, David 14
Cox, Brian 128, 129, 130, 136
The Cranberries 171
Crisp, Donald 10, 30, 87
Cristal, Linda 76
Cuchulain myth 147
Cullingford, Elizabeth Butler 15, 16, 130, 182ch4n10
Curtiz, Michael 171
Cusask, Cyril 101, 181n7, 182ch3n10
Cvetkovich, Ann 175n6

Dailey, Dan 81
Damon, Matt 166–7, 183–4n4
Darnell, Linda 45–6, 90, 178n31, 178–9n32, 178–9n33
Darwell, Jane 29, 34–6, **37**, 38–9, **40**, 41, 42, 90, 106
Daves, Delmer 180n25
Day-Lewis, Daniel 94, 95–7, **98**, 99–100, **101**, 102, 118–9, **120**, 121, 122–4, 127–30, **131**, 132, 133–4, 135–6, 181n5
December 7 47–8, 79
de Certeau, Michel 154, 185n18
DeMille, Cecil B. 71
Dempsey, Jack (William Harrison) 11, 13, 176n11
Dempsey, "Nonpareil" Jack 176n11
The Departed 83

Depression Era (in the U.S.) 34–5, 42
detective films 9, 92
Donovan's Reef 24, 66, 79, 80–1, 82, 86, 91, 94, 180n12, 181n29
Downfall 168
Doyle, Roddy 146–7
Dru, Joanne 90
Drums Along the Mohawk 9, 23, 28, 31–2, **33**, 34, 43, 50, 52, 62, 84, 86, 91, 93, 177n6, 177n12, 177n13, 178n21, 179n4, 180n16
Dwan, Allan 52
Dyer, Richard 67–8

Easter Rising of 1916 21, 98, 146
Eastwood, Clint 5, 83, 168, 177n15, 180n14
Ebert, Roger 49
Edwards, Mike 148, **149**
Eisenhower, Dwight 186n6
Erickson, Glenn 28
E.T. 104, 182ch3n13
Eyman, Scott 7, 23, 27–8, 30, 42, 50, 51, 56, 63–4, 71, 79, 179n7, 180n21

family (social) melodrama 6–7, 9, 15, 16, 92–3, 103, 122, 167, 175n4, 175n6
Farrell, Nicholas 148
Fassbender, Michael 169
Feldman, Allen 13, 114, 124–6, 183n18
Felski, Rita 115
feminism 1–3, 4, 14, 28, 32, 38, 61, 62, 81, 91, 123
The Field (1990 film) 5, 8, 10, 19, 84, 92, 94, 102, 114, 115–18, 123, 124, 128, 138, 181n5, 183n21
The Field (play) 116, 117
50 Cent (Curtis Jackson) 166
The Fighter 180n14
First Blood 176n16
Fisher, James T. 183n19
Fitzgerald, Barry 7, 28, 56, 58, 59, 62, 85, 178n16
Fitzgerald, Ciaran 124, 125, 127, 128, 133, 136
Flags of Our Fathers (film) 168
Fonda, Henry 10, 25, 28, 31–2, **33**, 34, 35–6, **37**, 38–9, **40**, 41–2, 43–5, 50, 51, 52, 71, 82, 177n12, 178n25, 178n26, 178n27, 178n29, 178n30, 181n2
Fonda, Peter 51
Forbes, Michèle 158–9
Ford, John: *The Battle of Midway* 47–8; *Chesty: A Tribute to a Legend* 177n7; *Cheyenne Autumn* 24, 79; cinematic style 5; conservatism of 12, 22, 49, 50–1,

52, 71, 79–80, 111, 179n5; *December 7* 47–8, 79; *Donovan's Reef* 24, 66, 79, 80–1, 82, 86, 91, 94, 180n12, 181n29; *Drums Along the Mohawk* 9, 23, 28, 31–2, **33**, 34, 43, 50, 52, 62, 84, 86, 91, 93, 177n6, 177n12, 177n13, 178n21, 179n4, 180n16; *Fort Apache* 5, 10, 21, 23, 24–5, **26**, **27**, 32, 43, 51, 55, 66, 67, 73–4, 75, 86, 87, 88, 89, 91, 94, 100, 175n4, 177n8, 178n25, 179n3, 180n25, 182n16; genre elements in films of 6–7, 52, 93–4; *The Grapes of Wrath* 7, 10, 13, 18, 23, 28, 29, 34–6, **37**, 38–9, **40**, 41–3, 47, 49, 87, 88, 90, 92, 93, 95, 105, 106, 110, 177n9, 178n18, 178n19, 178n20, 178n21, 178n22, 178n23, 178n24, 181n26, 182ch3n14; Hollywood's influence on 5–6, 23–4, 52, 78–9, 87; *How Green Was My Valley* 7, 9, 10, 13, 18, 23, 24, 28–31, 35, 36, **37**, 39, **40**, 42, 46–8, 50, 52–3, 55, 58, 66, 82, 85, 87, 88, 90, 91, 92, 93, 94–5, 102, 176n9, 177n9, 177n10, 177n11, 181n6; *The Hurricane* 85; *The Informer* 7, 26–7, 85, 90; Irish identity of 7, 21, 34, 54–5, 180n13; *The Last Hurrah* 7, 87, 88, 91, 181n27; *The Long Gray Line* 7, 55, 90; *The Long Voyage Home* 85; *The Man Who Shot Liberty Valance* 23, 44–5, 71–2, 78, 83, 85, 86, 87, 88, 89, 91, 94; militarism of 8, 10, 18, 21, 24–6, 42, 49, 86–7, 88, 89, 182n16; military service of 42, 46, 51, 175n7; *Mogambo* 91, 177n5, 180n17; *My Darling Clementine* 23, 43, 45–6, 52, 86, 88, 90, 91, 178–9n32, 179n33; narrative approach typical of 5, 46; *The Plough and the Stars* (1936 film) 21; progressivism of 6, 7, 8, 18, 22, 46–8, 79, 80, 87, 88, 89; *Quiet Man* 5, 7, 8, 12, 16, 18, 21, 22, 23, 24, 26, 30, 46, 51, 53–64, **65**, 66, 67, 68, 71, 78, 81, 82, 85, 87, 88, 91, 94, 100, 115–6, 126, 177n4, 177n8, 177n14, 179n10, 180n4, 180n15, 180n17, 180n18, 180n19, 180n20, 180n21, 180n22, 180n23, 181n28; relationship with Henry Fonda 43, 49–51; relationship with John Wayne 51–2, 64–6, 70–2, 82, 179n9; relationship with Katharine Hepburn 27–8, 63; relationship with Maureen O'Hara 63–4, 180n13, 180n19, 180n21, 180n22; representation of race 21–2, 24, 55, 72, 73–4, 75–6, 79, 81, 86, 88, 177n5, 177n13, 178n31, 178–9n32, 180n12, 180n25; representation of religion 29–30, 44, 46–8, 53, 58–9, 87, 176n9, 177n10; representation of social class 6, 7, 21–2, 28, 30, 34–5, 39, 41, 42, 48, 52, 53, 80, 86, 87, 90, 91, 94, 177n4, 177n9; representation of violence 33–4, 41, 43–6, 54, 56–7, 63–5, 73–5, 82, 88–9; representation of women 6, 8, 10, 18, 22, 24, 25–6, 28–30, 31–2, 34, 35–9, 42–3, 45–6, 54, 56, 59–63, 64, 75, 76–8, 79, 80–82, 90–1, 111, 177n9, 178n28, 178n31, 178–9n32, 179n33, 180n16, 180n17, 180n18, 180n19, 180n21, 180n22, 181n3, 182ch3n14; *The Rio Grande* 22, 23, 24, 66, 81, 86, 87, 91; *The Rising of the Moon* (1957 film) 7, 21, 55, 176n2; *The Searchers* 6, 11, 18, 23, 54, 65, 72, **73**, 74–7, **78**, 79, 81, 82, 83, 86, 87, 90, 91; sentimentality of 6, 53–4, 79; *Sergeant Rutledge* 24; *7 Women* 18, 23, 61, 79, 81, 91; *She Wore a Yellow Ribbon* 23, 50, 65, 86, 89, 179n5; *Stagecoach* 22, 85, 90; *The Sun Shines Bright* 85, 86, 87, 88, 90, 91; *They Were Expendable* 10, 67, 80, 85, 86, 87, 91, 94, 179n33; *This Is Korea!* 51; *Tobacco Road* 85, 90, 177n9; treatment of actors 30–1, 63–4, 111; *Two Rode Together* 76; *Wagon Master* 85, 86, 90; *The Wings of Eagles* 80–1; *Young Mr. Lincoln* 5, 13, 21, 23, 43–4, 46, 52, 66, 77, 88, 89, 90, 91, 93, 178n17, 178n26, 178n27

Fort Apache 5, 10, 21, 23, 24–5, **26**, **27**, 32, 43, 51, 55, 66, 67, 73–4, 75, 86, 87, 88, 89, 91, 94, 100, 175n4, 177n8, 178n25, 179n3, 180n25, 182n16
Foucault, Michel 182ch4n12
Freudian psychology 39, 113, 114, 182n7
Fricker, Brenda 95, 96, 97, 98, 99, 100, 102, 118, 161–2, 181n5
Friel, Brian 36

Gable, Clark 180n17
Gallagher, Michael 158
Gandhi (film) 13, 17, 176n16
Gandhi, Mohandas K. (Mahatma) 14, 139, 145, 153
gangster films 9
Gansel, Dennis 180n14
Gardner, Ava 91, 180n17
Garfield, John 134
Generation Kill 167
George, Terry 182ch4n11
Get Rich or Die Tryin' 166
Gibbons, Luke 23, 24, 54–5, 81, 179n11, 181n28
Gibney, Alex 167
Gibson, Mel 13, 177n15
Girlfight 180n14
Goodfellas 83

Graham, Stuart 157
Grand Illusion 51
Grant, James Edward 68, 82, 181*n*29
The Grapes of Wrath 7, 10, 13, 18, 23, 28, 29, 34–6, **37**, 38–9, **40**, 41–3, 47, 49, 87, 88, 90, 92, 93, 95, 105, 106, 110, 177*n*9, 178*n*18, 178*n*19, 178*n*20, 178*n*21, 178*n*22, 178*n*23, 178*n*24, 181*n*26, 182*ch*3*n*14
Great Famine (in Ireland) 11, 34–5, 105, 112, 116, 117, 138
The Great White Hope 133, 134–5
Green Zone 166–7, 186*n*2, 186*n*3
Greengrass, Paul: *Bloody Sunday* (film) 8, 10, 13, 19, 139, 140, 141, 142–5, **146**, 148, **149**, 150–2, 153, 154–5, 162, 165, 184*n*9, 184*n*10, 184*n*11, 185*n*12, 185*n*14, 185*n*15, 185*n*18, 185*n*19; *The Bourne Supremacy* 17, 166, 183–4*n*4; *The Bourne Ultimatum* 17, 166, 183–4*n*4; documentary stylistics of 8, 17, 140–2, 151, 154, 183–4*n*4, 184*n*5; genre elements in films of 142–3, 152, 154, 155, 161, 165–6, 167; *Green Zone* 166–7, 186*n*2, 186*n*3; Hollywood career of 17, 166; *Omagh* (film) 10–11, 13, 19, 139, 140, 141, 142, 155–61, **162**, 185*n*20, 185–6*n*22, 186*n*23; professional background of 8, 140, 183–4*n*4; representation of British military 148–9, 150; representation of religion 144, 145; representation of social class 145; representation of violence 139, 145, 150, 151, 154, 155–7; representation of women 10, 143, 144, 157, 158–60, 161–2; *United 93* 183–4*n*4
Greenwald, Glenn 170
Gregory, Lady Augusta 21, 176*n*2
Grenier, Richard 182*ch*4*n*13
Guthrie, Arlo 178*n*22
Gyllenhaal, Jake 166

Haggis, Paul 167
The Harder They Fall 12, 135
Harris, Richard 116–18, 181*n*5
Heaney, Seamus 11
Hellman, Lillian 68
Hemingway, Ernest 177*n*5
Hepburn, Katharine 27–8, 63, 111, 179*n*6
Herr, Cheryl 116–7, 182*n*9
Hetherington, Tim 167
Hiroshima bombing 171
Hiss, Alger 69
Hitchcock, Alfred 5, 16
Hollywood studio system 5–6, 23–4
hooks, bell 2, 16
Hounsou, Djimon 104, 105, 106–7, 108, **109**
How Green Was My Valley 7, 9, 10, 13, 18, 23, 24, 28–31, 35, 36, **37**, 39, **40**, 42, 46–8, 50, 52–3, 55, 58, 66, 82, 85, 87, 88, 90, 91, 92, 93, 94–5, 102, 176*n*9, 177*n*9, 177*n*10, 177*n*11, 180*n*20, 181*n*6
Howard, Ron 180*n*14
Hunger 169
Hunter, Jeffrey 73, 74–5, 77–8, 87, 88, 91
The Hurricane 85
Hurt, John 117
The Hurt Locker 167, 186*n*3

In America 10, 11, 18, 84, 92, 94, 102–6, **107**, 108, **109**, 110, 111–12, 115, 181*n*5, 182*ch*3*n*12, 182*ch*3*n*13, 182*n*15
In Bruges 169
In the Name of the Father 8, 10, 13, 19, 84, 92, 94, 102, 112, 113, 114, 115, 118–9, **120**, 121–2, 123, 128, 138, 158, 160, 162, 181*n*4, 181*n*5, 182*ch*4*n*11, 182*ch*4*n*13, 182–3*ch*4*n*14, 183*n*21
In the Valley of Elah 167
The Informer 7, 26–7, 85, 90
Inglourious Basterds 186*n*4
Into the West 182*n*4
Irigiray, Luce 127
Irish cinema (definition of) 7–8, 15, 17–8, 84, 173
Irish Republican Army (IRA) 10, 27, 53, 55, 115, 116, 118–20, 121, 123, 124, 126–7, 128–9, 130, 135–6, 137, 140, 144, 146, 147, 150–1, 152, 153–4, 160, 168, 169, 172, 182*ch*4*n*13, 184*n*8, 184*n*11, 185*n*12, 185*n*14, 186*n*23

Johnson, Ben 86, 90
Johnson, Jack 134
Johnson, Nunnally 34
Jones, James Earl 134–5, 153
Jones, Mary "Mother" 113
Jones, Shirley 91, 181*n*3
Jordan, Dorothy 76
Jordan, Neil 16, 147, 168, 176*n*8
Joyce, James 11, 101
Junger, Sebastian 167

Kazan, Elia 12, 126
Keane, John B. 116, 117
Kemper, Charles 86
Kennedy, John F. 179*n*7
Kiberd, Declan 113, 114, 119, 120–1, 122, 124, 182*n*3, 182*ch*4*n*12
King, Coretta Scott 14, 176*n*17
King, Martin Luther, Jr. 14, 145, 153, 176*n*17
Kurosawa, Akira 16
Kusama, Karyn 180*n*14

Lakoff, George 4
The Last Hurrah 7, 87, 88, 91, 181*n*27
The Last of the Mohicans 177*n*6
LeRoy, Mervyn 178*n*29
Letters from Iwo Jima 168
The Lieutenant of Inishmore 168
Llewellyn, Richard 180*n*20
Loach, Ken 168
The Long Gray Line 7, 55, 90
Long Kesh (Maze) prison hunger strikes (1981) 104, 138, 140, 147, 169
The Long Voyage Home 85
Ludwig, Edward 68, 69

MacArthur, Douglas 179*n*5
MacDowall, Roddy 10, 29, 30–1, 47, 87, 88, 94
The Magdalene Sisters 5
Maguire, Tobey 166
Malden, Karl 126
The Man Who Shot Liberty Valance 23, 44–5, 71–2, 78, 83, 85, 86, 87, 88, 89, 91, 94
Mankiewicz, Joseph L. 71
Martin, Jean 151
martyrdom 13, 25, 98, 138, 145–7, 173
Marvin, Lee 79, 86
Matewan 152–3, 185*n*16, 185*n*17
matriarchy 18, 62, 90, 102–3, 105–6, 109–10, 111
Mature, Victor 45, 86
Mbembe, Achille 147–8
McAnally, Ray 95, 96–7, **98**
McBride, Joseph 6, 7, 23, 24, 28, 50–2, 53, 63, 65, 68, 79, 81, 82, 111, 175*n*7, 179*n*2, 179*n*5, 179*n*7, 179*n*9, 179–80*n*11
McCabe, Ruth 94, 99–100, **101**, 102
McCain, John 185*n*21
McCarthy Joseph 51, 53, 69–70, 179*n*7
McCracken, Henry Joy 145
McDonagh, Martin 168–9
McElhinney, Ian 158
McGuigan, Barry 11, 132–3, 136–7, 183*n*24
McIlroy, Brian 16, 121, 123, 140, 155, 161
McLaglen, Andrew 63, 180*n*21
McLaglen, Victor 7, 56, 57, 58, 59, 61, 63, 85
McLoone, Martin 7, 16, 119, 122, 123
McQueen, Steve (film director) 169
McSorley, Gerard 123, 125, 128–9, 130, 136, 148, 157, 158–61, **162**, 183*n*22
The Messenger 167
Michael Collins (film) 147, 168, 176*n*8
Mies, Maria 4
Miles, Vera 44–5, 74, 75, 76–7, **78**, 89, 91, 178*n*28, 181*n*3

Million Dollar Baby 180*n*14
misogyny 42, 60, 81, 111, 170, 183–4*n*4
Mitchell, Thomas 85
Mogambo 91, 177*n*5, 180*n*17
Monaghan, John "Rinty" 11
Montgomery, Robert 86
Morris, Errol 142, 184*n*6
Morton, Samantha 103, 105–6, **107**, 109–10
Moverman, Oren 167
Mowbray, Alan 85
Mullan, Don 143, 158
Mullan, Peter 5
Mulvey, Laura 16
Muste, A.J. 80
My Darling Clementine 23, 43, 45–6, 52, 86, 88, 90, 91, 178–9*n*32, 179*n*33
My Left Foot 10, 18, 84, 92, 94–7, **98**, 99–100, **101**, 102, 181*n*5, 181*n*6, 181*n*7, 181*n*8, 182*ch*3*n*10, 182*ch*3*n*11
Mystic River 5

Naor, Igal 167
Napola (Before the Fall) 168, 180*n*14
nationalism 48, 68, 70, 138, 154, 163
Nesbitt, James 143–5, **146**, 149–51, 152, 153, 154–5
Nichols, Bill 141
non-sectarianism 13, 129, 132, 136, 157, 172
Nugent, Frank S. 61, 63, 177*n*8

Oates, Joyce Carol 13
O'Brien, Edmund 85
O'Casey, Sean 20, 36, 106, 177*n*9
O'Connor, Hugh 181*n*8
O'Connor, Sinead 171
O'Hara, Maureen 7, 21, 28, 29–30, 36, **37**, 39, **40**, 46, 52–3, 54, 57, 58–64, **65**, 66, 71, 81, 90, 91, 93, 111, 176*n*1, 178*n*16, 180*n*13, 180*n*19, 180*n*22, 181*n*3
Oldham, Will 153
Oliver, Edna May 32, 34, 91, 111, 178*n*21
Omagh (film) 10–11, 13, 19, 139, 140, 141, 142, 155–61, **162**, 185*n*20, 185–6*n*22, 186*n*23
Omagh bombing 137, 141, 155, 172, 185*n*20, 185–6*n*22
On the Waterfront 126, 129, 183*n*19
O'Neill, Margaret 142, 185*n*18
O'Toole, Fintan 169
The Ox-Bow Incident 178*n*27

pacifism 3, 12, 13, 14, 17, 18, 41, 56–7, 80, 87, 88–90, 106, 115, 118, 120–2, 125–6, 139, 145, 151, 152–3, 171–3
Pallette, Pilar 52

Parnell, Charles Stewart 145
The Passion of the Christ 13, 176n16
patriarchy 1–3, 4–5, 8, 9–11, 12, 14, 16, 18, 19, 22, 24, 26, 28, 29, 32, 36, 39, 41, 42, 46, 47, 53, 54, 56, 57, 58, 59–62, 64–6, 77–9, 82, 86–8, 92, 94–7, 99, 102–3, 110, 111, 112, 113–6, 118, 120–1, 123, 124, 125, 126–7, 128–32, 137–8, 169, 180n15, 181n8, 182n16, 182n6, 182n7, 183n20
Patriot Act 184n7
Patterson, Elizabeth 90, 177n9
Peace Process (in Northern Ireland) 127, 136, 143, 160–1, 172
peace studies 14–5
Peirce, Kimberly 167
Pettitt, Lance 120, 122
Pichel, Irving 48
Pidgeon, Walter 10, 29–30, **37**, **40**, 46–7, 50, 52–3, 87, 88, 89, 93, 95
Pigott-Smith, Tim 148
The Playboy of the Western World 21, 179n10
The Plough and the Stars (1936 film) 21
Pontecorvo, Gillo 151–2
Portman, Natalie 166
Postlethwaite, Pete 118, 119, **120**, 121–2
Power, Tyrone 87
Prevention of Terrorism Act of 1974 144

Qualen, John 35
Queensberry rules (in boxing) 176n10, 183n25
The Quiet Man 5, 7, 8, 12, 16, 18, 21, 22, 23, 24, 26, 30, 46, 51, 53–64, **65**, 66, 67, 68, 71, 78, 81, 82, 85, 87, 88, 91, 94, 100, 115–6, 126, 177n4, 177n8, 177n14, 179n10, 180n4, 180n15, 180n17, 180n18, 180n19, 180n20, 180n21, 180n22, 180n23, 181n28

Raging Bull 83, 133, 135
Ramírez Berg, Charles 6, 13, 15, 22, 24, 30, 52, 55, 57, 67, 93, 178n32
Rea, Stephen 17
Reds 17
Reed, Donna 91, 179n33
Renoir, Jean 51, 176n15
Requiem for a Heavyweight 12, 57, 135
Restrepo 167
Rich, Irene 25, **26**, **27**
The Ring 12, 57
Rio Grande 22, 23, 24, 66, 81, 86, 87, 91
The Rising of the Moon (1957 film) 7, 21, 55, 176n2
The Rising of the Moon (play) 176n2
Ritt, Martin 134

Robbins, Marty 178n22
Robson, Mark 12, 135
Rolston, Bill 147
Rossen, Robert 12, 57, 134
Royal Ulster Constabulary (RUC) 134, 137, 144, 148, 159, 160, 161
Russell, David O. 180n14

Sands, Bobby 147, 169
Sands of Iwo Jima 52
Sayles, John 152–3
Schatz, Thomas 9, 15, 74, 92–3, 103, 111–2, 161, 175n4, 178n28, 182n5
Scorsese, Martin 16, 83–4, 112, 135
screwball comedy 9, 176n15
The Searchers 6, 11, 18, 23, 54, 65, 72, **73**, 74–7, **78**, 79, 81, 82, 83, 86, 87, 90, 91
sectarianism 94, 133, 152
Sergeant Rutledge 24
7 Women 18, 23, 61, 79, 81, 91
Shame 169
Shane 180n15
Sharpeville massacre 152
Shaw, Fiona 99, 100, **101**
She Wore a Yellow Ribbon 23, 50, 65, 86, 89, 179n5
Sheridan, Jim 140, 143; *The Boxer* 8, 10, 11, 12, 13, 19, 84, 92, 94, 102, 113, 114, 115, 118, 122–30, **131**, 132–4, 135–7, 181n5, 183n16, 183n22, 183n23, 183n25, 183n26; *Brothers* (2009) 166; family background of 103, 104, 182ch3n12; *The Field* (1990 film) 5, 8, 10, 19, 84, 92, 94, 102, 114, 115–18, 123, 124, 128, 138, 181n5, 183n21; genre elements in films of 8, 19, 92–4, 102–3, 104, 122 133–4, 166, 167; Hollywood career of 17, 166; *In America* 10, 11, 18, 84, 92, 94, 102–6, **107**, 108, **109**, 110, 111–12, 115, 181n5, 182ch3n12, 182ch3n13, 182n15; *In the Name of the Father* 8, 10, 13, 19, 84, 92, 94, 102, 112, 113, 114, 115, 118–9, **120**, 121–2, 123, 128, 138, 158, 160, 162, 181n4, 181n5, 182ch4n11, 182ch4n13, 182–3ch4n14, 183n21; John Ford's influence on 18, 92, 99, 100–1, 105–6 115–6; *My Left Foot* 10, 18, 84, 92, 94–7, **98**, 99–100, **101**, 102, 181n5, 181n6, 181n7, 181n8, 182ch3n10, 182ch3n11; representation of religion 108, 119, 121, 181n8; representation of social class 94–5, 101–2; representation of violence 115, 118, 119, 121, 123, 124–6, 128, 130, 133, 135, 137, 183n21, 183n22; representation of women 8, 10, 16–7, 18–9, 92, 94–6, 97, 98, 99, 101–2, 103–4, 105–6, 108–10, 118, 123, 126, 130–1, 181n8, 183n23; senti-

mentality of 8, 94; theatrical career of 104, 182*ch*3*n*11
Shields, Arthur 7, 28, 30, 46, 56, 58, 177*n*11, 178*n*16
Silverman, Kaja 5, 16, 114, 129, 183*n*20
Simmons, Jean 180*n*15
Six Shooter 169
Slaughterhouse-Five 169–70
Soldier 027 148–9
Some Mother's Son 158, 182*n*4
Sophie Scholl – The Final Days 168
Spielberg, Steven 83, 104
Springsteen, Bruce 80, 181*n*26
Stagecoach 22, 85, 90
A Star Called Henry 146–7
Steinbeck, John 34, 42, 178*n*19, 178*n*20, 178*n*23
Stevens, George 48, 71, 180*n*15
Stewart, James 44–5, 76, 181*n*2
Stop-Loss 167
Stott, Ken 123, 124–5, 133, 134
Strode, Woody 71–2
Sullivan, John L. 11
The Sun Shines Bright 85, 86, 87, 88, 90, 91
Synge, J.M. (John Millington) 21, 101–2, 179*n*10

Tarantino, Quentin 186*n*4
Taxi Driver 83
Taxi to the Dark Side 167
Temple, Shirley 25, **26**, **27**
Terkel, Studs 171
They Were Expendable 10, 67, 80, 85, 86, 87, 91, 94, 179*n*33
This Is Korea! 51
Thompson, Emma 181*n*4
Tibbets, Paul 171
Tobacco Road 85, 90, 177*n*9
Toland, Gregg 178*n*24
Tone, Wolfe 145
Tracy, Spencer 87, 179*n*6, 181*n*2
Trevor, Claire 90
troubles (in Northern Ireland, 1960–1990s) 8, 11, 12, 16, 19, 102, 112, 113, 119–21, 123, 124–6, 127, 132, 136, 137, 140, 141, 143–6, 147–8, 154, 155–6, 159–60, 161–3, 169, 172, 173
Truman, Harry 179*n*5
Tunney, Gene 11
Two Rode Together 76

Uekrongtham, Ekachai 180*n*14
Ulster Volunteer Force (UVF) 137, 144
United 93 183–4*n*4
U2 (rock band) 154, 171–2, 186*n*5

Vietnam, Vietnam 79
Vonnegut, Kurt 169–70

Wagon Master 85, 86, 90
Walker, Rebecca 2
Walsh, Maurice 53, 63
war films 6, 10, 47–8, 67, 80–1, 86–8, 89, 139, 166–8, 170, 177*n*6, 177–8*n*15, 179*n*33
Watson, Emily 123–4, 127–30, **131**, 136
Wayne, John 7, 10, 12, 18, 22, 23, 24–5, **26**, 41, 42, 44–5, 50, 51–2, 54–5, 56–64, **65**, 66–8, **69**, 70–2, **73**, 74–6, 77–9, 81, 82, 85, 86, 87, 89, 93, 111, 165, 170–1, 178*n*28, 179*n*1, 179*n*3, 179*n*8, 179*n*9, 179*n*33, 180*n*19, 180*n*22, 181*n*2, 181–2*n*9
Welles, Orson 5, 6, 175*n*3, 181*n*2
Wellman, William A. 178*n*27
westerns 6, 15, 21, 22, 44–6, 52, 55, 74, 93, 139, 155 175*n*5, 177*n*6, 177–8*n*15, 180*n*15
The Whereabouts of Eneas McNulty 147
Widgery Report 142
Widmark, Richard 76
Wilde, Oscar 11, 63, 176*n*10
Williams, Rhys 85
Wills, Garry 49, 52, 60–1, 62, 70, 71–2, 73, 79, 111, 170, 179*n*1, 179*n*8
The Wind That Shakes the Barley 168
The Wings of Eagles 80–1
Wink, Walter 14, 139, 183*n*3
Winninger, Charles 87
Winston, Brian 141, 143
Wood, Natalie 72, 76, 78
World War II 9, 10, 18, 22, 24, 42, 44, 45, 49–50, 52, 58, 66, 70, 72, 79–80, 89, 92, 93, 105, 111, 112, 168, 170, 171
Wyler, William 16, 48, 71, 180*n*15

Yeats, W.B. (William Butler) 11
Young Cassidy 21, 177*n*3
Young Mr. Lincoln 5, 13, 21, 23, 43–4, 46, 52, 66, 77, 88, 89, 90, 91, 93, 178*n*17, 178*n*26, 178*n*27

www.ingramcontent.com/pod-product-compliance
Ingram Content Group UK Ltd.
Pitfield, Milton Keynes, MK11 3LW, UK
UKHW042002140426
5217IPUK00015B/939